CROSSROADS

Literature and Language in Culturally and Linguistically Diverse Classrooms

Carole Cox
California State University—Long Beach

Paul Boyd-Batstone
California State University—Long Beach
Long Beach Unified School District

Merrill,
an imprint of Prentice Hall
Upper Saddle River, New Jersey   *Columbus, Ohio*

Library of Congress Cataloging-in-Publication Data

Cox, Carole
    Crossroads : literature and language in culturally and
linguistically diverse classrooms / Carole Cox and Paul Boyd-
Batstone.
        p.   cm.
    Includes bibliographical references and index.
    ISBN 0-13-191578-9
    1. Language arts (Elementary)—United States.   2. Multicultural
education—United States.   3. Literature—Study and teaching
(Elementary)—United States.   4. Reader-response criticism—United
States.   I. Boyd-Batstone, Paul.   II. Title.
LB1576.C754   1997
372.64—dc20
                                            96-30761
                                                CIP

Cover photo: © Lawrence Migdale
Editor: Bradley J. Potthoff
Production Editor: Julie Peters
Design Coordinator: Karrie Converse
Text Designer: Linda Robertson
Cover Designer: Brian Deep
Production Manager: Patricia A. Tonneman
Director of Marketing: Kevin Flanagan
Advertising/Marketing Coordinator: Julie Shough

This book was set in Revival by The Clarinda Company and was printed and bound by
Courier/Westford, Inc. The cover was printed by Phoenix Color Corp.

 © 1997 by Prentice-Hall, Inc.
A Pearson Education Company
Upper Saddle River, NJ 07458

Photos by Stuart Spates

Printed in the United States of America

10 9 8 7 6 5 4 3 2

ISBN: 0-13-191578-9

Prentice-Hall International (UK) Limited,London
Prentice-Hall of Australia Pty. Limited, Sydney
Prentice-Hall Canada Inc., Toronto
Prentice-Hall Hispanoamericana, S.A., Mexico
Prentice-Hall of India Private Limited, New Delhi
Prentice-Hall of Japan, Inc., Tokyo
Pearson Education Asia Pte. Ltd., Singapore
Editora Prentice-Hall do Brasil, Ltda., Rio de Janeiro

Carole Cox

For my wonderful family: Stuart, Wyatt, Gordon and Elizabeth.

Paul Boyd-Batstone

To Nancy and Kathryn, my family, my life, my loves.

Preface

This book is an exploration of the crossroads of reader-response and second language acquisition theories and research as a foundation for practice. It provides a model for teaching with literature that supports language and literacy development for students learning English as a first or second language.

We have provided a balance between theoretical and practical dimensions in the area, and tried to showcase literature-based reader-response approaches to teaching. To communicate this content to readers, we have laid out important background information and issues and integrated them with narrative, interpretive case studies from the points of view of both a researcher engaged in teaching and a teacher who carries out research. You will hear the two distinct voices of the researcher/teacher (Carole Cox wrote Chapters 1–6) and teacher/researcher (Paul wrote Chapters 7 and 8), often speaking together, as well as those of the children and the families they have written about.

We believe all children—children who come to school already speaking English and those learning it as a new language—deserve the best that literature-based instruction has to offer. We advocate an inclusive, response-centered approach to language and literacy development for all students.

Organization of the Text

The text is organized in three parts. Part 1, Literature and Language Theory Into Practice, begins with a conversation between the text's two authors about a real classroom experience (Chapter 1), maps out the crossroads of reader-response theory and second language acquisition theories and research as a foundation for practice in the context of current social constructivist approaches to teaching (Chapter 2), and bridges theory to practice by showing a model for student-centered and response-centered instruction that supports first- and second-language and literacy development (Chapter 3).

Part 2, Case Studies of Children, describes and interprets the language and literacy development of three children from kindergarten through fifth grade: a native English speaker (Chapter 4), a native Spanish speaker and English learner (Chapter 5), and a bilingual student fluent in Spanish and English (Chapter 6). Readers are asked to reflect on the lives of these students both at home and at school in terms of their own classroom practices.

Part 3, Literature and Language Crossroads in a Bilingual Classroom, gives a third-grade bilingual teacher's perspective on the crossroads of reader-response and language acquisition. Reflecting on his own practices, he provides a picture of what reader-response looks like in action (Chapter 7) and answers the "how-to" questions vital to putting theory into practice in nontechnical language with richly detailed examples (Chapter 8).

Special Features

"A Thought from Carole/A Thought from Paul"   Throughout the text, the authors provide commentary on each other's writing, and make connections between practice and theory.

Part openers   An overview of each of the three main parts of the text provides a summary of the chapter content as an advanced organizer for readers.

Things to Think About/Things to Do   Each chapter ends with a list of things to think about as a way of guiding the reader's reflection on the chapter content, and a list of things to do in the classroom to put the ideas in the chapter into practice.

Further Reading   Each chapter includes an annotated list of further readings for readers who want to know more about topics addressed in the chapter.

Suggestions for the monolingual teacher   Specific ways to integrate content instruction across the curriculum with special consideration for monolingual teachers in diverse classroom settings are provided throughout.

Children's work   Many examples of children's artwork and written work illustrate the content of Chapters 7 and 8.

Photographs   Most of the photos were taken in Paul's bilingual class, showing—not just telling—what he writes about.

Appendix: Word Processing and Authoring Tools   This overview highlights the application of authoring tools in a response-centered learning environment.

Acknowledgments

From Carole Cox

Thanks to Linda Scharp McElhiney at Merrill for her immediate interest in this book, and Brad Potthoff for seeing it through to completion. All the reviewers' ideas were excellent and most useful and we thank them: Christian Faltis, Arizona State University; Terry Piper, Saint Mary's University; Barbara A. Schaudt, California State University, Bakersfield; Gail Tompkins, California State University, Fresno; and Janet Towell, California State University, Stanislaus.

Our conversations reflecting on Louise Rosenblatt's transactional theory gave us a place to stand in mapping the terrain of classroom experiences with regard to teaching with literature and we are ever grateful to her. We have found that there is nothing more practical than a good theory such as hers.

While the children in the case studies must remain anonymous, I must acknowledge them. Their ideas and insights into literature and life are among the most important presented in the book. My longitudinal study of children's responses to literature which resulted in the case studies in Chapters 4–6 was partially funded by a California State University—Long Beach Scholarly and Creative Activities Award. This book would never have happened if Paul hadn't let me into his classroom, and been such a good friend and collaborator.

And as usual, I owe my family for the time I spend writing in my office and their love and warmth when I go home. My husband, Stuart Spates, took all the photographs in the book, and many more, and has always helped me look at things with new eyes.

From Paul Boyd-Batstone

Thanks to Linda Poderski and Julie Peters for their careful editing and guidance in the formation of the book. I especially want to say thank you to my students at Edison School who daily challenged me to teach, listen, and learn with them. Thank you, Carole Cox, for envisioning this book and my part in it from a sketch on the back of a napkin. Carole's mentoring and prodding to seize the day instilled in me the confidence to be a co-author.

Most of all, thanks to my wife, Nancy, who carved out time for me to write with our lively three-year-old daughter, Kathryn, clamoring for attention.

Contents

PART 1   Literature and Language Theory into Practice   1

    CHAPTER 1   The Story of Javier and the Turnip   3

Meet the Authors   3
    Carole Cox   3
    Paul Boyd-Batstone   4
    The Authors Meet   4
A First Visit to Señor B.-B.'S Third-Grade Class   6
    An Overview of a Bilingual Classroom   6
Teaching with Literature in a Bilingual Class   10
    A Literature Group Conference: *The Rabbit and the Turnip*   10
    A First Conversation between Carole and Paul   14
Changing Thinking about Teaching with Literature   16
    A New Literature Plan   16
    What Happened to Javier and the Turnip?   19
Things to Think About   19
Things to Do   20
Further Reading   20
References   21

    CHAPTER 2   Mapping the Crossroads of Reader-Response and Second Language   23

Reader-Response Theory   23
    The Reader or the Text?   24

Reader-Response Theories Influential in Education   24
Second-Language Acquisition Theory   27
    Grammar or Communication?   27
    Second-Language Acquisition Theories Influential in Education   29
Theoretical Crossroads   34
    Transmission or Social Construction of Knowledge?   34
    Reader-Response Theory and Second-Language Acquisition   37
Things to Think About   41
Things to Do   42
Further Reading   43
References   43

**CHAPTER 3   Teaching with Literature and English Language and Literacy
            Development   49**
Text-Centered Approach   49
    Learning Part to Whole   50
    Meaning in the Text   51
    Standardized Assessment   51
Response-Centered Approach   52
    Learning Whole to Part   52
    Meaning Transacted between the Reader and the Text   54
    Authentic Assessment   54
Two Ways to Teach with Literature   55
    A Text-Centered Lesson from a "Literary" Basal Reader   55
    A Literature Group Forms in a Response-Centered Classroom   57
    Comparison of Text-Centered and Response-Centered Classrooms   59
Integrated, Literature-Based Teaching   60
    Read   61
    Respond   62
    Ripple   66
Literature and Learning English as a Second Language   70
    Second-Language Literacy   71
    Honoring Students' Voices   72
Things to Think About   74
Things to Do   74
Further Reading   75
References   76

PART 2   Case Studies of Children   79

CHAPTER 4   The Native English Speaker: Case Study of Anne   81
Meet Anne   81
Background and Home Influences   82
Language Development: Native English Speaker   83
Anne as a Student   83
Anne's Response Process Style: Challenges the Text   88

Things to Think About   91
Things to Do   91
Further Reading   92
Reference   92

CHAPTER 5   The English Learner: Case Study of Juan   93
Meet Juan   93
Background and Home Influences   94
Language Development: English as a Second Language   95
Juan as a Student   96
Juan's Response Process Style: Makes Personal Connections   100
Things to Think About   105
Things to Do   106
Further Reading   107
Reference   107

CHAPTER 6   The Bilingual English/Spanish Speaker: Case Study
                     of Eduardo   109
Meet Eduardo   109
Background and Home Influences   110
Language Development: Fluent Bilingual in English and Spanish   111
Eduardo as a Student   111
Eduardo's Response Process Style: Tells His Own Stories   116
Things to Think About   120
Things to Do   121
Further Reading   121
Reference   121

PART 3   Literature and Language Crossroads in a Bilingual Classroom   123

CHAPTER 7   Reader-Response in a Bilingual Classroom   125
Description of the Site   127
A Morning in Paul's Class   128
   Classroom Setup   128
   Whole-Group Instruction, Individual Space, and Small-Group
   Work   129
   Planning for the Next Day: Responding to Needs,
   Solving Problems   143
Conclusion: Authors, Artists, and Explorers   146
Things to Think About   149
Things to Do   149
Further Reading   149
References   150

CHAPTER 8   Components of Response-Centered Instruction   151
Preparation and Planning for the Literature Cycle   154
   Language and Literacy Development Options   155
   Language and Literacy Sources   158

Materials and Tools for a Literature Cycle   158
The Literature Cycle   162
    Choosing and Using Literature   162
    Forming Literature-Response Groups   164
    Conducting a Response Forum   168
    Conducting Subsequent Response Forums   178
    Putting on the Group Presentation   181
Conclusion   187
Things to Think About   188
Things to Do   188
Further Reading   188
References   189

Word Processing and Authoring Tools Software   191

Index   195

Literature and Language Theory into Practice

The three chapters in this section of the book present a literature-based, response-centered approach to language development in the elementary classroom, especially as it applies to culturally and linguistically diverse students.

Chapter 1 sets the stage with an introduction to the authors, an explanation of how they came to collaborate together, and a very telling story about a third-grade bilingual student named Javier and a turnip.

Chapter 2 maps out the crossroads of reader-response theory and second-language acquisition theory as a foundation for practice. Because books on second-language education do not usually address teaching with literature, we see great benefit in joining ideas from these two fields as they pertain to language and literacy development for culturally and linguistically diverse students. We discuss these ideas in the context of current social constructivist approaches to teaching.

Chapter 3 brings ideas about second-language education into the picture of student- and response-centered instruction and provides a model for integrated, literature-based teaching that supports language and literacy development for students learning English as a first or second language.

CHAPTER ONE

The Story of Javier and the Turnip

Because this book has grown out of our five-year ongoing conversation about teaching with literature and language and literacy development, we think we should introduce ourselves to you, explain how our conversation started, how we have kept it going, and how we came to collaborate on this book. Although we have written the book together, you will hear our separate voices in three ways. First, we wrote separate chapters: Carole wrote Chapters 1 through 6; Paul wrote 7 and 8. Second, some of the book is written as conversation between us. Third, we make comments throughout that begin with a special heading: *A Thought from Carole* or *A Thought from Paul*. In this way, the book reflects the conversational character of our five-year ongoing collaboration on research and writing about teaching with literature and language and literacy development, which began one day about a third-grade boy named Javier and a turnip.

MEET THE AUTHORS

Carole Cox

Carole is a former elementary teacher, now a professor at California State University, Long Beach (CSULB). She teaches university classes in language arts and reading methods for preservice teachers earning the Cross-Cultural Language and Academic Development (CLAD) California elementary credential, which provides specialized study in second-language acquisition for teaching in culturally and linguistically diverse classrooms.

Carole's research focuses on the development of children's responses to literature from a reader-response perspective—specifically, Louise Rosenblatt's transac-

3

tional model of the reading process (1938/1983). She began looking at children's responses to film (Cox, Beach, & Many, 1989) and later film and literature with Joyce Many (Cox & Many, 1989a, 1989b) when she was a professor at Louisiana State University in Baton Rouge. She and Joyce collaborated on the edited book of research *Reader Stance and Literary Understanding* (Many & Cox, 1992), and Joyce has described this work and her own (Many, 1994), grounded in Rosenblatt's theory in the newest edition of *Theoretical Models and Processes of Reading* (Ruddell, Ruddell, & Singer, 1994).

Carole is now in the seventh year of a longitudinal study of the development of children's responses to literature. She began looking at the responses and reading of a group of 57 kindergarten students in 1989 (Cox, 1994) in Long Beach. They are now in sixth grade, and she is still collecting data on fifteen. Three of them are the subjects of the case studies you will read in Chapters 4, 5, and 6.

When these students were in third grade, Carole met Paul, began spending time in his bilingual Spanish/English classroom, and started reading to his third graders as well. She is still collecting data on seven of these students. You will read about them in Chapters 1, 2, 3, 7, and 8.

Paul Boyd-Batstone

Paul is an experienced Spanish/English bilingual teacher who has worked as a mentor teacher and training specialist at the Center for Language-Minority Education and Research at California State University, Long Beach, under the direction of Dr. J. D. Ramirez. Paul is in the doctoral program at the Claremont Graduate School's Center for Educational Studies and will soon start gathering data for his dissertation in his own classroom.

Paul has been a frequent presenter at conferences on second-language acquisition and teaching in a bilingual classroom (e.g., California Mentor Teacher Conference) and has written about his experiences (Boyd-Batstone, 1996); and he and Carole have presented together on teaching with literature and language and literacy development at conferences of the National Council of Teachers of English, International Reading Association, and Teachers of English to Speakers of Other Languages.

Paul was named 1993 Bilingual Teacher of the Year for the Los Angeles County Office of Education. He is also a songwriter and musician.

The Authors Meet

One reviewer of an earlier draft of this book said, "I would like to hear the voices of Carole and Paul speaking together and speaking out together more often in the text. I believe that readers might like to know more about how they came to collaborate and to be able to do so for so long, as well as how they went about writing this text together."

A Thought from Carole   In 1991, I was writing a reading methods textbook called *Teaching Reading with Children's Literature* with Jim Zarrillo (Cox & Zarrillo, 1993). I was up to the chapter on teaching reading in culturally and linguistically diverse classrooms and was looking for a teacher of language-minority students who took a literature-based and student-centered approach to write about. This was at the same time that all teacher education programs in California were undergoing revision to meet the new CLAD guidelines, and we held a meeting at California State University, Long Beach, with experienced teachers in the field working with language-minority students.

After I heard Paul comment on what was happening in education with whole language, I thought he might be the teacher I wanted to write about. He seemed very cautious when I asked him, but I was very determined. Meanwhile, I talked with Ron Reese, head of the bilingual program in the Long Beach Unified School District, about Paul. He was an unabashed fan of Paul and highly recommended that I visit his classroom. I wanted to see firsthand how a bilingual teacher would use literature and perhaps apply some of the big ideas driving whole language in his classroom.

I knew when I walked into his room that it was the right place to be to write about a student-centered classroom. I just hoped he wouldn't mind me hanging out there awhile to get enough material to write about what he was doing in a meaningful way for other teachers. I tried to be quiet and not get in the way. I also was really interested to see how he would use literature in his bilingual third-grade class.

A Thought from Paul	I first met Carole in 1991 at a meeting I was invited to at California State University, Long Beach. A group of experienced teachers were asked to speak to the teacher education faculty about what new teachers needed to know to be successful in the public schools. We spoke about teaching. Much of it centered on the efforts to meet the needs of language-minority children.

I had worked in various capacities in the Long Beach Unified School District, including being a Spanish/English bilingual teacher at the primary grades, a bilingual/English as a second-language (ESL) specialist, a Title VII grant coordinator for a Cambodian bilingual program, and a third-grade bilingual teacher at the time of the meeting with the faculty at CSULB. While teaching, I had grown to set aside the teacher's guide with language arts instruction. I had become disenchanted with mechanistic approaches to developing literacy and found answers to the challenge of teaching with the writings of Stephen Krashen, Jim Cummins, and Ken and Yetta Goodman.

I remember one professor asking the teachers about how the whole-language movement was being received by classroom teachers. I responded by saying that I thought whole language had set everybody on his or her ear and that it appeared to me that few people understood what Ken and Yetta Goodman advocated as a central tenet: that language instruction begins with the child. It was apparent to me that many people labeled techniques as "whole language" that were no more than kinds of global ways of dealing with print.

At the end of the session, Carole introduced herself and asked whether she could observe my classroom. I had the sinking feeling of someone who had been shooting off at the mouth and then had to perform. I inquired what she was studying, and she invited me to her office and offered me a copy of her text (*Teaching Language Arts*, now in second edition, 1996), some articles, and another book that she had coedited on reader-response (Many & Cox, 1992).

At that point, I had never even heard of reader-response theory. Whole language at that time was providing the most helpful way to understand developing literacy, but it did not address differing models of teaching with children's literature. I told Carole I would look over her writing and get back to her about coming to my classroom.

During the following week, I looked over the materials Carole had provided me. I was impressed to read such a comprehensive treatment of language development in theory and practice. I was surprised at how far ahead of the current thinking about literacy Carole's work was. That's when I became very nervous, wondering what this professor could actually gain by observing in my classroom. I was afraid to call her back, but Carole took the initiative to call me and set up a time to come to my classroom.

On the day of the first observation, I had no idea that our collaboration would lead to writing a book together. All I was worried about at the time was that my students would embarrass me in front of this college professor. I wanted everything to go smoothly so that I would look like a competent bilingual teacher. Some of my students, however, had other ideas about what was going to happen in the classroom that day. Their responses to the story we were reading about a rabbit and a turnip initially set me on my ear but ultimately generated a major shift in my thinking about developing language and literacy with children's literature.

A FIRST VISIT TO SEÑOR B.-B.'S THIRD-GRADE CLASS

An Overview of a Bilingual Classroom

This description of Señor B.-B.'s class in June 1991 is taken from Carole's field notes of her first visit there. (Paul asked his students to call him Señor or Mr. B.-B. after he became tired of the students innocently referring to him as Mr. Boys' Bathroom.) She describes the room environment, daily schedule, mathematics/content areas, and language arts/reading instruction.

Room environment

Paul's classroom at Edison Elementary School in Long Beach is in the older part of the building, Art Deco circa 1930s. It's one of those bigger, high-ceilinged rooms with many coats of beige paint. It's survived many children as well as earthquakes.

The first thing I noticed was a sheet of chart paper (see Figure 1.1) with a Literature Plan on it hanging on a clothesline. It was a cluster with "Literature Plan" in the middle, surrounded by three satellites: "Art Project," "Creative Ideas" (another story, song, poem, Big Book, computer book), and "Writing Analysis" (1, 2, 3).

A Thought from Carole

I liked the child-centered buzz in Paul's class right away. I was excited to see a plan for teaching with literature that could incorporate students' ideas and responses as creative ideas and art projects, rather than simply follow the teacher's guide for the reading series used in the district. I'll admit to wondering about the label "Writing Analysis 1, 2, and 3." Did it mean that the students would only write about three predetermined topics (e.g., the literary elements such as setting, plot, and characters) or about the order of the events in the story? Such analysis is a common practice in writing about literature. It does, however, reflect a traditional and text-centered view of teaching with literature. My acknowledged bias for a reader-response approach is that students first be given the opportunity to reflect and talk or write about what they were thinking during reading. I was interested to see what would happen when Paul's students wrote about literature, what kind of approach he would take.

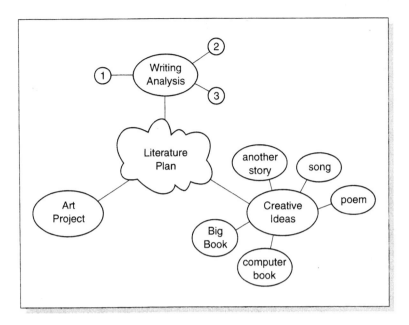

FIGURE 1.1 A literature plan

Paul listens to José on the first day that Carole visited his student-centered classroom. Notice Paul's original Literature Plan on the right.

The walls of the room are covered with student work, a Diego Rivera poster and pictures of Mexico, a calendar, the alphabet in cursive, and school memos. Songs that Paul's students have written are on large sheets of chart paper above two chalkboards where they can be easily seen and read by everyone for sing-alongs.

On one side of the room is a vintage computer, the Literature Plan display, and Paul's chair in front of a chalkboard next to a plastic rolling cart with supplies. His guitar leans next to the chair. Stacks of magazines (e.g., *National Geographic*) and catalogs are on the floor, and paperback books in Spanish and English line the chalk tray: *Ramona la Chince* by Beverly Cleary, *Sideways Stories from Wayside School* by Louis Sachar, and *Las Telaraña de Carlota* by E. B. White. A table in front of his desk in the corner is home to In and Out boxes full of interactive journals. Under the table are plastic tubs with each child's literature folder.

A clothesline strung in front of the window wall holds various Literature Plans in use. Papier-mâché models of the planets hang in front of a mural of the solar system on the same long wall. Models of volcanoes sit on the floor nearby in front of a volcano mural.

On the third wall are a sink, a cloak room, another museum-quality PC, and student writing taped to a supply cupboard with the title "Escritura Excelente." On the last long wall in front of the room are bookshelves, a copy of a Frida Kahlo self-portrait by the class artist Gustavo, a long chalkboard, and a wooden clothes drying rack with Big Books the class has made of interviews they have conducted with class visitors. The one prominently displayed is of Bubba, Paul's dog.

Daily schedule

The following list is a schedule of daily events:

8:40–9:40	Mathematics/Content Areas in Spanish
9:40–10:50	Language Arts in Spanish/English
Recess	
	Back-to-Back Reading in Spanish/English
11:00–12:00	Half of the class (other half on playground)
Lunch	
12:40–1:50	Other half of the class (others on playground)
Recess	
2:00–3:00	Mathematics/Content Areas in Spanish

Mathematics/content area instruction (Spanish)

A set of mathematics books rests on a shelf, with an In/Out box for mathematics homework and classwork on top of it. Above it on the chalkboard, Paul has written an assignment of page numbers and problems and a special "Problem of the Week: Conduct an Opinion Survey on 'What is your favorite pet?'" Directions for conducting this survey are in a folder on the shelf below the chalkboard.

The students are using textbooks, which are in Spanish (maps in the social studies text are in English), and some of the same texts in English that could be used, depending on the language level of the student. Paul also uses a hands-on inquiry approach to science and social studies. Students are working on papier-mâché models of the planets, a mural of the solar system, and reports, written in Spanish, about a planet. They are also working in groups building models of types of volcanoes. One child reports to me that the volcanoes will "actually work." The students are also mapping locations of the volcano types in three parts of the world: Mexico, Hawaii, and the continental United States. Near the area where they are working on the models, mural, map, and reports is a rolling cart with books on space and volcanoes, primarily in Spanish and Spanish/English. The cart also has references: maps, an atlas, and encyclopedia volumes.

For more on mathematics/content area learning in Paul's class, see the Box 3.1 in chapter 3, "Integrating Content Instruction with Literature-based Instruction: Mathematics, Social Studies, Science."

Language arts/reading instruction (English/Spanish)

Paul organizes the students for a seventy-minute language arts period from 9:40 to 10:50, centered around literature groups. After that is a school-adopted schedule of back-to-back reading—half the class at a time while the other half is on the playground—continuing the literature groups. He gives directions to all in Spanish as they begin an *escritura rapida*/quick write about their stories. These are adaptations of children's books in a bilingual Spanish/English basal reader, newly dubbed "literary readers." They brainstorm prompts for these (in parentheses below).

1. *Katy No Pocket*   (mechanics)
2. *Ratona Osa*   (foxes)
3. *Poinsettia and Her Family*   (about her house)
4. *The Rabbit and the Turnip*   (turnips)
5. *A Special Trade*   (grandparents)

After five minutes of writing, they read to a partner. A volunteer from each table reads to the whole class. The quick writes are written and read in Spanish.

Paul then discusses the various Literature Plans with each group, moving from table to table as the groups get organized. Some are making a mural; others, a five-foot cobalt blue painted apron for *Katy No Pocket*, masks for a play, and puppets; others, writing a puppet play. They are all talking animatedly. Each student has a literature folder with work in progress handy.

Paul next meets with one of the groups: *Ratona Osa*. They are writing a puppet play. Paul has made a cluster around the title "Los Animales" on a sheet of chart paper. The students name all the characters in the story. Each character gets its own cluster. Around it, the students talk about what that character will say: an extended, intense discussion of who and how many characters and what they will say. The play is then cast, and the names of the students are written in each character's cluster. Then a discussion of puppet making takes place.

Paul moves from group to group, checking progress. Students are all over the room: writing scripts; making paper bag puppets, masks, stick puppets; helping each other; referring back to the story text and pictures to extend through their projects; doing "writing analysis." They are always talking and interacting with each other in both Spanish and English about stories, the art-making process, the writing process, and procedures. They are encouraging to each other. It is not a quiet room. It hums, not roars, with the sounds of students actively engaged in listening, talking, reading, writing, creating projects, and sharing ideas. Many are missing recess.

TEACHING WITH LITERATURE IN A BILINGUAL CLASS

Paul's basic approach to teaching with literature is to use these literature groups, Literature Plans, and a combination of self-directed student learning and conferences between himself and the groups. Paul schedules conferences with the groups according to the following plan, which covers the language arts block of time plus the two back-to-back reading periods.

	Time	M	T	W	Th	F
Whole Group	10:00	1	4	1	4	—
Half the Group	11:15	2	5	2	5	Free
Half the Group	1:15	3	6	3	6	Free

Although the conference I describe next followed the format he had been using, it is significant because things didn't go the way he had planned. And because they didn't, Paul and I started our ongoing five-year conversation about teaching with literature and language development.

A Literature Group Conference: *The Rabbit and the Turnip*

Paul held this conference with *The Rabbit and the Turnip* group in English. The story is a Russian folktale about a rabbit who finds a turnip in the snow and gives it to another hungry animal, who passes it on to another, and so on until it comes back to the rabbit, who shares it with the other animals. Copies of the literary readers were handed out.

The heading "Writing Analysis" was on the back of the Literature Plan chart for this group. Paul had divided the paper into three sections with the titles "The Setting," "The Problem," and "The Characters." He had already recorded the group's ideas about setting and characters in a cluster on the chart during other conferences. The setting cluster included "The rabbit lives in a house" and "There is snow in the mountains." The characters cluster included each character's name with a remark: Little Rabbit—"Little Rabbit went out to look for food. He found a turnip." Only the section on the problem remained.

Paul: We need to talk about the problem. Take a minute and talk with each other. What would you call the problem in the story?

One child starts to speak very softly, and Paul leans forward to listen. Another child says, "Talk like at recess." Paul laughs out loud.

Child: Little rabbit . . .
P: Help her out. What's the problem with the turnip?
C: Threw in the snow.
P: Why is that a problem? Let's think. The turnip was in the snow. What's the big problem?
C: He gave to the donkey.
P: Why?
C: Because . . .

(Paul writes on the chart while saying: "Little rabbit gave turnip to little donkey. Why?")

C: Because they don't have anything to eat.

(Paul writes this on the chart, too.)

P: Let's focus on eating.

(One child lights up and starts talking excitedly.)

C: Oh! The problem is they was cold.
C: They could put it in the microwave.
P: (Laughing). But do you think it was a problem because it was cold?
C: Yeah!
P: What time of year was it?
C: Navidad!

Paul writes on the chart "It was wintertime and Christmastime." Then he tells the group to go back and read page 248 in the story. He apparently wants them to understand that the problem was that it was winter and the animals were hungry. They read for a few minutes until one child speaks.

C: Oh. The rabbit ate the turnip.
P: How does he feel?
C: Happy.
P: Why?
C: The turnip was at his door again. It was a gift.
P: What happens at Christmastime?

(While Paul is trying to guide the students in the direction of identifying the problem found in the story itself, Javier takes a sudden detour by identifying the problem he's having with his personal reading of the story. The real problem for him is the lack of authenticity in the story.)

Javier: The turnip was white and not red.

Paul meets with *The Rabbit and the Turnip* literature group but has trouble getting the students to identify the problem in the story.

P: Is that a problem?

J: Yeah. No good. My Grandpa has a farm in Mexico and grows turnips and carrots and vegetables. That turnip's (in the story) no good.

P: OK! You know more than I do. Then the illustrator didn't draw the turnip right. You might want to write about the turnip and how it should be.

(Paul then summarizes what they've said, including Javier's response.)

P: (Writing on the chart) There are a few problems. The turnip's in the snow. The rabbit gave it to the donkey because there was nothing to eat. The turnip was at the door. The illustrator didn't draw it right.

(Paul continues the discussion, apparently still hoping to reach a consensus among the group about the problem in the story.)

P: Who was hungry in the story?

C: Little sheep.

C: Little donkey.

C: Little doe.

P: Everybody's hungry. Can we say that?

C: Yeah.

P: Everybody's hungry. It's Christmastime.

(They are close to a consensus, but Javier derails the discussion again by challenging the text.)

J: Maybe the animals couldn't find anything because of the snow. But where did he find the turnip if there's snow all over?

P: This is a toughie. Talk it over and see if we can figure out. Javier, you said something: "The rabbit ate and the others didn't. That's not fair."

C: They're poor and don't have enough to eat.

P: OK. You're saying, "Everybody's hungry."

C: Not enough turnips to go around, for the animals.

(Javier jumps the rails again and instead of just stating the problem, he offers a solution and rewrite of the story.)

J: They could have cut the turnip in half so more people could have it!

P: What a good solution. Let's do a quick summary and start the play.

(Paul reads and points to what he's written about the problem on the chart.)

P: You need to write about the problem later on today and tomorrow. Let's talk about masks.

(Now they plan a play of the story, and Paul shows them how they might make masks.)

Meet Javier wearing his donkey mask for a play of *The Rabbit and the Turnip* in Paul's class.

I honestly wondered why Paul, an obviously student-centered teacher, stayed focused on the idea of "the problem" in the story as long as he did. He seemed delighted when Javier brought his personal interpretation of the story to bear and triggered the richest part of the discussion up to that point. Paul made a final attempt, however, to focus the students' attention to the problem at the same time he celebrated the richness and honesty of Javier's response drawing on his personal experience with turnips.

I didn't know Paul well enough to come right out and ask him why he focused on the story problem rather than use open questions and prompts—"What did you think of the story?" or, "Tell about any similar experiences you've had," for example—and I liked what I saw so much in his classroom that I didn't want to seem to be critical and perhaps unwelcome later. I didn't have to wait long, however, for the issue of The Problem of the Story versus The Problem Javier Was Having With the Story to come up: only until the lunch bell, when we started talking, to be exact.

During lunch, we began to talk about what happened in *The Rabbit and the Turnip* group and subsequently started a conversation we are still having about what's important in teaching with literature and language and literacy development.

A First Conversation Between Carole and Paul

This is not actually our first conversation, but one we just had about it. We tried to re-create it, and it didn't work. We do remember it as important and as the beginning of our collaboration.

Carole: I remember you seemed frustrated by the way the conference went, and I was hoping you weren't irritated because I was there and we started talking about what happened. It seemed to me that the problem was that those students just weren't going to talk about what you wanted them to, and I wondered why you persisted.

Paul: I was frustrated with my students and embarrassed at first because they refused to comply with my inquiry about the problem of the story. Having sat in an in-service training about the use of literary readers that stressed the importance of story grammar, I thought that I was engaging the students in a significant exploration of the story. Teaching the problem of the story made sense to me. There was a nice logical progression in story grammar. We would establish the setting first, then the characters, order the events of the story, identify the problem, and finish with the solution. I could have each literature group work through those elements and feel that I was covering the ground of the literature. It all fit on paper and gave me a kind of handle on that elusive subject of language arts. Nevertheless, what fits on paper does not always match the reality of my students. What my students helped demonstrate was that the meaningful aspects of the story were far more personal than the abstractions of story structure or analysis.

Carole: Like Javier and the turnip?

Paul: With the turnip story, the problem was so obvious that it was almost stupid to have a conversation about it. In fact, I remember you and I concurred that it was a stupid story. But I was going to be the responsible teacher and plow through it.

Carole: Would you have stayed with it as long as you did if I hadn't been there? I sensed a tension, and it didn't fit with what I'd seen of your teaching style up to that point.

Paul: I was very aware of being observed by a professor. But I would probably have come back to it the next day. Javier has been a really difficult child to work with. And today he was really sabotaging the group. Every time I asked what the problem was, he'd start giggling or kicking another student or generally disrupting the discussion.

Carole: Until he got to express his own problem with the story.

Paul: I remember asking you what you would have done.

Carole: I said something about just asking an open question instead of focusing on "the problem." You got the best response from anybody—and it turned out to be Javier, the behavior problem—when he ignored what you were really asking for—the problem in the story—and started talking about the problem he was having with the story. An authentic response.

Paul: The discussion became engaging when I got fed up with the structure piece and threw it back on the students. When I finally let Javier tell me the problem with the whole story in general, he finally got to bring his grandfather into the story and tell his own story about the turnip farm in Mexico. What's most important here? Is it that he could identify that everybody was starving, or that he began to see a relationship between himself and the story, or that he had a valid critique of this story—the misrepresentation of turnips in it. Maybe he knew something that the author didn't.

Carole: Did you have similar struggles with other aspects of story structure?

Paul: Yes. The most difficult was the whole idea of the events in the story. Rarely did the students ever talk about the order. It was always a battle getting past what happened first, second, next. Sometimes just dealing with characters of story is a struggle. They don't want to talk about all of them.

Carole: I remember feeling that we had a meaningful exchange going here and asking you whether you had ever read any reader-response theory. Like Louise Rosenblatt's transactional theory—the idea that meaning isn't found in the text alone or in the reader, but is a transaction between the reader and the text.

Paul: When you first started talking about it, I didn't have a clue to what you meant. The meaning isn't found in the text? Now it's so obvious having this thing hanging in front of your face—a student like Javier telling about his grandfather. At the time, the most important piece seemed to be to plow through this story so that I covered all my bases: the story elements. Seems so obvious now, but not at the time. I do remember you waving your hand around and talking about a "to and fro" between the reader and the text.

Carole: I sensed you were intrigued. It certainly resonated with what had happened that day. I also thought "OK, I know something he doesn't. I'll use this opportunity to ask about second-language acquisition and education." I was feeling undereducated about bilingual education at this time, and because we were revising our program to more fully address the needs of teachers of language-minority students, I thought I might as well get it from the horse's mouth. This is obviously a great teacher who also happens to be a bilingual teacher and is wrestling with what to do about literature, something I know about. Maybe we each had something to offer the other. I was eager to learn firsthand about bilingual education, to spend more time in this room, and thinking that I didn't know nearly as much as I should about what went on in a bilingual classroom.

Paul: Yes, I remember being embarrassed because I hadn't heard of Rosenblatt, so I said, "Oh yes, Rosencrantz and Guildenstern." You get the joke?

Carole: I get it, Paul.

CHANGING THINKING ABOUT TEACHING WITH LITERATURE

After lunch, a child from *The Rabbit and the Turnip* group came up to Paul with his paper about the problem with *The Rabbit and the Turnip* and said "he didn't get it." Paul said, "Aha," and shared with the child that we'd been talking about it being a dumb story and said, "Why don't you write a better story?"

A New Literature Plan

The next time I visited Paul's class, he was trying something new for his Literature Plan chart. He did not section off the side of the chart where he recorded the students' ideas about a story into separate parts for character, events, setting, and problem.

He said they had so much to say when he began by doing everything at once, and he simultaneously encouraged them to talk about anything and everything. Evidently it was working better. It cut down conference time if they did it all at the same time. He also began by just asking them to "talk about the story," rather than about the conventions of literature. Paul's expression is "Talk to me." And then he waits for the ideas and language to emerge.

From the ideas that Paul recorded on the chart, the group members did four pieces of writing on self-selected topics generated during their open discussions of literature (e.g., Javier writing about life on a turnip farm) instead of three pieces of "writing analysis" based on the literary elements (e.g., the problem).

Curious George *Literature Plan*

Gustavo took over leading the *Curious George* discussion and recording their responses because Paul was needed by another group. Because the approach was not a teacher-directed, text-centered one in which Paul (the teacher) would be necessary because he knew what the answers were (e.g., What is the problem in the story?), this was possible. Now Paul's approach was to generate and record the students' ideas about the story, what they were thinking about while reading, and how it related to their own ideas and life experiences. Gustavo could now guide the

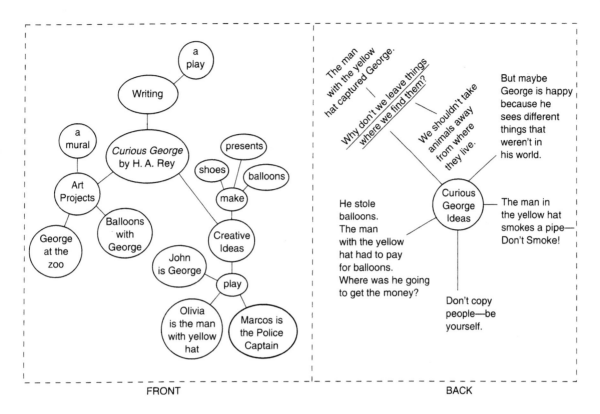

FRONT   BACK

FIGURE 1.2 *Curious George* literature plan

group because his ideas were as important as the teacher's (or those in the teacher's guide). See Figure 1.2.

More conversations between Carole and Paul

Before I left the first day, I told Paul I'd bring him a copy of Louise Rosenblatt's first book, *Literature as Personal Exploration* (1938/1983). I also took this opportunity to ask him what he'd recommend as reading in the field of second-language education. He gave me his copy of a book published by the California State Department of Education, *Schooling and Language-Minority Children: A Theoretical Framework* (1981). He asked me whether I'd read *What's Whole in Whole Language* by Ken Goodman (1986), and I said yes.

After this, Paul and I really began to explore the crossroads between reader-response theory and teaching with literature, and theories of second-language acquisition and education in our conversations. I continued to observe, take notes, and participate in his classroom. And, during lunch periods, we talked a lot about what it all meant.

Although we each came from a different experiential background and theoretical orientation, we found that reader-response theory provided a common ground and vocabulary for talking about children's responses to literature and life, teaching with literature, and language and literacy development. Paul showed me obvious connections among key ideas of reader-response and second-language acquisition theories and how he would apply them in his literature-based teaching.

The common interest we shared was a drive to understand more about the importance of children's voices in the classroom. We never seem to tire of talking about how it plays out in children's language and literacy development. We listen for their voices through response to literature and film, through drama and dance and Shakespeare that Carole does with children, through songs and writing that Paul does in his bilingual classroom. We hear it in informal conversations or chance remarks or the serendipitous metaphor spoken by a child that can become a central focus in learning to speak a second language, to write in two, or to become the raw material for a song or poem or drama, or simply an image that sustains thought and talk beyond a teacher's expectations. It compels us both.

All this talking has led to two consequences. One is that both of our spouses have put time limits on our telephone conversations. The other is that we figured we might as well write a book exploring the crossroads of reader-response theory and language and literacy development. It would probably take less time than all our conversations.

That hasn't been true, but through our conversations and writing, we have gained a deeper and richer understanding of processes that will always elude total understanding. But isn't that what makes them so intriguing in the first place? This book, then, is our effort to talk with each other, as well as with other teachers, about mapping the crossroads of literary understanding and teaching with literature, and language acquisition and second-language education.

Two caveats. First, this book is not intended to be a comprehensive treatment of all theories of second-language acquisition, ESL or bilingual methodology, reader-response theory, or methods of teaching with literature. Our discussion has always focused on the application of Rosenblatt's transactional theory to teaching with literature—in this case, Paul's third-grade bilingual Spanish/English classroom. Furthermore, we see oral language development as a naturally occurring by-product of student- and response-centered literature-based teaching across the curriculum, in combination with related literacy experience. It appears quite seamless to us, so we have not broken the discussion into separate parts for listening, speaking, reading, writing, and content area instruction. We see them as an integrally related whole.

Second, we live in Long Beach in Los Angeles County, where the largest number of language-minority students are native Spanish speakers. Paul has always been a teacher in a bilingual Spanish/English classroom, and classroom descriptions in this book reflect this. Of the three case studies of children that Carole writes about from her research, one child is an English-only speaker, and the other two are bilingual Spanish/English.

Keep in mind, however, that reader-response and second-language acquisition theories have been broadly applied across cultural and linguistic groups and in the multilanguage classroom where the teacher only speaks English but uses approaches that foster English language and literacy development. To address the needs of (1)

English-only teachers of language-minority students and (2) content area instruction, Paul has provided ideas in special boxed sections of Chapters 3, 7 and 8.

What Happened to Javier and the Turnip?

What Paul did with Javier's response to the story *The Rabbit and the Turnip* reflects his orientation as a student-centered teacher, but clearly applied to teaching with literature. After his students just "didn't get" what they were supposed to say in response to the question "What's the problem in the story?" and after our conversation about what should be the focus of a literature discussion, Paul did what he did in every other aspect of his teaching: He recognized and validated Javier's challenging the text concerning turnips: "The turnip was white and not red. No good. My Grandpa has a farm in Mexico and grows turnips and carrots and vegetables. That turnip's no good" and, "Maybe the animals couldn't find anything because of the snow. But where did he find the turnip if there's snow all over?"

Paul argues that the challenge for the educator of language-minority students for purposes of learning to speak English, maintaining their native language, becoming literate in both, and succeeding academically is to create the environment that invites students like Javier to share their lives and knowledge in the classroom. He points out the parallel between reader-response theory and second-language education. Learning becomes a two-way undertaking when transactional instruction happens in the classroom. Listening to students as they respond to a text becomes the first act of instruction.

Paul encouraged Javier to share more about turnips and his grandfather with the group. Javier brought a pile of photographs of his family's ranch in Mexico, showing him riding a mule with his brother, working the land, and harvesting turnips. Paul helped him make a display of the ranch pictures and write about life on their turnip ranch.

In this instance, Paul made a clear shift from a text-based approach of asking the students to focus on the story to a reader-response approach to teaching with literature by focusing on the student's personal experience of the story. He encouraged Javier to draw on his own life experiences as a rich environment for spoken language and literacy development. And a story became more than just a means to an end of gaining word knowledge, or even knowledge of the world, to the real purpose of literature as a means of self-knowledge.

THINGS TO THINK ABOUT

1. If you have not had experience teaching limited-English-proficient students, think about the beliefs you had about what might go on in a class in which students were learning English as a second language. How do they compare with the description of Paul's class in this chapter?

2. If you have had experience teaching limited-English-proficient students, compare your knowledge of these students with the description of Paul's class in this

chapter. How are they alike or different? What tentative conclusions can you draw from your comparison?

3. As you read the description of Paul's class and Carole's thoughts about them, what did you think about the way Paul taught and Carole's ideas?

4. What do you think is the most important thing to do when teaching with literature? How does your idea compare with Paul's or Carole's?

THINGS TO DO

1. Visit a bilingual classroom, especially during a time when the teacher is using literature and/or teaching language arts and reading. Observe and take notes on the following: room environment, daily schedule, mathematics/content areas, language arts/reading. Write up your observations, inserting your thoughts along the way prefaced with *A Thought from (your name)*.

2. Do the activity in #1 in another class and compare the two, especially with regard to teaching language and literacy and the role of the student and the teacher. If you are teaching, write up your own class and compare them with either your observation in another class or Paul's class.

3. Sketch a cluster for the Literature Plan you might use in your own class. It could be different from the one Paul used. For example, if I did a Literature Plan, it would definitely have a heading for drama/media. What might yours look like? What ideas about language and teaching with literature would it reflect?

4. Read the books that Carole and Paul exchanged to inform each other about their respective interests in reader-response theory—specifically, Louise Rosenblatt's transactional theory and second-language education, as well as the book they had both read on whole language:
   On reader response theory (transactional theory): Rosenblatt, L. M. (1983). *Literature as personal exploration*. New York: Modern Language Association. (Original work published 1938)
   On second-language education: California State Department of Education. (1981). *Schooling and language-minority children: A theoretical framework*. Los Angeles: Los Angeles State University.
   On whole language: Goodman, K. (1986). *What's whole in whole language*. Portsmouth, NH: Heinemann.
   Jot down your own ideas about these books, their possible application in the classroom, and compare your ideas with those of Carole and Paul in this book.

FURTHER READING

Freeman, D. E., & Freeman, Y. S. (1994). *Between worlds: Access to second-language acquisition*. Portsmouth, NH: Heinemann.

Illustrated with many examples of student work, this book discusses theory in the context of classroom practice with strategies that support second-language learners. It addresses the issue of cultural and social contexts of second-language learning and the importance of tapping into students' life experiences and working with students' families and the community.

Gallas, K. (1994). *The languages of learning: How children talk, write, dance, draw, and sing their understanding of the world.* New York: Teachers College Press.

Although this book is not focused specifically on learning English as a second language, Paul and I both like this richly descriptive case study of the author's experience as a teacher/researcher in her own class. It focuses on the power of stories and narrative and the individual voices of students in a student- and response-centered classroom.

Whitmore, K., & Crowell, C. (1994). *Inventing a classroom.* York, ME: Stenhouse.

This is a description of a third-grade Spanish/English bilingual classroom with a whole-language approach. The format is similar to the format in this book because you hear the voices of the two authors—a researcher (Whitmore) and a classroom teacher (Crowell), each of which presents a personal perspective on what is happening in the classroom. The book challenges the notion that teaching second-language learners is somehow problematic or that a great deal of direct instruction of skills or a narrow curriculum is required.

REFERENCES

Boyd-Batstone, P. (1996). Learning to walk together in a third-grade bilingual classroom: From transmission to transactional instruction with literature. In N. Karolides (Ed.), *Reader response in elementary classrooms: Quest and discovery* (pp. 46–53). Hillsdale, NJ: Erlbaum.

California State Department of Education. (1981). *Schooling and language-minority children: A theoretical framework.* Los Angeles: California State University.

Cox, C. (1994, April). *Young children's responses to literature: A longitudinal study.* Paper presented at the annual meeting of the American Educational Research Association, New Orleans.

Cox, C. (1996). *Teaching language arts: A student- and response-centered approach* (2nd ed.). Needham Heights, MA: Allyn & Bacon.

Cox, C., Beach, R., & Many, J. E. (1989). Response to film art: Commonalities within a community of young viewers. *Arts and Learning Research Journal, 6,* 61–68.

Cox, C., & Many, J. E. (1989a). Personal understanding from film and literature: Different paths reaching comparable heights. *Arts and Learning Research Journal, 7,* 29–37.

Cox, C., & Many, J. E. (1989b). Worlds of possibilities in response to literature, film, and life. *Language Arts, 66*(3), 287–294.

Cox, C., & Zarrillo, J. (1993). *Teaching reading with children's literature?* Upper Saddle River, NJ: Merrill/Prentice Hall.

Goodman, K. (1986). *What's whole in whole language?* Portsmouth, NH: Heinemann.

Many, J. E. (1994). The effect of reader stance on students' personal understanding of literature. In R. B. Ruddell, M. R. Ruddell, & H. Singer (Eds.), *Theoretical models and processes of reading* (4th ed., pp. 653–667). Newark, DE: International Reading Association.

Many, J. E., & Cox, C. (Eds.). (1992). *Reader stance and literary understanding: Exploring the theories, research, and practice.* Norwood, NJ: Ablex.

Rosenblatt, L. M. (1983). *Literature as personal exploration.* New York: Modern Language Association. (Original work published 1938)

Ruddell, R. B., Ruddell, M. R., & Singer, H. (Eds.). (1994). *Theoretical models and processes of reading* (4th ed.). Newark, DE: International Reading Association.

CHAPTER TWO

Mapping the Crossroads of Reader-Response and Second Language

Here are some ideas Paul and I talked about as we began to explore the crossroads of reader-response theory and teaching with literature and second-language acquisition and education. These ideas lay a foundation for the rest of the book. This is not intended to be a comprehensive discussion of reader-response or second-language acquisition theories. When Paul and I began our conversation, I was intensely interested in doing research on the application of Louise Rosenblatt's transactional theory to teaching with literature. Paul had been primarily influenced by the work of James Cummins and Stephen Krashen as they applied to teaching in a bilingual classroom, as well as the field of whole language. For a more complete discussion of other ideas in each of these fields, see the reference list at the end of this chapter.

READER-RESPONSE THEORY

All literary critics hope to explain how people make meaning when they read literature. Not all critics focus on the same aspects of the reading event, however. Although literary criticism may seem far removed from the classroom, it has, in fact, greatly influenced how literature has been taught and continues to do so. Knowledge of these theories may not be explicit in teachers' minds, but often the theories guide instruction implicitly if they were reflected in the way teachers were taught literature. With something as significant and also ephemeral as literature, it's important that teachers know not only what to do but also why they are doing it. Or there may be nothing more practical than a good theory.

The Reader or the Text?

Reader-response criticism emerged during the twentieth century with a new emphasis on the reader, in contrast with the emphasis in the nineteenth and early twentieth centuries on biographical and historical background and in the late 1930s and 1940s of the "New Criticism" on the text itself.

The Text

The New Criticism changed literary scholarship when a new group of critics shifted the focus of attention to the works themselves, especially the use of figurative language and metaphor (Brooks & Warren, 1938; Wellek & Warren, 1949). This school of literary criticism reflected a positivistic epistemology, which sought to create "an objective, empirical and systematic foundation for knowledge . . . [where the] . . . ideal pursued is knowledge in the form of a mathematically formulated universal science" (Held, 1980, p. 164). Applied to literature, this meant that the New Critics sought to impose a universal system of structure upon a text. This shift in epistemological and literary theory influenced the way literature was taught in college and subsequently in K–12 reading and literature instruction.

The New Critics rejected the idea that the author's intention ("the intentional fallacy") or the reader's response ("the affective fallacy") had much bearing on the meaning of a text. Instead, they maintained that meaning could be found within the text itself. The reader's subjective response was not important either. Most important was a careful analysis of the text's language (e.g., figurative language)—not just what it "said," but the way it was said and what it symbolized. A proper reading of a text was like a careful dissection of a frog in biology class. Reading literature was more like science than art although a literary work was viewed as a carefully constructed work of art that must be dissected and the parts carefully analyzed for the whole to be fully understood and appreciated. This view, incidentally, coincided with the heavy influence of behavioral psychology in education.

The Reader

The first reader-response theorists, I. A. Richards (1935) and Louise Rosenblatt (1938/1983), predated the New Critics, but their ideas did not influence instruction until a reaction to the strict formalism of the New Criticism in the late 1960s. Reader-response theorists argued the active role of the reader in the construction of meaning while reading. Because meaning is a creation of individual and unique readers, not everyone would agree on a single, "correct" meaning of a text.

Reader-Response Theories Influential in Education

Reader-response theory is not essentially new. Louise Rosenblatt's landmark first book, *Literature as Exploration*, was initially published in 1938. It did not gain an influence in education until the 1960s, well after the new critical orientation of the 1940s had predominated literature instruction in the United States. The most widely referred to reader-response theory in education is Louise Rosenblatt's transactional theory of the literary work (Clifford, 1991; Cox, 1996; Cox & Zarrillo, 1993; Farrell & Squire, 1990; Hungerford, Holland, & Ernst, 1993; Karolides, 1992, 1996; Probst, 1988). The transactional theory is a well-established piece of the whole-language movement (Goodman, 1992, 1994).

The Transactional Theory

In a recent explanation of her ideas, Rosenblatt (1994) begins by defining "the reader" for a new generation of educators. The definition is the same one she first wrote in her landmark book in 1938:

> Terms such as "the reader" are somewhat misleading, though convenient, fictions. There is no such thing as a generic reader or a generic literary work; there are in reality only the potential millions of individual readers of individual literary works . . . the reading of any work of literature is, of necessity, an individual and unique occurrence involving the mind and emotions of some particular reader. (Rosenblatt, 1938/1983, p. 1057)

Transacting with the text. The transactional theory focuses on the active role of the reader in creating meaning from a text, or literary work. She describes this creation of meaning as

> a complex, to-and-fro, self-correcting transaction between reader and verbal signs which continues until some final organization, more or less complete and coherent, is arrived at and thought of as corresponding to the text. The "meaning"—whether, e.g., poem, novel, play, scientific report, or legal brief—comes into being during the transaction. (1986, p. 123)

Rosenblatt describes this process as a "two-way transaction," a "live-circuit" between the reader and the text. She borrowed the term *transaction* from John Dewey (1938), who defined it as a reciprocal relationship among the parts in a single situation. This is in contrast with the term *interaction*, which involves two separate entities acting on one another.

Each reading event is unique, involving a particular reader, text, and context and occurring at a particular moment in time. Both the reader and the text are two aspects of a totally dynamic situation. A reader may read the same text at different times and under different circumstances or in a different mood, and the result would be a new and different meaning. Reader and text are not two separate entities, but rather are factors in a total situation. The reader activates and draws from a linguistic-experiential reservoir, paying selective attention to those physical, personal, social, and cultural factors that enter into the reading situation and that will eventually be organized and synthesized into "meaning." Rosenblatt uses William James's (1890) phrase for reading as a "choosing activity."

Reader stance. According to Rosenblatt (1978), although all reading occurs as experienced meaning, readers assume a stance, or focus their selective attention in different ways. *Stance* represents a reader's readiness to organize thinking about what is read according to a more efferent or more aesthetic framework. The reader's adoption of a stance, either conscious or unconscious, guides the "choosing activity" in the stream of consciousness. Any text can be read efferently or aesthetically, and readers move back and forth on a continuum from efferent to aesthetic, eventually settling on one predominant stance.

During a more efferent reading, the reader's focus is on the information he or she will take away from the text, or the more public aspects (e.g., reading the label on a bottle of prescription medicine to find the correct dosage). During a more aesthetic reading, the reader's focus is on the lived-through experience of the reading event, or the more private aspects (e.g., reading a novel and picturing yourself as one of the characters). A more efferent reading focuses on what is in the text; a more aesthetic reading focuses on the associations, feelings, attitudes, and ideas that the text arouses in the reader. The lived-through experience of the work during the aesthetic transaction constitutes the "literary work." Rosenblatt calls this the "evocation" and "the poem" (not to be confused with a poetic text). And evocation, she argues, should be the center of literature response and interpretation, and discussions and instruction, both during and after the reading event.

Most readings are a mix of both stances, and any text can be read more efferently or more aesthetically (e.g., reading the sports page to find out who won a baseball game and what the score was, or reading the same page and imagining yourself as a player in the game). Readers may adopt a different stance toward the same text at different times and different situations: reading *Romeo and Juliet* in high school or college to study for a test on it in English; or reading it for pleasure and savoring the beauty of the language; or perhaps reading it while in love, thinking about whom they love.

Rosenblatt maintains that, for most experiences with literature, "our primary responsibility is to encourage the aesthetic stance" (1982, p. 275). Yet a study of teachers who were self-described as making the shift from a basal reader to literature-based reading instruction showed that they were still using a more efferent, less aesthetic, teacher- and text-centered approach (Zarrillo & Cox, 1992).

Other reader-response theories

No unilateral view is held by all reader-response theorists. The importance of the text, as well as the reader, varies among reader-response theorists such as David Bleich, Norman Holland, Wolfgang Iser, James Britton, D. W. Harding, and Stanley Fish. Contemporary literary theorists have also focused on the importance of cultural and social influences. Feminist, Marxist, and African American and other ethnic critics draw on reader-response theory, as well as other perspectives, in describing literary understanding. For more on reader-response theories, see Richard Beach's *A Teacher's Introduction to Reader-Response Theories* (1993), in which he provides a historical overview and a discussion of individual theories that he groups according to the major emphasis of each one: textual, experiential, psychological, social, and cultural.

SECOND-LANGUAGE ACQUISITION THEORY

Like literary theory, second-language acquisition theories often present contrasting views of how both a first and a second language are learned and have had varying effects on second-language instruction. Historically, the development of theory and approaches to second-language instruction have included an emphasis on grammar-translation approaches in the nineteenth century; behaviorist approaches, such as the audiolingual method in the mid-twentieth century; Noam Chomsky's notion of innate language ability and a universal grammar; and communicative approaches that influence second-language education today, especially Stephen Krashen's monitor model and James Cummins's description of dimensions of language proficiency with regard to bilingual education (Crawford, 1993; Richards & Rodgers, 1986). This is not intended to be a comprehensive overview, but rather a description of the major ideas that have most influenced practice.

Grammar or Communication?

Viewed very broadly, approaches to learning a second language have ranged on a continuum from those that are predominantly grammar-based to those that are predominantly communicative-based.

Grammar

Grammar-based instruction has focused on accuracy in grammar usage. The goal of this type of instruction is to learn grammar or to produce grammatically correct sentences in a limited communicative context. This approach may seem familiar if you took a foreign language class in high school or college in which you used a textbook with sequential chapters on a language grammar system (e.g., present tense verbs, then past tense verbs; regular verb endings, then irregular verbs), did exercises at the end of the chapter in which you practiced these language forms, and were largely graded on written tests. You may have learned set dialogues with other students or the teacher using the form. Your teacher taught lessons on the forms, corrected the exercises, and graded the tests. You probably spent less time actually communicating with the teacher or other students in the language, and little of that time would have been spent on communicating things of interest to you. The focus of instruction was on the grammar of the language as content.

Different grammar-based methods of language instruction have emphasized different strategies. From the nineteenth century through the 1950s, the grammar-translation approach dominated. Rules of grammar were taught by translating a text—which aptly illustrated that rule—from the foreign language into the student's first language. Lists of words, and sentences unrelated by meaning but illustrating the rule, were also used. Instruction was in the first language, and communication in the language was not important.

With the advent of World War II and a need to learn languages quickly, the audiolingual method was used by the military and began to replace grammar-translation. It was related to the work of structural linguists, such as Bloomfield

(1933) and Fries (1945) in the 1930s and 1940s, who carefully listed and described the structure of languages. It also meshed well with behaviorism, the ruling learning theory of the period. This method used a sequence of oral patterned dialogues that were practiced and memorized through many repetitions to teach grammatical structures. Listening and speaking were emphasized over reading and writing, but still scant attention was paid to students' creative language production. A student's job was to repeat and memorize. Pronunciation was important and was often practiced with tapes and earphones in language laboratories. The direct, or Berlitz, method used more dialogue but still with a focus on a grammatical aspect of the language taught inductively in formal exchanges between the teacher and the student.

In the 1960s, cognitive methods focused on learning all the parts of a language, in order, from part to whole (e.g., letter sounds, then words, then phrases, then sentences) through structured lessons and drill of these subskills. By this time, the Chomskyan revolution in linguistics had occurred, replacing the predominance of structural linguistics. Noam Chomsky's (1957) theory of a transformational-generative grammar, which maintained that language had two levels—a deep and a surface structure—led to teachers leading students through sentence-recombining drills to understand grammar. These drills were used extensively by English teachers as well. Chomsky, however, did not suggest this use of his theory and, in fact, questioned it. His idea that humans had an innate cognitive ability to learn language was probably more influential in that it offered a direct challenge to behavioral psychology, the learning theory that predominated in schools when grammar-based methods were prevalent. Chomsky critiqued B. F. Skinner and behaviorism, maintaining that language was not learned through imitation and repetition because the ability of humans to produce sentences they had never heard before proved the creative nature of language production.

Support for his ideas came from psycholinguistic research that described the commonalities of children's natural speech development over time and across languages. Chomsky's theory of innateness prompted interest in psycholinguistic research in children's language development in the 1960s and 1970s, particularly regarding the stages and rate of acquiring language structures (Cazden, 1972; Chomsky, 1969; Menyuk, 1963; Strickland, 1962), and opened the field of second-language education to methods that used students' own ideas and language production, or communicative-based methods, rather than behavioristic grammar-based methods that relied on imitation, repetition, memorization, and drills of skills.

Communication

Communicative-based approaches currently used in many elementary classrooms apply methods relevant to the functional language needs of students who are learning to live in language environments different from those of their homes. The goal of this type of instruction is for students to be able to communicate messages in the language they are learning and to use it for meaningful purposes. Swain (1986) argues that the opportunity to engage in meaningful oral exchanges of "comprehensible output" in the classroom or community is an essential component of second-language acquisition. In conveying meaning when speaking, the speaker also learns the structure and form of the language.

Language forms will be learned, then, but the emphasis of instruction is on language as a medium of communication and on using language to learn, rather than as a subject to study. Teachers using this approach encourage students to initiate language events and to use language for functional and creative experiences and products. The teacher creates contexts in which this can occur. Much time is spent on students' ideas and interests as a focus of language and literacy experiences.

A focus on communication rather than on grammar in language teaching was supported by sociolinguistic theoretical positions and research in the 1970s and 1980s (Cook-Gumperz, 1979; Halliday, 1975; Lindfors, 1987; Tough, 1977; Wells, 1981), which argued for the importance of the social aspects of language learning, and in several cases criticized Chomsky for his lack of attention to it. Dell Hymes (1974) argued that being proficient means demonstrating *communicative competence:* knowing how to use a language for specific purposes in real-life situations; and Michael Halliday (1975) defined language as "'meaning potential,' that is, as sets of opinions, or alternatives, in meaning, that are available to the speaker-hearer" (p. 63).

Several communicative models of second-language education have evolved—for example, those of Breen and Candlin (1979), Widdowson (1978)—"use" (communication) versus "usage" (analysis), Wilkins's idea of a notional-functional syllabus (1976), and Krashen's (1981) monitor model. For more on comparative second-language acquisition theories, see Ellis's discussion (1986).

Second-Language Acquisition Theories Influential in Education

The work of Stephen Krashen (1981) and James Cummins (1981) bears special consideration in this discussion because of its influence on classroom practices. Much has already been written explaining and applying (Baker, 1993; Cooper, 1993; Faltis, 1993, Holt, 1993; Piper, 1993), as well as criticizing, these theories (Bowerman, 1982; Lieberman & Lieberman, 1990; McLaughlin, 1987; Maratsos, 1983). Following is a description of the key ideas, especially as they pertain to crossroads with reader-response theory and classroom practices, the focus of this book.

Here's a comparison of the major emphases of the two instructional approaches; it shows the contrast between traditional and predominantly grammar-based language learning and predominantly communicative-based language acquisition, especially Krashen's ideas about second-language instruction.

Language Learning (grammar-based)	Language Acquisition (communicative-based)
1. Focus is on language forms.	1. Focus is on meaningful instruction.
2. Success is based on mastery of language forms.	2. Success is based on using language to get things done.
3. Lessons are organized around types of language forms and structures: teacher-directed activities.	3. Lessons are organized around ideas and interests of students: student/response-centered activities.

4. Error correction is essential for mastery.

5. Learning is a conscious process of memorizing rules, forms, and structures.

6. Emphasis on production skills may result in anxiety in early stages.

4. Errors in form are acceptable.

5. Acquisition is unconscious and occurs through exposure to comprehensible input.

6. Emphasis on letting language production emerge naturally results in low anxiety.

The Monitor Model

Krashen's monitor model (1981) has been influential but controversial, particularly the dichotomy he has drawn between the acquisition and learning of a second language (McLaughlin, 1978; McLaughlin, Rossman, & McLeod, 1984). His model has five hypotheses. For a review of Krashen's critics, see *An Introduction to Second-Language Acquisition Research* (Larsen-Freeman & Long, 1991).

Acquisition versus learning. Second-language learning involves two distinct processes: (1) language acquisition, or the subconscious, natural way people learn language by using it for real communication; and (2) language learning, or conscious knowing about a language, as when people are able to describe the rules. On the one hand, people *acquire* a second language the same way they *acquire* a first language: through the successful communication of meaningful messages. Children acquire their first language this way, picking it up naturally as informal, subconscious, implicit knowledge that formal teaching doesn't help. So do people who live or travel in foreign countries. On the other hand, people *learn* language by studying grammar and rules as in a foreign language class. Language *learning* is formal, conscious, explicit knowledge that formal teaching helps.

Natural order. Grammatical structures are acquired in a predictable order—some early and some late. Not everyone acquires these structures in exactly the same order, however, nor do people acquire them in a second language in exactly the same order that they acquired them in the first language.

The monitor. Conscious learning about a language has a limited function in second-language performance. The rules of language that we learn don't make us more fluent speakers, but only check or fix what we've acquired. Fluency is the result of what we acquire in natural communicative situations. Also, to use the monitor function successfully, three conditions must be met: (1) The speaker must have time (if the conversation is rapid, thinking about the rules may disrupt it), (2) the speaker must be thinking about the rule, and (3) the speaker must know the rule. The monitor is only used for self-correction, and many people learn a language without conscious knowledge of the rules.

Comprehensible input. We acquire (not learn) language by understanding input that's a bit beyond our current level of proficiency—or, i (what we know) + 1 (what we learn). To progress to the next stage in language acquisition, we must understand language that's somewhat more difficult than what we already know. (Compare this idea with Vygotsky's "zone of proximal development" in the next section.)

Characteristics of comprehensible input include (1) language that's already known to the student, together with some not yet acquired; (2) contextual clues, such as objects in familiar situations; (3) paralinguistic clues, such as gestures and facial expressions; (4) linguistic modification, such as intonation, repetition, paraphrasing, simplification, clear pronunciation, and reduced speed; (5) topics about which students have prior knowledge; (6) meaningful and interesting topics for students; and (7) language does not need to be grammatically sequenced.

Students learn a second language when they obtain comprehensible input in a low-anxiety situation, when they are presented with interesting messages, and when they understand those messages.

The affective filter. Comprehensible input is necessary but not sufficient for language acquisition to take place. Affective factors, called the affective filter, determine how much of the raw material of language (the comprehensible input) will be processed. Acquisition will be limited when the affective filter is high, as when students are nervous, not motivated to speak the new language, and lacking self-esteem. Acquisition will increase when the affective filter is low, as when students have low levels of anxiety but high levels of motivation and self-confidence.

Krashen (1985) argues that grammar-based instruction has not helped students function in normal communicative contexts or acquire language and use it for meaningful purposes:

> We acquire when we obtain comprehensible input in a low-anxiety situation, when we are presented with interesting messages, and when we understand these messages. Comprehensible input has been the last resort of the language teaching profession. We have tried nearly every other possibility—grammar teaching, dialogue memorization, pattern drills, and expensive awkward machines. None of these approaches attempts to provide the essential ingredient—comprehensible input. (p. 10)

Role of Primary Language

Teachers who aren't bilingual concentrate on methods of English language development grounded in second-language acquisition theory when teaching language-minority students—for example, Krashen's communicative-based monitor model. Current research by J. David Ramirez and others (Ramirez & Merino, 1990; Ramirez et al., 1991), however, suggests that this be done in conjunction with primary language support for academic achievement in other subjects with a late-exit bilingual maintenance program (classes taught in students' first languages, K–12) for maximum school success. Students' first languages can be maintained through the use of bilingual teachers, aides, paraprofessionals, and school staff; cross-age tutoring and grouping; and flexible scheduling and team teaching among bilingual and monolingual teachers in a school.

The ideas of Canadian linguist James Cummins about the role of primary language have greatly influenced ideas about the education of language-minority students in the United States. Several of his key ideas pertain not only to language

Native Spanish-speaking students learning to read and write in their first language is an example of primary language support for academic achievement and self-esteem.

development and academic achievement but also to implications for the application of reader-response theory.

Dimensions of language proficiency. Cummins (1981) identified two dimensions of language proficiency: communicative language skills and academic language skills. *Communicative language skills* are those used in daily social speaking situations, such as children talking on the playground. *Academic language skills* are those used in school tasks, such as taking notes when the teacher is talking and writing answers to a test question using the information.

The relationship between these two dimensions of language proficiency is often illustrated with an iceberg and the adage about being deceived in seeing only its tip. The tip represents communicative language skills. In other words, teachers can hear basic communicative competence but can be misled in thinking that a student has also developed the academic language skills necessary for success in complex school tasks.

Context-embedded instruction. Proficiency in both dimensions of language is determined by the amount of *contextual support present.* Cummins calls this proficiency *context-embedded communication.* In it, meaning is actively negotiated between speakers and supported by many contextual clues, such as when deciding whose turn it is in playing a game. In *context-reduced communication*, there are few clues as to meaning—for example, answering a teacher's questions after a lecture. Each type of communication task also has a level of cognitive demand. Little thought is required in cognitively undemanding tasks, such as taking your turn in a game. Cognitively demanding tasks such as writing a five-paragraph essay, however, are more difficult. According to Cummins (1984),

> A major aim of schooling is to develop students' ability to manipulate and interpret cognitively-demanding context-reduced text. The more initial reading and writing instruction can be embedded in a meaningful communicative context (i.e., related to the child's experience), the more successful it is likely to be. The same principle holds for second-language instruction. (p. 136)

Common underlying proficiency. A teacher must ensure that language-minority students are able to develop both communicative and academic language skills in English and in their primary languages. This doesn't mean, however, that the task

In Paul's bilingual class, José likes to read his favorite book—*Rumpelstiltskin*, illustrated by Paul O. Zelinsky—in both Spanish and English at the same time! This is an example of additive bilingualism.

will take twice as much time and effort. These students are able to manage the linguistic demand of more cognitively difficult, context-reduced school tasks because of a *common underlying proficiency* for both languages; that is, developing the ability to perform cognitively demanding tasks in context-reduced situations in one language is a basis for performing similar tasks in another language.

For example, bilingual students who read well in one language usually also read well in the other language. This ability is called *additive bilingualism*. The opposite is also true and is called *subtractive bilingualism*. Cummins calls this the *linguistic threshold hypothesis:* For bilingual students, the degree to which proficiency in both the first and second languages is developed is positively associated with academic achievement.

Level of Bilingualism	Academic Effect
1. Proficient bilingualism: High levels in both languages	Positive
2. Partial bilingualism: Native-like ability in one of the languages	Neither positive nor negative
3. Limited bilingualism: Low levels in both languages	Negative

Bilingual education remains controversial, the subject of a continuing debate both inside and outside the educational system. For discussions of the conflict surrounding it, see Baker (1993), Lessow-Hurley (1996), McGroarty (1992), and the entire March 1992 issue of *Educational Researcher*.

THEORETICAL CROSSROADS

Transmission or Social Construction of Knowledge?

The conceptual landscape within which to situate the theoretical crossroads of reader-response theory and second-language acquisition theory can be drawn from a social constructivist view of learning. Reader-response and social constructivist theories are often linked in discussions of student-and response-centered teaching. This perspective contrasts with the more traditional teacher- and text-centered teaching, with its origins in the "New Critical" literary theory that came about when a transmission model of learning was developed and applied in American classrooms.

Transmission Model

A traditional teacher- and text-centered classroom reflects the psychological theory of behaviorism and a transmission model of teaching. Educational applications of B. F. Skinner's behaviorist learning theory were popular in the 1950s. Early behaviorists, particularly Ivan Pavlov, conducted experiments with animals in laboratories. You may have heard of Pavlov's dogs, who salivated in response to the ringing of a bell that signaled mealtime. Behaviorists believe that learning follows a formula of stimulus-response conditioning, according to which acceptable responses are reinforced.

In a classroom based on a behaviorist view of learning, teaching language is based on the belief that children learn through a process of environmental conditioning and by imitating adult models. Teachers condition students' learning by modeling behaviors that the students are to imitate. If the students imitate those behaviors correctly, they receive positive reinforcement, such as praise or rewards. If they don't, they receive negative reinforcement, such as criticism or even punishment.

According to this traditional behaviorist approach, language learning is not believed to be instinctive. Moreover, language is supposedly learned in small increments, or skills. Mastering those skills means that a person learns them, one by one, and builds a repertoire until he or she can read and write. For example, children learn to read by first mastering the letters of the alphabet, then combine letters to master words, and then combine words to master sentences. Learning to read is thought to be a step-by-step, cumulative process, each step building on the previous one. The basal readers used to teach reading in this way have "scope and sequences" of these skills, prepared for each grade and building on the grade before.

Text-centered views of how students read and understand literature mesh well with the behaviorist, transmission model of learning and developing language. Assuming that literary meaning is found in the text means there is a set of knowledge about the literary conventions such as genre and style and literary elements. It is separate from a student's individual experience of a literary work. To facilitate a true understanding of the work—the meaning within the work itself—the teacher's job is to transmit the knowledge of literary conventions bit by bit until the student builds up enough of a repertoire of these to fully understand what he or she has read. For example, an elementary teacher explains that stories have main characters that carry the action of the stories. Then students are asked to identify the main characters and what they do in a particular story. The teacher can verify the students' knowledge of this literary convention by testing: asking students to define a main character and to identify the character in a story. Teachers who reflect this model of learning, language development, and understanding literature explain many literary conventions and genre, assign specific books or stories for reading that exemplify these conventions and genre, use worksheets or guides for students to practice learning them, and can verify "literary knowledge" through testing or grading book reports.

Social Construction

The *constructivist theory of learning* or cognitive development put forth by Jean Piaget (1973, 1977) maintains that learning is an active process in which the learner constructs meaning. This idea is also behind John Dewey's (1938) famous expression "learning by doing," which means that we discover or construct concepts by actively participating in our environments.

Piaget believed that children can construct a view of reality that's based on what they learn as they mature and also what they experience in their lives. In other words, they learn throughout their lives by exploring and discovering new things. Learning is a process of adding new bits of information to what one already knows. Given this, it is important that the teacher be aware of how children learn and develop and that he or she provide an environment and initiate experiences that help children engage in the active construction of meaning and knowledge about themselves and the world.

According to Piaget, language acquisition is an aspect of general cognitive development. Although he believed that thought (or cognition) and language were interdependent, he maintained that language development is rooted in the more fundamental development of cognition. In other words, conceptualization precedes language. These ideas were based on his observation of children at play. Through manipulating objects, children demonstrate that they understand concepts and can solve problems without verbalizing them. Children learn to understand language as they first assimilate and then accommodate language symbols to their symbolic structures, or schema. In the search for meaning, children symbolize before they verbalize.

Piaget viewed the adult's role in teaching language as creating situations in which children discover meaning themselves. According to the constructivist view, language will follow experience. To support language development, teachers provide students opportunities for self-discovery in the classroom, such as group work with materials for writing and art.

The *social interactionist theory* of Lev Vygotsky (1962) proposes that children learn through meaningful interactions with their environments and other people and that these are essential factors in the development of new knowledge. Whereas Piaget suggested that children's learning is an individual, internalized cognitive process that does not depend on adult support, Vygotsky emphasizes the social, contextual nature of learning and language. For example, children learn to talk by listening to their parents, siblings, and others and eventually talking back. Similarly, children learn to read and write by having others read to them, by participating in shared storybook readings and writing events, and by eventually reading and writing on their own.

A key idea in Vygotsky's (1978) theory is the *zone of proximal development:* "the distance between the actual developmental level as determined by independent problem solving and the level of potential development as determined through problem solving under adult guidance or in collaboration with more capable peers" (p. 76). This means that children learn when they are supported by others who know more than they do—for instance, teachers, parents, and peers. A parallel idea is Krashen's "i + 1."

Environment plays a more prominent role in social interactionist theories than in cognitive constructivist theories. Social interactionist theory assumes that language acquisition is determined by the interaction of physical, linguistic, and social factors, any and all of which may vary greatly for each child. Vygotsky (1978, 1986) believes that interaction with the environment, especially with adults and older children, plays a critical role in children's language development. As summarized by Vygotsky, "Language is a major stimulant for conceptual growth, and conceptual growth is also dependent on interaction with objects in the environment. Moreover, adults (and older children) have a role in stimulating language growth through a variety of means" (p. 11, quoted in Pflaum, 1986).

This stimulation should take place within the zone of proximal development, the center around which the child forms thought complexes (similar to schema) or symbolic structures. Piaget (1973, 1977) also identified the importance of connecting new experiences to prior knowledge and organizing that new information. His ideas differ from those of Vygotsky, however, in that Piaget believed that children verbalize structures that have already developed through firsthand experiences with objects in the environment. Vygotsky sees the verbal interaction between adult and child as the primary means by which a child achieves potential meaning through language. He clearly puts great emphasis on the role of the teacher in the cognitive and linguistic development of the child.

The key ideas in Piaget's cognitive constructivist theory and Vygotsky's social interactionist theory have been loosely grouped together as a social constructivist perspective on language and literacy learning. The social constructivist framework also often takes into account the unique cultural aspects of each classroom (Spindler, 1982), as well as the role of the family and the cultural and linguistic background of each child (Heath, 1983). On the basis of this framework, learning occurs in a particular context, which will vary from class to class and year to year (Green & Meyer, 1990). For instance, ideas and expectations will never be exactly the same. The teacher will initiate experiences, observe students, and set expectations based on the uniqueness of each child, group, and class. Reader-response theory in many ways mirrors the social constructivist perspective on language learning in that it describes reading as an active, social, and individual process unique to each reader.

Reader-Response Theory and Second-Language Acquisition

Both reader-response and second-language acquisition theory cover a lot of ground, not to mention social constructivism. The points at which they seem to cross, however, especially as this pertains to teaching with literature and second-language education, are how they describe the role of students, language, the teacher, and the classroom in student- and response-centered instruction (see Table 2.1). The following discussion draws mainly from Rosenblatt's transactional theory of reader-response and the work of Krashen and Cummins on second-language acquisition.

The Students

Transactional theory describes reading as experienced meaning, a two-way transaction between the reader and the text. The focus of the reader's attention is on a personal evocation of the text while reading, what Rosenblatt refers to as "the poem." This emphasis on the lived-through experiences of readers affirms the importance of the role of the reader/student in constructing meaning from a text and is similar to the great importance placed on students' prior knowledge and life experience among the second-language acquisition theorists Cummins and Krashen.

TABLE 2.1 Theoretical crossroads

Reader-Response	Second Language
Student	*Student*
Reading as experienced meaning	Student prior knowledge and life experience valued
Personal evocation of a text	
Affirms important role of reader	Low-anxiety environment required
Each response is unique and individual	Self-esteem and motivation to speak important
	Language and culture of each learner respected
Language	*Language*
Embodied in transactions between individuals and social and natural context	Acquired as it is used in meaningful communication contexts
Not self-contained, ungrounded, ready-made code	Not learned via rules of grammar and pronunciation
Activation of reader's linguistic-experiential reservoir	Words acquire sense from context
Both primary language and English are funds of knowledge	Role of primary language essential for learning English and academic achievement
Also, texts in other languages and from other cultures	
Teacher	*Teacher*
Listens to students	Focuses on meaning
Invites students' personal responses to texts as meaning construction	Comprehensible input: key is student background knowledge
Learning from literature dependent on social and cultural context of students' lives	Context-embedded communication: students' lives are the context, basis for cognitively demanding learning
Classroom	*Classroom*
Students' voices a prerequisite	Students' voices are goal
Silence while listening and thinking understood	Silent period is expected
Responses to text a starting point	Acknowledge and tap into prior knowledge
Multiple and diverse responses expected	Diversity celebrated
Conversations among students encouraged and valued	Cooperative, collaborative atmosphere essential

A pertinent idea here is Krashen's notion of a low-anxiety environment for language learning, in which students are motivated to speak and are confident. In a response-centered discussion, motivation and confidence are highly likely because students' ideas or images about a literary text are welcomed. They are, in fact, a necessary part of talking and writing about literature. As in a text-centered approach, questions are often a test of knowledge of the text itself. A common fear among students is not knowing the "right answer." The result is that students may not speak because they are afraid that their answers aren't the right ones (e.g., the teacher's idea about the text).

In a reader-response type discussion, the atmosphere is more of a conversation with friends than an oral test. Responses that might be acceptable in a reader-response type (e.g., "That turnip's no good") would not be in a text-centered type. The point is that language development would not be inhibited because students lacked interest or confidence or the formal language or rhetoric necessary to answer analytical questions about a text.

Each student would respond in a unique way, no matter his or her level of English proficiency. Each should be allowed to respond in his or her native language or English or a combination of the two. What's important is that students are actively engaged, as explained in Piaget's constructivist theory (1973, 1977).

The Language

Drawing on the field of semiotics (Pierce, 1933, 1935), which explains the importance of the context of language, Rosenblatt maintains that language is "not . . . a self-contained, ungrounded, ready-made code of signifiers and signifieds, but as embodied in transactions between individuals and their social and natural context" (1986, p. 122). An essential idea in her transactional theory is that of the activation of the reader's "linguistic-experiential reservoir" as the means to construct new meanings and experiences while reading. This concept takes into account both the first and second language as funds of knowledge for the bilingual learner, as well as reading texts in languages other than English or produced in other cultures. The emphasis here is on the unique, lived-through experience of each individual reader.

Second-language acquisition theorists, such as Cummins and Krashen, who advocate a communicative approach maintain that acquisition of the target language emerges from students' own experiences, which should be the focus of language instruction, as opposed to language learning, with its focus on rules of grammar and pronunciation dispensed by a teacher.

Vygotsky, too, emphasizes both the social context and the individual's role in language development (1962). Words, like literary interpretations, acquire sense from the context in which they appear: "sense of a word" is "the sum of all the psychological events aroused in our consciousness by the word" (p. 46). Conversations about literature with a reader-response focus center around the student and encourage the student to draw on his or her own language, culture, and life experiences as a basis for language and literacy learning, rather than on the text itself or what might be learned from it. Both language and learning are centered in the student's own experiences.

The role of primary language, as described by Cummins, is important here. Proponents of bilingual education maintain that although it may seem to defy common sense, creating a bilingual and bicultural classroom and school community will increase students' self-esteem and academic achievement, which in turn is what provides a supportive environment for learning English.

The Teacher

The teacher with a reader-response theoretical orientation would invite students' personal responses to texts, encouraging the personal construction of meaning. This type of teaching reflects the belief that learning from literature is dependent on the social and cultural context of students' lives. Such a teacher would listen to students. An initial transaction with literature would become an invitation to the students to bring life experiences into the classroom. Not simply the text, but also students' responses to a literary text are the starting point for language and literacy experiences.

Two ideas from second-language acquisition parallel this perspective. One is Cummins's idea of *context-embedded instruction*. Students' lives, cultures, and language experiences constitute the context necessary for second-language learning at a cognitively demanding level. Another is Krashen's idea of *comprehensible input*. This is a key to second-language acquisition; the key to teachers providing this comprehensible input is tapping into students' background knowledge, which occurs naturally in response-centered instruction.

A father brings his mariachi band and plays music with his son in response to Paul's open invitation to students' families to come to school and share their lives.

Other linguists have described the nature of teachers' or caretakers' input, demonstrating that it consistently focuses on meaning rather than on form (Cook-Gumperz, 1979; Shugar, 1978; Snow, 1986; Wells, 1981). This focus supports the idea that students will be empowered to use language for meaningful purposes when the teacher focuses on what they are trying to say, as explained in Vygotsky's (1962) social interactionist theories, rather than on a text, such as a basal reader.

The Classroom

Reader-response theory suggests that student voice is essential to learning from literature in both a literal and a figurative sense. Response is individual and not tied to one agreed-upon meaning of a text. Silence while thinking about a text is understood. When they are expressed, students' responses to texts are the starting point, rather than ending point, for further discussion and language and literacy experiences. A response-centered classroom is an environment for rich discussions and exchanges between teachers and students, students and students, and students and texts. Multiple interactions are possible, creating a richly layered environment for experiencing literature and learning language. In such a classroom, you would not see a simple question-answer ratio of one teacher question to one student answer that could be verified by the text. Students might ask as many questions as the teacher. The teacher might share his or her own responses to the text and add personal life experiences to the mix. The atmosphere would be more like a warm, steamy, tangled, tropical rain forest than a cool, dry, formal, English garden. Multiple and varied responses and interpretations of a text, rather than a single consensus, are expected. Above all, conversations among students are encouraged and valued.

In both a literal and a figurative sense, student voice is the goal in second-language instruction. A silent period is expected, however, and students are not forced to speak before they are ready. Listening and speaking are of primary importance; reading and writing come later. In transactional teaching, students are encouraged to talk about their responses to literature, a part of which is listening to others respond. Answers to efferent type questions ("What color shoes did Dorothy have on?") are neither forced nor the focus of a discussion. Reader-response theory emphasizes the importance of the reader's personal response. When the reader does speak, the teacher acknowledges and taps into student prior knowledge and creates a classroom environment to make this happen. Cooperative, collaborative learning, such as student conversations when working in groups, is a part of the picture. Cultural and linguistic and personal diversity is expected and celebrated.

THINGS TO THINK ABOUT

1. Think about your own experiences with reading and literature while you were in grades K through 12 or even through college. What theory or theories did the teaching of your various teachers reflect?

2. Did you ever use Cliff Notes to prepare for an exam or to write a paper on a work of literature? If you did, think about the emphasis of the exam questions or paper assignment. Would it reflect a New Critical or a reader-response approach? Why do you think so?

3. Think about a recent book or poem you have read or movie you have seen. On the basis of your thoughts, what was the stance you took toward this work: primarily efferent or primarily aesthetic? Why do you think so?

4. Think about how you were taught a second language in high school. What approach did your teachers take: grammar-based or communicative-based? Why do you think so?

5. On the basis of your own experiences and the theory and research in this chapter, what do you think about the role of primary language support and bilingual education?

THINGS TO DO

1. Louise Rosenblatt's definition of **the reader** is given at the beginning of the chapter. Without referring back to it, write down your own definition of the reader. Then pick a teacher you had in K through 12 and write down what you think that person's definition of the reader was, given the way he or she taught with literature. Compare all three definitions and write down two or three teaching implications for each and compare those.

2. Jot down a few ideas about any or all of the following that apply to any experience you may have had learning a language other than your native language:
   a. Learning English as a second language
   b. Learning a second language other than English in high school or college
   c. Learning a new language while visiting or living in another country
   d. Learning the language of your students if you are a native English speaker and they are native speakers of a language other than English
   Compare each of these in terms of how you actually learned to speak and use a new language for real purposes.

3. Ask three teachers their views on primary language support and bilingual education for limited-English-proficient students. Compare what they say with the theory and research in this chapter and your own views.

4. Observe in a classroom where the majority of students are limited English proficient (LEP). Take notes on what you see. Write down what theories of second-language acquisition you think the teaching reflects. Write down some of your own ideas about teaching LEP students.

5. Using the notes you took in #4 above, analyze what you saw in relation to each of the following ideas:
   a. Learning as the transmission of knowledge: behaviorism
   b. Learning as the social construction of knowledge: Piagetian and Vygotskian views

FURTHER READING

Beach, R. (1993). *A teacher's introduction to reader-response theories.* Urbana, IL: National Council of Teachers of English.

Written for teachers to both introduce and demystify the field of reader-response literary criticism, this book discusses the theories from the perspective of the author's personal readings of literature, as well as making connections with classroom practice. This is the best overview around for teachers.

Larsen-Freeman, D., & Long, M. H. (1991). *An introduction to second-language acquisition research.* White Plains, NY: Longman.

This book is an excellent, comprehensive, and accessible overview of key topics in second-language acquisition theories and developmental and instructional aspects. It provides an extensive bibliography and suggestions for further reading.

Lessow-Hurley, J. (1996). *The foundations of dual language instruction* (2nd ed.). White Plains, NY: Longman.

This book provides an overview of theory, research, and discourse from several areas of scholarship and inquiry on issues related to dual language instruction: historical and international perspectives; program models; language aspects, development, and ability; primary language instruction for limited-English-proficient students; second-language instruction; culture and academic success; and legal foundations and politics of bilingualism.

Many, J., & Cox, C. (Eds.). (1992). *Reader stance and literary understanding: Exploring the theories, research, and practice.* Norwood, NJ: Ablex.

This is a book of readings by researchers who have investigated key ideas in response to literature: theoretical perspectives on reader stance and response; students' perspectives when reading and responding; and interaction in the classroom among teachers, students, and literature. It provides recommendations for instruction.

Ramirez, A. G. (1995). *Creating contexts for second-language acquisition: Theory and methods.* White Plains, NY: Longman.

A current, comprehensive, and practical overview of both theory and practice, this book has ideas and examples for language and literacy instruction for second-language learners and addresses the role of culture in second-language learning.

REFERENCES

Baker, C. (1993). *Foundations of bilingual education and bilingualism.* Philadelphia: Multilingual Matters.

Beach, R. (1993). *A teacher's introduction to reader-response theories.* Urbana, IL: National Council of Teachers of English.

Bloomfield, L. (1933). *Language.* New York: Henry Holt.

Bowerman, M. (1982). Start to talk worse: Clues to language acquisition from children's late speech errors. In S. Strauss & R. Stavey (Eds.), *U-shaped behavioral growth* (pp. 97–113). San Diego: Academic Press.

Breen, M., & Candlin, C. (1979). Essentials of a communicative curriculum. *Applied Linguistics, 1*(2), 90–112.

Brooks, C., & Warren, R. P. (1938). *Understanding poetry.* New York: D. Appleton Century.

Cazden, C. (1972). *Child language and education.* New York: Holt, Rinehart & Winston.

Chomsky, N. (1957). *Syntactic structures.* The Hague, The Netherlands: Mouton.

Chomsky, N. (1969). *The acquisition of syntax in children from 5 to 10* (Research Monograph No. 52). Cambridge, MA: MIT Press.

Clifford, J. (Ed.). (1991). *The experience of reading: Louise Rosenblatt and reader-response theory.* Portsmouth, NH: Boynton/Cook.

Cook-Gumperz, J. (1979). Communicating with young children in the home. *Theory Into Practice, 18,* 207–212.

Cooper, J. D. (1993). *Literacy: Helping children construct meaning.* Boston: Houghton Mifflin.

Cox, C. (1996). *Teaching language arts: A student- and response-centered classroom* (2nd ed.). Needham Heights, MA: Allyn & Bacon.

Cox, C., & Zarrillo, J. (1993). *Teaching reading with children's literature.* Upper Saddle River, NJ: Merrill/Prentice Hall.

Crawford, J. (1993). *Bilingual education: History, politics, theory, and practice* (2nd ed.). Los Angeles: Bilingual Educational Services.

Cummins, J. (1981). The role of primary language development in promoting educational success for language-minority students. In *Schooling and language-minority students: A theoretical framework* (pp. 3–49). Los Angeles: California State University.

Cummins, J. (1984). *Bilingualism and special education: Issues in assessment and pedagogy.* San Diego: College-Hill.

Dewey, J. (1938). *Experience in education.* New York: Collier.

Ellis, R. (1986). *Understanding second-language acquisition.* Oxford, UK: Oxford University Press.

Faltis, C. (1993). *Join fostering: Adapting teaching strategies for the multilingual classroom.* Upper Saddle River, NJ: Merrill/Prentice Hall.

Farrell, E. J., & Squire, J. R. (Eds.). (1990). *Transactions with literature.* Urbana, IL: National Council of Teachers of English.

Fries, C. (1945). *Teaching and learning English as a foreign language.* Ann Arbor: University of Michigan.

Goodman, K. S. (1992). I didn't found whole language. *Reading Teacher, 46*(3), 188–199.

Goodman, K. S. (1994). Reading, writing, and written texts: A transactional sociopsycholinguistic view. In R. B. Ruddell, M. R. Ruddell, & H. Singer (Eds.), *Theoretical models and processes of reading* (4th ed., pp. 1093–1130). Newark, DE: International Reading Association.

Green, J. L., & Meyer, L. A. (1990). The embeddedness of reading in classroom life: Reading as a situated process. In C. Baker & A. Luke (Eds.), *The sociology of reading* (pp. 141–160). Amsterdam, The Netherlands: Benjamins.

Halliday, M. A. K. (1975). *Learning how to mean*. London, UK: Edward Arnold.

Heath, S. B. (1983). *Ways with words: Language, life, and work in communities and classrooms*. New York: Cambridge University Press.

Held, D. (1980). *Introduction to critical theory: Horkheimer to Habermas*. Berkeley: University of California Press.

Holt, D. (Ed.). (1993). *Cooperative learning: A response to linguistic and cultural diversity*. Chicago: Center for Applied Linguistics and Delta Systems.

Hungerford, R., Holland, K., & Ernst, S. (Eds.). (1993). *Journeying: Children responding to literature*. Portsmouth, NH: Heinemann.

Hymes, D. (1974). *Foundations in sociolinguistics: An ethnographic approach*. Philadelphia: University of Pennsylvania Press.

James, W. (1890). *The principles of psychology* (2 vols). New York: Henry Holt.

Karolides, N. J. (Ed.). (1992). *Reader response in the classroom: Evoking and interpreting meaning in literature*. White Plains, NY: Longman.

Karolides, N. J. (Ed.). (1996). *Reader response in elementary classrooms: Quest and discovery*. Mahwah, NJ: Erlbaum.

Krashen, S. D. (1981). Bilingual education and second-language acquisition theory. In *Schooling and language-minority children: A theoretical framework* (pp. 51–79). Los Angeles: California State University.

Krashen, S. D. (1985). *Inquiries and insights: Essays in language teaching, bilingual education, and literacy*. Hayward, CA: Alemany.

Larsen-Freeman, D., & Long, M. H. (1991). *An introduction to second-language acquisition research*. White Plains, NY: Longman.

Lessow-Hurley, J. (1996). *The foundations of dual language instruction*. White Plains, NY: Longman.

Lieberman, I. Y., & Lieberman, A. M. (1990). Whole language versus code emphasis: Underlying assumptions and their implications for reading instruction. *Annals of Dyslexia, 40*, 51–76.

Lindfors, J. W. (1987). *Children's language and learning* (2nd ed.). Upper Saddle River, NJ: Merrill/Prentice Hall.

Maratsos, M. (1983). Some current issues in the study of the acquisition of grammar. In P. H. Mussen (Ed.), *Carmichael's manual of child psychology* (Vol. 3, 4th ed.). New York: Wiley.

McGroarty, M. (1992). The societal context of bilingual education. *Educational Researcher, 21*(2), 7–9, 24.

McLaughlin, B. (1978). The monitor model: Some methodological considerations. *Language Learning, 28*, 309–332.

McLaughlin, B. (1987). *Theories of second-language learning*. London: Edward Arnold.

McLaughlin, B., Rossman, T., & McLeod, B. (1984). Second-language learning: An information-processing perspective. *Language Learning, 33*, 135–158.

Menyuk, P. (1963). Syntactic structures in the language of children. *Child Development, 34*, 407–422.

Pflaum, S. W. (1986). *The development of language and literacy in young children.* Upper Saddle River, NJ: Merrill/Prentice Hall.

Piaget, J. (1973). *To understand is to invent: The future of education.* New York: Grossman.

Piaget, J. (1977). *The development of thought: Equilibration of cognitive structures* (A. Rosin, Trans.). New York: Viking.

Pierce, C. S. (1933, 1935). *Collected papers* (Vols. 3 and, 6) (P. Weiss & C. Hartshorne, Eds.). Cambridge, MA: Harvard University Press.

Piper, T. (1993). *Language for all our children.* Upper Saddle River, NJ: Merrill/Prentice Hall.

Probst, R. E. (1988). *Response and analysis.* Portsmouth, NH: Boynton/Cook.

Ramirez, J. D., & Merino, B. J. (1990). Classroom talk in English immersion, early-exit and late-exit transitional bilingual education programs. In R. Jacobson & C. Faltis (Eds.), *Language distribution issues in bilingual schooling* (pp. 61–103). Clevedon, UK: Multilingual Matters.

Ramirez, J. D., Yuen, S. D., & Ramey, D. R. (1991). *Final report: Longitudinal study of structured English immersion strategy, early-exit and late-exit transitional bilingual education programs for language-minority children* (Prepared for the U.S. Dept. of Education, Executive Summary No. 300-87-0156).

Richards, I. A. (1935). *Practical criticism: A study of literary judgment.* New York: Harcourt Brace.

Richards, J. C., & Rodgers, T. S. (1986). *Approaches and methods in language teaching.* Cambridge, UK: Cambridge University Press.

Rosenblatt, L. M. (1978). *The reader, the text, the poem: The transactional theory of the literary work.* Carbondale: Southern Illinois University Press.

Rosenblatt, L. M. (1982). The literary transaction: Evocation and response. *Theory Into Practice, 21,* 268–277.

Rosenblatt, L. M. (1983). *Literature as personal exploration* New York: Modern Language Association. (Original work published 1938)

Rosenblatt, L. M. (1986). The aesthetic transaction. *Journal of Aesthetic Education, 20,* 122–128.

Rosenblatt, L. M. (1994). The transactional theory of reading and writing. In R. Ruddell, M. Ruddell, & H. Singer (Eds.), *Theoretical models and processes of reading* (4th ed., pp. 1057–1092). Newark, DE: International Reading Association.

Shugar, G. W. (1978). Text analysis as an approach to the study of early linguistic operations. In C. Snow & N. Waterson (Eds.), *The development of communication* (pp. 78–94). Chichester, UK: Wiley.

Snow, C. E. (1986). Conversations with children. In P. Fletcher & M. Garman (Eds.), *Language acquisition: Studies in first language development* (2nd ed., pp. 69–89). Cambridge, UK: Cambridge University Press.

Spindler, G. (1982). *Doing the ethnography of schooling.* New York: Holt, Rinehart & Winston.

Strickland, R. J. (1962). *The language of elementary school children* (Bulletin of the School of Education, No. 4). Bloomington: Indiana University.

Swain, M. (1986). Communicative competence: Some roles of comprehensible input and comprehensible output in its development. In J. Cummins & M. Swain (Eds.), *Bilingualism in education* (pp. 16–28). White Plains, NY: Longman.

Tough, J. (1977). *The development of meaning.* London, UK: Allen & Unwin.

Vygotsky, L. S. (1962). *Thought and language* (F. Hanmann & G. Vakar, Eds. & Trans.). Cambridge: MIT Press.

Vygotsky, L. S. (1978). *Mind in society.* Cambridge, MA: Harvard University Press.

Vygotsky, L. S. (1986). *Thought and language.* Cambridge: MIT Press.

Wellek, R., & Warren, R. (1949). *Theory of literature.* New York: Harcourt Brace.

Wells, G. (Ed.). (1981). *Learning through interaction: The study of language development.* London, UK: Cambridge University Press.

Widdowson, H. (1978). *Teaching language as communication.* Oxford, UK: Oxford University Press.

Wilkins, D. A. (1979). *Notional syllabuses.* London, UK: Oxford University Press.

Zarrillo, J., & Cox, C. (1992). Efferent and aesthetic teaching. In J. Many & C. Cox (Eds.), *Reader stance and literary understanding: Exploring the theories, research, and practice* (pp. 235–249). Norwood, NJ: Ablex.

CHAPTER THREE

Teaching with Literature and English Language and Literacy Development

Literature-based teaching is a growing curricular movement. Curriculum has shifted from traditional, text-centered approaches that use basal readers and textbooks for other school subjects such as social studies and science to a response-centered approach that uses whole, meaningful texts such as children's literature and children's own writing. This new curriculum approach is used for developing English language and literacy for students learning English as both a first and a second language and to integrate the curriculum (Cox & Zarrillo, 1993; Cullinan, 1987, 1992). This shift has meant that teachers change not only the type of texts they use but also the way they use them (Langer, 1992).

In this chapter, we compare two approaches to teaching with literature: the more traditional, text-centered approach and the more current response-centered approach. Each is described in terms of underlying assumptions about learning, meaning in literature, and assessment. A classroom example of each is described to show theory in practice and as a basis for comparing the roles of the teacher and the student in each approach, followed by characteristics of integrated, literature-based teaching and implications for students learning English as a second language.

TEXT-CENTERED APPROACH

A text-centered approach reflects the behaviorist tradition of learning described in Chapter 2. Most of us have spent many hours in a classroom like this: in rows, raising a hand to speak, listening to the teacher give directions, knowing that the correct response was the one the teacher wanted, doing the same worksheet as everyone else, and knowing that you were grouped according to ability in reading even though the groups might be called The Lions, The Tigers, and The Bears—everyone knew which was the high, middle, and low group. Reading was taught with a class set of graded, basal readers. Students in a group read the same stories and answered the teacher's questions about them. Emphasis was placed on learning discrete skills along with reading the stories. Literature such as a library book was only read if you finished all your work and had some extra time.

Learning Part to Whole

This type of approach reflected a *transmission model* of teaching grounded in behaviorism, a learning theory that was made popular in the 1950s by B. F. Skinner and that continues to influence education today. As applied to reading, it reflects a linear model, familiarly called a "bottom-up" or "part-to-whole" approach. First, the reader learns to recognize letters, followed by words, and then words in context, until he or she finally begins to understand what's read (Gough, 1976; LaBerge & Samuels, 1976).

The *linear model* is the theory behind the basal reader, sequential approach to teaching reading. According to this approach, the reading process is broken down into a series of smaller to larger subskills that should be taught in a certain order. These skills are grouped under such headings as Readiness, Word Recognition, Word Meaning, and Comprehension. *Basal readers* are used; these are graded sets of books that have hierarchies of objectives and activities. The commercial basal reader program has been the dominant method of reading instruction in elementary schools (Langer, Applebee, Mullis, & Foertsch, 1990). A basal reader program consists of a set of graded books used by a class or by groups within a class. All the books include selections of stories that form the core of the reading lessons. The teacher follows directions in the teacher's guide for covering the separate subskills thought necessary in learning reading and related speaking and writing skills. Students complete workbooks and skillsheets to practice the skills taught during the teacher-directed lesson planned in the teacher's guide.

Patrick Shannon (1988), among others, has criticized basal readers because they have reduced reading to a kind of management system that certifies students' minimum reading competence. He maintains they are widely used because schools want to show they have a standardized way of judging reading competence. Commercial materials make this possible by using a sequence of testable objectives, a teacher's manual to guide instruction in meeting these objectives, and a test that demonstrates whether instruction has succeeded. This approach has also been criticized because it inhibits instructional innovations by predetermining teachers' decisions and limits the amount of attention paid to individual students (Goodman, Shannon, Freeman, & Murphy, 1988).

Newer basal reading systems have recognized the widespread use of literature-based instruction and used excerpts or intact selections of children's literature in what are called *literary readers*. Nonetheless, they still take a text-centered approach and take time that could be spent on self-selected, voluntary reading (Krashen, 1993; Morrow, 1992).

Meaning in the Text

In a classroom with a traditional, 'New Critical orientation to literature study, whether the teachers explicitly know that this is the guiding theory behind their instruction or simply do what they themselves did in literature classes, analysis of the text is most important. The key idea is that meaning is in the text and the reader's job is to find it.

With this text-based approach, the most important things are understanding the language and structure of the story and how the literary elements of setting, character, plot, problem, mood, theme, and so on work together. The underlying assumption is that if children understand the significance of the language and the story structure and elements, they will come to a clear and "correct" understanding of the story itself. In general, this is an understanding that other readers will share. Reaching a single, agreed-upon meaning of a story is the goal of instruction. Teaching strategies such as introducing and defining literary terminology, analyzing the language and structure of the story, and using these to answer the teacher's questions or to write book reports reflect this text-based approach.

Materials such as a set of readers for the whole class (basal readers in elementary school; literature anthologies in middle and high school) and a teacher's guide with definitions, plot summaries, analyses of the stories, classification by genre, and questions that help students focus on a "close reading" or analysis of the text are used.

Standardized Assessment

Standardized testing is the focus of assessment in a teacher-, text-centered classroom. Standardized tests are based on the behaviorist, transmission model of learning. *Learning* is described in this model as a set of subskills that can be separated, taught, mastered, and tested. Multiple-choice tests reflect this model of learning. These kinds of tests can pinpoint what skill a student has difficulty with and can make a reliable comparison of his or her ability with that of other students. These tests cannot, however, explain what went wrong in the learning process. Here are the basic principles of standardized testing.

1. Information is gathered with paper-and-pencil tests.
2. Tests are given only periodically.
3. One test, given at a single point in time, determines evaluation.
4. Specific problems can be identified but not in context.
5. Subskills, rather than process, are the focus.
6. Forms include multiple-choice, true/false, matching, and short-answer questions.
7. Teachers make no decisions about which tests are used.
8. Attempts to "teach to the test" may not support learning.
9. Testing disrupts the classroom schedule.

A belief in the value of standardized testing may also lead a teacher to believe that asking questions with only one answer reveals whether a student is learning and thereby influences the way questions and answers are used in the classroom. Or, the teacher's questions are a kind of continual test to determine whether students "were listening" and whether they can repeat the answer the teacher has in mind.

RESPONSE-CENTERED APPROACH

A response-centered approach is reflected in the example of Paul's Spanish bilingual class described in Chapter 1. Paul uses literature to teach English as a second language and reading and writing in both languages by organizing students into literature groups for reading, listening, talking, writing, and art making in rich social and interactive situations. Many of the literature-based experiences in his class extend across the curriculum, so students are learning subject matter content as well as developing spoken language and literacy. Most important, Paul centers his teaching around the responses of his students transacting with literature, encouraging them to draw on their own lives and experiences to make sense of what they are reading and as a basis for language and literacy development in both Spanish and English.

Learning Whole to Part

The shift to literature-based reading grounded in reader-response theory is supported by the whole-language movement, which advocates a greater role for both literature and teachers in reading instruction, as opposed to basal readers with teacher's guides (Altwerger, Edelsky, & Flores, 1987; Goodman, 1986). Whole language is not a method, but rather is a set of applied beliefs with regard to language development, curriculum, learning, teaching, and the community. Edelsky, Altwerger, and Flores (1991) describe it as a "professional theory in practice," drawing from the fields of psychology, child development, psycholinguistics and sociolinguistics, literary theory, composition theory, and the theory of literacy. The term *whole language* can mean many things to many people and remains—like bilingual education—controversial. For a critique of whole language, see Moorman, Blanton, and McLaughlin (1994) and four responding articles in the October/November/December issue of *Reading Research Quarterly*.

Here are key assumptions underlying the response-centered approach. Language and literacy learning is an active, constructive process that takes place when students are truly engaged in what they're doing and focused on the discovery of meaning. The constructivist learning theory of Jean Piaget described in Chapter 2 explains that children learn by adding new experiences to old ones and by constructing new understandings of themselves and the world.

It follows that children learn to use language by using it—listening, speaking, reading, and writing. Children must first explore and discover for themselves, which is essentially an individualized and internalized process. And even though all children go through approximately the same stages of cognitive development, each child is unique and will develop personal understanding at his or her own rate. The teacher's job is to encourage and support this natural development by initiating hands-on experiences. Research by Walter Loban (1979) has also demonstrated that language modes function together as children learn to use and control language. He found a strong correlation among reading, writing, listening, and speaking abilities. According to Loban, the most important element in learning to use language is to use it: "The development of power and efficiency with language derives from using language for genuine purposes and not from studying about it. The path to power over language is to use it, to use it in genuinely meaningful situations, whether we are reading, listening, writing, or speaking" (p. 485).

Language and literacy learning is a social, interactive process that take place when students work collaboratively with each other and the teacher. The social interactionist theory of Vygotsky, described in Chapter 2, explains that children construct new knowledge by first interacting in context with adults, other children, and materials and tasks in the environment; later, they internalize what they've learned. Teachers and more capable peers build "scaffolds," according to Jerome Bruner (1983), to help learners construct new knowledge based on the foundation of what children already know. According to this view, the teacher's job is to observe, demonstrate, and support students' efforts and to organize instruction so as to include time for collaboration among students and with the teacher.

Reading is a two-way transaction between a reader and a text during which meaning is created, according to Rosenblatt's transactional theory, described in Chapter 2. Readers draw on prior experiences, a stream of images and ideas that flow through their minds while reading. In response-centered teaching, the teacher initiates experiences with literature but also observes each student's personal response to a story. The teacher uses these responses as a basis for extending experiences with literature and language and literature activities.

Kenneth Goodman has described five key ideas about whole language relevant to literacy (1986):

1. Literacy develops from whole (big chunks) to part (small increments) during functional, meaningful, relevant language use.

2. Readers construct meaning while reading, drawing on their prior learning and experience.

3. Readers predict, select, confirm, and self-correct as they make sense of print.

4. Three language systems interact in written language: the *graphophonic* (sound and letter patterns), the *syntactic* (sentence patterns), and the *semantic* (meanings). They work together and cannot be isolated for instruction.

5. Comprehension of meaning is always the goal of readers. In a whole-language classroom, literature and other authentic texts such as children's writing are the material for reading, and the teacher makes decisions about how reading is taught.

Meaning Transacted Between the Reader and the Text

In a classroom with a reader-response orientation, young speakers and readers have more choice and control and an opportunity to use their voices in response to literature. It also gives them more responsibility. Although the teacher may initiate experiences with literature, as in the organizing of language arts/reading around literature groups, he or she does not set predetermined outcomes, such as having everyone agree on what the story meant or doing a book report that must include sections on setting, plot, character, mood, and theme.

Rather, the teacher encourages students to respond openly and aesthetically, drawing on their fund of prior experiences and impressions while reading to construct a personally meaningful interpretation of the text. The focus of learning and teaching is on the students' responses, not on the text itself or the teacher's ideas (which are often based on the teacher's guide prepared by a publishing company). More efferent analysis of a text emerges from the more aesthetically oriented discussion and activities that come first.

Students can choose from a range of response options to literature. These include speaking a personal response in a discussion with the teacher or other students, writing (e.g., their ideas about a story, another story, a poem, or a song), drama (e.g., acting out a story or writing and producing a play or puppet show), art making (e.g., drawings, murals, models, masks, puppets), media (e.g., creating a storyboard for a videotaped version of the story or a new story created as a result of reading), or special events (e.g., writing an original story based on literature and making a Big Book version to read to a class of younger students), or presenting a play or singing a song for the school and parents.

Materials for language and literacy development include many children's books in both English and the child's primary language, and other authentic texts: children's own writing, charts made by a teacher, magazines, newspapers, advertisements, and media texts—videos, CD-ROM, cassette tapes, or CDs.

Authentic Assessment

Authentic, contextualized performance assessment reflects a holistic model of the social construction of meaning. Authentic assessment is continuous, embedded in classroom contexts, and includes information from teacher observations, anecdotal records, checklists, conferences, and student work (e.g. art, writing, journals, reading records, projects, portfolios).

Herman, Aschbacher, and Winters (1992) contrast the older behaviorist, transmission model of teaching and testing with the more current constructivist, holistic model:

> No longer is learning thought to be a one-way transmission from teacher to students, with the teacher as lecturer and the students as passive receptacles. Rather, meaningful instruction engages students actively in the learning process. Good teachers draw on and synthesize discipline-based knowledge, knowledge of student learning, and knowledge of child development. They use a variety of instructional strategies . . . [and] involve their

students in meaningful activities . . . to achieve specific learning goals . . . Good teachers constantly assess how their students are doing, gather evidence of problems and progress, and adjust . . . accordingly. (p. 64)

Here are the basic principles of authentic assessment:

1. Information is gathered by teachers and students.
2. Ongoing, daily observations are made.
3. Multiple sources of information are used.
4. Information is considered in the context of process.
5. Artifacts (writing, art, journals, tapes) and rich descriptions (anecdotal records, checklists) are used.
6. Teachers and students make decisions about assessment.
7. Information is gathered as part of the classroom schedule.

TWO WAYS TO TEACH WITH LITERATURE

Let's look into two classrooms in the same school that reflect different perspectives on how children learn, develop language and literacy, and use literature. The school has a high percentage of language-minority students, primarily native Spanish-speaking Mexican American children. Let's look at the experience of one student in the two classrooms. Anne is a native English-speaking child whose experiences with literature are described in more detail in Chapter 4. Pay particular attention to who is doing the talking in each classroom, a fundamental issue in both first- and second-language acquisition.

A Text-Centered Lesson from a "Literary" Basal Reader

Anne's first-grade classroom teacher uses literature to teach reading but usually teaches whole-class lessons with a class set of literary readers—a newer generation of the basal reader with excerpts of children's books. Each child has the same reader and a "pupil response booklet" with prompts for students to write after reading. The teacher uses a teacher's guide with ideas for teaching with literature provided by the publisher.

Teacher Asks Questions About Anna Banana and Me

Before directing students to read the excerpt from *Anna Banana and Me*, the teacher asks, "Are any of you ever afraid when you try something new?" Students answer this question for a full ten minutes, each child always responding to the teacher. Anne does not participate. Then the teacher says, "Today, we're going to learn something about a person who follows someone else's action when the person was unsure and afraid. I think it's exciting to read about somebody who has some of the same feelings we do." She hands out paperback copies of the excerpted book that comes with this reading series. First, she directs the students to look at the title and then asks a series of questions: "What does it say? What is she? How do you know she's friendly?" She tells them to notice that the author and the illustrator are related, what technique the illustrator uses (black ink and watercolor), and the title page and dedication page. Anne still says nothing.

After the teacher reads the book aloud, she says: "The story had a lot of messages." She tells the students that the people who made the reader wrote some questions of students in the teacher's guide and that she has written them on a sheet of chart paper. She reads them aloud and asks the students to answer each of them:

1. Where do you think they are?
2. What does Anna Banana say about feathers?
3. Why does the boy go home?
4. Why does she visit him?
5. What kind of building does he live in?
6. What is he doing?
7. Why does his voice echo?
8. How do you think the boy is feeling about Anna Banana?

(The teacher points out that this last question doesn't have a right or wrong answer.)

9. What's something in the story that makes you think that?

Finally, she asks what she calls a "thinking question": "How does she suddenly become brave?" The children offer many tentative answers to this question. Anne finally raises her hand and answers in a rather uncompromising way: "Because Anna Banana told him the feather was magic and made him brave." The teacher says: "Here is a big question. WAS IT MAGIC?" Anne answers: "Yes, because it really made him brave." The teacher says: "Anne says the feather was magic. What do the rest of you think?" Answers include (1) in the story, but not in real life; (2) sort of, not really; (3) sort of, but different; (4) I think that it's not real, but he thought it was, and then it was, but not really.

It is clear the teacher wants the students to "learn" the difference between "real and make-believe" and to come to the consensus that magic could happen in a story but not in real life. The students appear to sense that she is waiting for this answer. After no one disagrees that magic can't happen in real life, Anne speaks again: "I think he really believes that the feather is magic and it will make it happen. When I throw a coin into a wishing well, I believe my wish will come true." She says this in a rather uncompromising, even matter-of-fact, way. She apparently has not been swayed by the teacher's implied answer or the lack of support from other students. After this teacher-directed question-and-answer period, the teacher gives the students a writing prompt: "If the feather were really magic, I would . . ." She tells them to go to their seats and write.

This is an example of a text- and teacher-centered approach to teaching with literature. Did you notice that the teacher did most of the talking and that the students rarely interacted with each other?

A Literature Group Forms in a Response-Centered Classroom

In third grade, Anne also spends time in another teacher's room. It is a bilingual Spanish/English classroom taught by Paul. During a period called "integration," throughout the school, native English-speaking students like Anne and limited-English-proficient students from bilingual classes go to each other's classrooms.

If you remember from Chapter 1, Paul made a shift from a text-based to a student-, response-centered approach to literature-based teaching. He chose not to do directed, whole-class teaching with a literary reader basal series although they are available as one of the many sources of reading material in his room. Paul reads aloud from a wide range of literature and other material and encourages students to do self-selected, wide independent reading and to read and work together in literature groups. Frequently, books that students read and discuss become a focal point for integrated learning across the curriculum.

Students Respond to Encounter *in a Bilingual Class*

One literature group has been reading and learning about Puerto Rico. The librarian, who works closely with Paul by paying attention to what his students are reading and learning about, offers Alfredo several books about the Caribbean. One book is *Encounter* by Jane Yolen, a story of Columbus's arrival and meeting the Taino. The narrator's voice in the story is that of a Taino child.

This particular literature group meets in a circle. Alfredo begins by telling them: "I went to the library and got this book and read it. It's a sad story about how Columbus brought disease to the Taino people. They wanted to get along with him, but he killed them off."

Paul approaches the group with Anne and asks whether she can join them. They agree. After asking them what they are doing, he asks whether Anne can read *Encounter* aloud to them because Alfredo is very interested in the book, which is in English, and Anne is an "expert English user." (He wants Anne to feel like part of the group.) Anne reads it aloud; Alfredo, Fabiola, Eddie, and Laura listen. Paul confers with another group and then moves about the room, conferring and interacting with other groups and students. He returns to this group when Anne finishes, suggesting they might all talk about the book. They begin an animated and lengthy discussion, pointing and referring to the dramatic and somber illustrations by David Shannon. Paul notices this and joins them.

Paul: Tell me about the book.
Alfredo: He was little, a child. He was Taino, and Christopher Columbus was Italian, sent from Spain.

Anne: He took the Taino as slaves and came back for more.

Paul: What happened to the rest of the Taino?

Alfredo: Many died. Only one survived in the story.

Paul: Why?

Alfredo: Because . . . (he reads part of the story and points to a picture with knives).

Paul: Tell me more about the boy.

Anne: He had a dream, and when he woke up . . .

Alfredo: (finishing Anne's sentence) . . . the boy saw them and thought their skin was funny (points to picture of Columbus's crew), but he was afraid.

Paul: Why do you think?

Alfredo: 'Cause he has his people and land taken away.

Paul: Have any of you ever had things taken away?

Anne: We were robbed. TV, VCR, my dad's tools, and our bikes.

Eddie: My mom was washing clothes and put them outside to dry, and they were taken. They stole my overalls.

Laura: (to Anne) How did they get in your house?

Anne: Don't know.

(Every student shares an experience of having something stolen.)

Paul: So you've all been robbed, and the child in this book has been robbed.

Anne: Yeah. Of his own people.

Alfredo: They took him away from his land.

Paul: Did he ever come back?

Anne: Let me read the last page (pointing to picture of child as an old man, telling the story).

Paul: What is he thinking?

Eddie: Of his people.

Paul: Tell me more.

Laura: He's wondering what they were doing (pointing to picture of Columbus's ships drawn as huge birds of prey).

Anne: His dream about the ships.

Paul: Look at the picture (a white bird like a ship). He is—he's dreaming of a ship.

Anne: My favorite picture is his dream of flying ships.

Fabiola: They look like parrots. My favorite picture is this one.

Paul: Do you ever have dreams?

The discussion continues, with students sharing their dreams, especially bad ones. The talk shifts to books with dreams, such as *There's a Nightmare in My Closet, The Alligator under My Bed,* and *The Wreck of the Zephyr.* Paul says, "We should write about our dreams." They also talk about the picture of the bird/boats in the boy's dream in *Encounter* and about old horror movies, and Alfredo talks at length about a story he heard in Mexico about being thrown into a hole with fire if you said a bad word.

Paul suggests they think about their discussion and something they could do in their literature group, perhaps about Christopher Columbus or dreams. Paul lists, on a sheet of chart paper, ideas they generate:

1. Make a story about what happened.
2. Do it on the computer like a book.
3. Make a musical play with songs.
4. Write poems about dreams of boats, or dreams, or boats.
5. Get some biographies of Christopher Columbus and read them.

This is what the students actually did.

1. Read other books about Christopher Columbus.
2. Made a comparison chart of several books about Christopher Columbus and his meeting the Taino people because they found these books had very different perspectives.
3. Invited a teacher in the school who had studied in Puerto Rico to talk to the class about the Taino and other native people of Puerto Rico.
4. Did a play of *Encounter* (Alfredo played Christopher Columbus with mixed feelings. He had the lead part, but with Richard III overtones.)
5. Wrote poems about dreams, boats, and the ocean.

This is an example of a student-, response-centered approach to teaching with literature. Did you notice that students did almost all the talking in a student-led discussion of *Encounter* and that Paul joined them as co-discussant, rather than as director?

Comparison of Text-Centered and Response-Centered Classrooms

Keep these two classrooms in mind as you consider a comparison of the roles of the teacher and the students in a teacher- and text-centered approach and a student- and response-centered approach, the latter in a bilingual Spanish classroom. Think about the conceptual differences with regard to teaching with literature and English language and literacy development.

The Teacher

Text-Centered Approach
Makes all decisions for what is to be learned.
Uses basal readers, textbooks, and commercial materials.
Follows teacher's guide for basals and textbook series.
Emphasizes part-to-whole learning.

Follows a sequence of skills to be mastered.

Bases assessment on questions with one right answer.

Response-Centered Approach

Provides opportunities for independent learning.

Uses children's literature and student writing.

Listens to students; honors student voice.

Emphasizes whole-to-part learning.

Uses ideas/interests of students to generate thematic learning.

Bases assessment on individual growth and development.

The Students

Text-Centered Approach

Are passive recipients of learning.

Imitate what teacher has modeled.

Follow directions of teacher or textbook.

Do the same assignments as other students.

Are grouped by ability.

Are assessed on mastery of skills in hierarchical order.

Response-Centered Approach

Learn by doing, active engagement, personal response.

Make choices: what to read, how to respond, what to learn.

Work in groups; discover things on their own.

Interact, cooperate, collaborate, plan on their own.

Are grouped by interests and compatibility.

Are assessed individually, negotiated with teacher.

INTEGRATED, LITERATURE-BASED TEACHING

Response-centered, literature-based classrooms in which learning focuses on students' responses do not all look the same, but many share a social constructivist view of learning and the transactional model of the reading process. Such classrooms are organized to provide time, opportunities, and an environment for students to read, respond, and *ripple*—develop further language and learning experiences to ripple out across the curriculum, like waves from a pebble thrown into a pond.

Language learning across the curriculum occurs within the context of content areas such as social studies, science, mathematics, and music and the arts (Froese, 1994). It is based on three principles: (1) All genuine learning involves discovery,

(2) language has a heuristic function (language as a means to learn), and (3) using language to discover is the best way to learn it (Bullock, 1975).

In a student- and response-centered classroom, language across the curriculum means an integrated approach to teaching. Students ask questions, identify and solve problems, use research and study skills, and discover the interconnectedness of subject matter. Teachers plan experiences to enable students to do this. Both teachers and students initiate themes of learning or identify a topic of interest for individual inquiry. Students collaborate, and teachers mentor them.

Thematic teaching goes back to the Socratic method of organizing instruction around meaningful questions. Today you will see such terms as *theme study, theme cycles* (Altwerger & Flores, 1994), *thematic units,* and *integrated, cross-curricular, thematic teaching. Whole language* generally means integrated teaching. I (Carole) have called these "ripple effects of response-themed learning" (Cox, 1996) because I know they are not totally planned ahead by the teacher, but like a pebble thrown into a pond, send out ripples of their own that can extend across the curriculum, depending on the ideas, interests, and experiences of students—for example, when students in Paul's third-grade bilingual class formed a literature group around the book *Encounter* and continued to read, listen, think, talk, write, research, and act out ideas about Columbus, the Taino people, and their own experiences with dreams.

Read

Literature-based teaching means creating a room environment and classroom library and scheduling time and opportunities for reading.

Room environment

Classroom reading corners or libraries have designated spaces for shelves and book displays, tables, comfortable chairs (or floor pillows, bean bag chairs, or mats) or a rocker for the teacher. Students' work is displayed on bulletin boards, tables, or shelf tops. Art and writing materials are available.

Time for reading

Time for reading can be done in several ways.

Reading aloud. Reading aloud can happen several times a day, to the whole class or a group, from picture books or chapter books, for sheer enjoyment or in connection with a theme such as Christopher Columbus and the Taino people in *Encounter.*

Shared reading. Students participate in reading by following along in their own copy of a chapter book or by reading the text of a Big Book, guided by the teacher, or by reading a teacher-made chart of poems or songs, which can also be written on sentence strips and used in a pocket chart.

Buddy reading. Students read in pairs. They may be reading for information to use for a project they are working on, such as comparing different perspectives on

Time for self-selected, wide independent reading in Spanish and English is a key to effective literature-based teaching in Paul's bilingual class.

Columbus, or simply because they like the same book and each other or for one to share a favorite book with a friend.

Sustained silent reading. Everyone in the class, including the teacher, reads a self-selected book silently.

Wide independent reading. Students self-select books and read widely for interest and enjoyment, or they may read widely on a theme of interest. Much wide independent reading can take place when students work in literature groups during fairly large blocks of time.

Respond

Students respond to literature in many ways. One of the most natural is through discussions, talking together and with the teacher.

Talking Together

Provide time and opportunities to talk before, during, and after reading, for the whole class, small groups, or one-to-one conferences, in what Peterson and Eeds (1990) describe as "grand conversations." This is some of the richest time for students to reflect on their own responses as a basis for planning further response-centered activities.

Questions: Aesthetic and efferent. The types of questions a teacher asks direct students to take a predominantly aesthetic or efferent stance toward any text. Ideally, the teacher should first direct students to take an aesthetic stance toward literature. Out of these broader, richer aesthetic responses leading to the development of personal meaning, more efferent concerns can emerge, such as developing explanations, attention to print and language, and content and analysis.

Here are questions and prompts based on students' responses (Cox, 1996; Cox & Zarrillo, 1993): First, the more aesthetic, which direct students to focus on the personal evocation of a text; and then, the more efferent, focused on the text itself, which tend to emerge from the more aesthetic.

Aesthetic

What do you think about the story?

Tell anything you want about the story.

What did you wonder about?

What was your favorite part?

Has anything like this ever happened to you? Tell about it.

Does the story remind you of anything? Tell about it.

What would you change in the story?

What else do you think might happen in the story?

What would you say or do if you were a character in the story?

Efferent

What was the main idea of the story?

What did the author mean by _____ ?

What was the problem in the story?

How did the author solve the problem?

Retell your favorite part.

Tell the order of the story events.

Describe the main characters.

Explain the characters actions.

What other stories are like this one? Compare and contrast them.

How did the author make the story believable?

Is the story fact or fiction?

How do you think the characters felt?

Writing in Response Journals

Response journals are an important component of response-centered teaching with literature. Students can write in these before, during, and after reading. The journals can trigger discussions when talking together about books, during conferences with the teacher, or while buddy reading.

Students can just write, or the teacher can suggest questions and prompts to get them started. The questions and prompts listed here are primarily aesthetic, to encourage students to focus on the lived-through experience of the book.

Questions and prompts for response journals. What were you thinking about while reading? Tell about it.

What was your favorite part of the story? Tell about it.

Did you wonder about anything? Tell about it.

What else do you think might happen?

Has anything like this ever happened to you? Tell about it.

Write anything you want about the story.

Double entry literature response journals. Some teachers suggest double entry journals, in which students write down the part of the story that interested them on one side and their thoughts about that part on the other side.

Left Side	**Right Side**
Interesting part of book	Response to the part

Response journals are important in assessing students' engagement with and understanding of literature. They provide an authentic, ongoing record of students' interests, responses, and personal explorations of literature.

Response Options

Here are other options for students to respond to literature. These should be flexible, with options for individuals and groups. The teacher should ask the students for ideas but be cautious about directing students to write or do a project after reading every book. Probably the best thing to do after reading a book is to read another one.

Read another book. If students enjoyed or were intrigued with a topic in a book, the teacher should observe their responses, talk with them, and help them find more books of the same topic, genre, or author. Some students who read *Encounter* went on to read biographies of Columbus and looked for books about the Taino and Puerto Rico and books with a dream theme.

Read, talk, draw, write. Younger students especially can draw in response to a book read aloud or in a literature group, talk about the book or their pictures, and either write or give dictation for a title and a caption.

Literature as a Model for Writing

Students draw on their own experience when writing by using a literary form.

Story dramatization. Students talk about the characters and how they act, analyze the story structure, and play the story. Students in the *Encounter* literature group wrote a script based on the book and produced it as a play.

Reader's theater. Any printed text can be adapted for reader's theater: picture books, excerpts from chapter books, traditional literature, and poetry (Shel Silverstein's *A Light in the Attic* or *Where the Sidewalk Ends* are both excellent sources).

Storytelling. Students can retell the story in their own words and also use a flannel board, props, music, and so on. Traditional literature is excellent for storytelling.

Puppetry. Students can choose to make puppets to play a part of the story or the whole story or can create their own story based on a story's characters and puppets they make.

Making puppets and producing a play are excellent response options to literature.

Art making. Options include drawing, painting, collage, constructions, murals, posters, mobiles, dolls, puppets, props for storytelling, costumes and backdrops for drama, and masks.

Media making. Students can create a filmstrip, slides, or overhead transparencies of a story, or their own version of the story, by drawing directly on clear film stock with permanent pens. They can also respond to literature in a variety of ways by videotaping: role-play characters, play a scene or dramatize the whole story, do their own version of the story, do mock interviews with story characters.

Computers. Students can write responses, stories, or scripts, make books, or create hypertexts with print, visuals, and sound in response to literature.

Constructions. Students can build three-dimensional constructions of the story world on a cardboard or Styrofoam base or in a box with one side cut away. They can make dioramas or scenes or landscapes, houses or buildings or boats from a story, or papier-mâché constructions.

Bookmaking. Students can write and make books based on their response to the story or a new version: stapling pieces of paper together with a construction paper cover, Con-Tact paper books, fold-a-books, pop-up books, and so on.

Ripple

The teacher should listen to students' responses and questions during literature discussions. These will often indicate a theme, a focal topic of interest, a pebble that will set off a ripple effect of learning experiences (Cox, 1996). Ideas from students' response journals may also be a source of worthy topics. One easy way for a teacher to develop these is to start, on a sheet of chart paper, a running list of ideas and questions about a book. Another way is to do a cluster or web of student ideas.

Literature Groups

Literature groups are formed when students have a common interest in a book or theme and enjoy working together. Literature groups can be formed to read, write, and discuss the book with the teacher. Or, they can be formed for a longer period of time, even several weeks or a month, for a ripple effect of response-themed learning. These groups require some self-direction on the part of students, who take responsibility for control of their own learning.

Other names for literature groups are book clubs, literature circles, and reading workshops. Although there is no single way to do this, these groups do share certain characteristics:

1. Groups are based on mutual interests: one book, several, or a theme.
2. Groups are flexible and can change membership, amount of time they meet, or focus.

3. Groups are social, cooperative, and collaborative.

4. Groups can be led by a teacher or students.

5. Groups are student- and response-centered and allow ample time and opportunity to read, talk, write, play, and carry out further experiences with literature.

Content Instruction

For Paul's ideas about teaching in the content areas in a literature-based classroom, see Box 3.1.

BOX 3.1

Integrating Content Instruction with Literature-Based Instruction: Mathematics, Social Studies, Science

Content instruction in mathematics, social studies, and science can be integrated quite naturally with literature-based instruction. It is not a substitute for daily, systematic instruction. The rule of thumb, however, is not to force the subject area into the story; rather, let the story dictate what concepts may emerge. Forcing content instruction into a discussion of a story is more of a distraction from a good story than a helpful instruction. Additionally, drawing story characters on worksheets in an attempt to tie a story to student work in other subject areas is no more than a superficial connection between dubious teaching and literature-based instruction. Nevertheless, mathematics, social studies, and science content may be meaningfully integrated with literature-based instruction in numerous ways. The following examples of integration are actual occurrences in Paul's classroom of literature-based instruction that incorporated content areas. Also notice suggestions for successful instruction.

Suggestions for successful integration of mathematics with literature-based instruction

- Do not force mathematics into a story; maintain daily systematic mathematics instruction.
- Let the story and the subsequent student discussion dictate the mathematics concepts to explore.
- When students are writing their own versions of a story, ask for details that involve mathematics: How many? How much? What size? What is the average? How much time did it take?
- When a student expresses an opinion about "what most people think," ask him or her to test that opinion with a survey.
- Look for opportunities to measure dimensions by creating sets and props for plays, life-size animal creations, or mapped-out distances.

Examples

A. *Robbery, Money, and Math:* Two students, Carmina and Rosalinda, were reading one of the Encyclopedia Brown stories in which he solved a robbery case. The girls wanted to write their own version of the story, so I suggested that they keep a detailed record of the money involved.

What they wrote opened with a fast-food business that began the day with $75.45 in the cash register. Before the robbers arrived on the scene of the crime, twelve customers had come buy to purchase food. To know how much money the fast-food business had made to that point, the students created a menu, priced the items, itemized what was purchased by the customers, and added the total sales to the starting amount.

The girls figured that the robbers would be too hurried to deal with the coins in the till, so they figured the amount stolen on the basis of bills. They also included that, prior to being captured, the robbers spent some of the money to purchase a Christmas tree and decorations; the girls subtracted this amount from the total.

Figuring out how much money the fast-food business recovered at the end of the story turned into a complex series of calculations. The students' version of a robbery was not only an entertaining story but also included detailed information of how much money was made, lost, and recovered in an adventurous day. The students authentically responded to the story, integrated mathematics concepts, and developed written language.

B. *Mathematics as the Language of Inquiry:* A natural way to incorporate mathematics concepts with literature-based instruction is to ask students to conduct an opinion survey related to a story. One such example grew out of a discussion of *Henry Huggins,* by Beverly Cleary. While discussing the story about Henry's adventures with various pets such as the dog Ribsy or the fish, José and Johnny speculated what most people would like to have as a pet. This comment opened the way for conducting a seven-step opinion survey:

1. Form a research question (What is your favorite pet?).
2. Hypothesize the outcome.
   a. Establish the range of choices to five or six pets plus "other" for an open choice.
   b. Estimate which pet will be the class favorite.
3. Collect the data.
   a. Devise a way to record responses.
   b. Start asking the question.
4. Organize the data.
   a. Use a table.
   b. Represent the data on a graph.
5. Write down observations.
   a. Record what the graph tells you in sentence form.
   b. Notice any interesting information.
6. Interpret the data.
   a. Calculate the percentages for each pet. Use this formula: (# of votes in a category/Total # of responses) x 100 = _____ %
   b. Compare your results with your original hypothesis. Were you on the mark? How far off was the hypothesis? Why?
7. Report the findings to the class in writing.

The entire inquiry process is a systematic way to naturally integrate dealing with data with literature-based instruction. The process has several instructional benefits: (1) It maintains the integrity of the story of Henry Huggins, (2) written language is developed, and (3) the students learn an open-ended research technique they can apply to numerous inquiry situations.

C. *Measurement and Animals:* While studying Lynne Cherry's *The Great Kapok Tree* (1991), I suggested that the students re-create a life-size version of the different animals in the story. Eduardo's group selected the boa constrictor. They went to the library to research the actual length of an adult boa constrictor and found that the snake ranged in size from ten to fifteen meters in length.

Initially, Eduardo was not impressed by such small numbers. He said, "Oh, that's not very long." So I replied by asking him to take hold of one end of a string. With a meterstick and pieces of masking tape, we marked off each meter. As the string lengthened, Eduardo stepped back until he wound up outside the classroom and down the hall a way. He finally realized the dimensions of this great snake. It was remarkable to see the light bulb go on with use of string and tape as a concrete manipulative.

This concrete way of measuring the length of the boa constrictor in meters had the benefits of building mathematical understanding and giving the students a metered string to accurately measure butcher paper to paint a life-size boa constrictor.

Suggestions for successful integration of social studies with literature-based instruction

- Social studies begins with the story of our lives. Look to touch students' experience with story.
- Compare and contrast opposing stories of the same individual or event.
- Challenge the author. Question the sources for the author's information.
- Interview any knowledgeable person as an expert on his or her own story.
- Validate the life story that each child brings by making his or her life the object of writing and study in the class.

Examples

A. *Biographical Research:* When reading historically based literature, a natural way to incorporate social studies is to research and record the biography of a character in the story. In my classroom, one group of students read Ingri and Edgar D'Aulair's (1955) book *Columbus;* another selected Jane Yolen's (1992) book *Encounter.* The two groups came up with radically different perceptions of Christopher Columbus. The polarization provided a unique opportunity to take a second look at the story of Christopher Columbus.

B. *Interviewing an Expert:* While reading Pura Belpre's (1987) story based in Puerto Rico, "La Gaviota Roja," I remembered that one teacher in the school was Puerto Rican. I mentioned that fact to the students, who in turn invited her to speak to the class. The students formulated questions about the island and its history, took notes during the interview, and wrote up the information in the form of a Big Book.

C. *Recording Your Story:* Whenever possible, I ask students to record their own stories as they relate to the text. This involves interviewing family members or relating a personal account and capturing the story in written form.

Suggestions for successful integration of science with literature-based instruction

- Focus on the processes of science and look for ways to apply those processes where appropriate.
- Combine illustrations with writing to provide for comprehensible input.
- When a story exhibits a wide variety of objects or life forms, allow the scientist inside each child to order them with classification.
- Bring real-life objects or life forms to the classroom whenever possible.

     ▲ Encourage detailed observation in the form of drawings and written expression.
     ▲ Keep reference material at the ready, such as field guides.
     ▲ Compare and contrast examples of objects and life forms in their appearance and/or life cycles.

Examples

A. *Classification:* Barbara Cooney's (1988) *Island Boy* provided Baudelio and Carmen a wonderful opportunity to identify and classify East Coast sea birds as they tried to understand which birds were cormorants in the story. They used a bird watcher's guide as a reference tool and created a poster with the various birds grouped according their unique characteristics.

B. *Detailed Observation:* Sylvia and Laura started reading *Top Secret* by John Reynolds Gardiner (1984), the hilarious story of a boy who invented "human photosynthesis" for a science project. He eventually turns his skeptical teacher, Mrs. Green, into a tree. I suggested that the girls take a closer look at leaves through the microscope to detail the components of leaves that photosynthesize. They drew pictures of the leaves from the microscope observations and labeled the significant parts.

C. *Recording Life Cycles:* The cycle of birth, change, and death is recorded in a myriad of ways in children's literature, whether it is Eric Carle's *The Very Hungry Caterpillar* (1969), the family on Tibbets Island in *Island Boy* (1988) by Barbara Cooney, or plant life in Brenda Guiberson's *Cactus Hotel* (1991). Recording that cycle can take the form of creating a Big Book accompanied by illustrations.
A unique way to document the cycle in the story is to begin with a large tagboard circle (eighteen inches in diameter). Cut a doughnut hole in the middle of the circle (approximately one inch in diameter). Identify the number of stages in the cycle, add one extra for a title page, and cut the circle into corresponding equal parts. Draw the animal or plant at each stage of the cycle on the pieces of the circle. Label each stage. Write an explanation of each stage on a separate card and glue it to the appropriate segment of the circle. Reattach each segment, in order, with cloth tape, allowing for a half-inch space between segments. Accordion fold the pieces so that the title page segment is on top. The final product documents the life cycle.

LITERATURE AND LEARNING ENGLISH AS A SECOND LANGUAGE

It is important to understand the underlying assumptions for the literature-based approach used by a teacher of English-language learners like Paul, described so far in vignettes about Javier and the turnip in Chapter 1, and earlier in this chapter about students in a literature group responding to *Encounter* and reading and talking about Columbus and the Taino people.

Second-Language Literacy

The principles of language acquisition and learning to read are the same, whether a child is learning to read in a first or a second language. Constructivist learning theory (described in Chapter 2) defines how people learn anything, including how to use language. Basically, children learn to speak and read and write by building increasingly sophisticated understandings about language and the world. Children learning to speak and read and write in English build their knowledge of English on both their emerging understanding of English and their first language.

One report (Johnson, 1992) has shown that only 60 percent of teachers of non-native English speakers hold well-defined theoretical beliefs about how children learn a second language, but most of those who do, practice a communicative-based approach with an emphasis on rich social interaction in their classes. These teachers rarely concur with a grammar-based behaviorist view.

Current theory and research supports the idea that children should learn to read in their primary language, and reading and writing experiences in the primary language support second-language acquisition (Hudelson, 1987; Krashen, 1991). Perhaps more important, the ability to read and write in a language other than English should be maintained throughout the child's schooling (Cummins, 1989). The effectiveness of "maintenance" bilingual programs with the goal of producing biliterate students has been well demonstrated (Cummins, 1989; Hakuta & Gould, 1987; Krashen & Biber, 1988). Furthermore, English-language learners can successfully learn to read and write in English while learning to speak it (Edelsky, 1986).

Stephen Krashen puts forth a strong argument for learning to read by reading—especially what he calls "free voluntary reading" (FVR)—in his book *The Power of Reading* (1993). He maintains this is true for students who are learning English as a second language. According to Krashen, "Free reading is one of the best things an acquirer can do to bridge the gap from the beginning level to truly advanced levels of second-language proficiency" (p. x). His review of the research shows the following:

1. Free reading is a powerful tool in language education, a missing ingredient in first language arts, and in second-language acquisition as well.

2. Students who read more in their second language also write and spell better in that language.

3. Learning to read in one language helps students learn to read in a second language.

4. Reading provides knowledge of the world and subject matter knowledge that supports second-language acquisition.

5. Pleasure in reading the first language will transfer to pleasure in learning to read the second language.

Evidence also supports a social interactionist perspective applied to learning a second language. Positive effects have been found as a result of the social context of group participation in literature-based teaching (Raphael & Brock, 1993), as well as parent participation in literature-response groups themselves to help teach their children how to read and write (Ada, 1988).

In a review of studies on teaching English as a second language, especially reading, Jill Fitzgerald (1995) makes several thought-provoking comments:

> The sketch of what goes on in ESL reading instruction might be considered by many reading educators as disheartening. The probable emphasis on word recognition (at least in the lower grades) . . . is inconsistent with a current focus in the literacy field on helping students to create and apprehend meanings with texts—a focus that is espoused by many reading educators and that is evidenced in reading theories which are currently widely embraced by the literacy-research community (e.g., Rosenblatt, 1978; Rumelhart, 1985). Likewise, such emphasis is contrary to instructional implications arising from at least two current predominant theories of second-language learning, namely a cognitive theory (e.g., McLaughlin, 1987) and the Monitor Model (Krashen, 1981). According to these views, instruction should center on meaning. Indeed, Krashen has explicitly outlined a "communicative approach" for use in second-language instructional settings which derives from the Monitor Model (Krashen, 1981). (p. 143)

In addition to the focus on letter and word skills, Fitzgerald notes that we might be concerned about the lack of spoken interaction in classrooms, especially using a discourse style compatible with students' cultural backgrounds. Both of these tendencies are in conflict with current views of literacy learning. She also suggests that the emergent literacy research in the field indicates that benefits can be gained by teaching speaking and literacy together and that reading instruction that is effective for native English speakers is also effective for children learning English as a second language.

Honoring Students' Voices

Teachers who use a text-centered approach often ignore the importance of students' voices. For students learning English as a second language, voice should be the primary goal in both a literal and a figurative sense. Research documents, however, that the content of reading instruction for students learning English as a second language has tended to allow for little interaction and to focus mainly on word recognition with an extraordinary emphasis on drill, as much as half of the time; when understanding was a focus, the emphasis was on literal, factual information. Furthermore, the emphasis on drill over discussion was greater for the lower reading groups (Delgado-Gaitan, 1990; Diaz, Moll, & Mehan, 1986; Mace-Matluck, Hoover, & Calfee, 1984).

Children, both native English speakers and those learning English as a second language, whom I have read to and observed over a seven-year period have demonstrated a natural freedom and eagerness to read and to talk about their responses to literature. This display seems significant when thinking about the future of teaching with literature in elementary schools. Children's ability and independence is not fully acknowledged in the development of the new "literary" basals, in which questions and prompts are provided for the teacher on the assumption that children

Paul listens to a student's ideas as they compose a group song in response to literature, an example of an interactive teaching style in a bilingual classroom.

need them to proceed further in their personal explorations of literature. I have found children capable of asking and answering their own questions, at length.

I also see an inherent conflict between the nature of literature as an art form that can lead to enjoyment, knowledge of the world, and self-knowledge and traditional text-centered methods that ignore the authenticity and diversity of children's unique and personal voice responses to it. Encouraging children to respond authentically and aesthetically and accepting diversity of responses could provide a rich medium of growth for language and literacy development for students learning English as a first or second language. Studies of students learning English as a second language have shown the effectiveness of interactive teaching styles, especially those that are compatible with home-discourse styles with a focus on meaning (Au & Mason, 1983; Delgado-Gaitan, 1990). A study of Hispanic kindergartners in a bilingual program and their teacher during storybook read-aloud time in English revealed a much higher level of participation by students when the teacher was less directive and more interactive and responsive to the students (Battle, 1993). Unfortunately, evidence suggests that many ESL and bilingual programs have "passive learning environments," meaning that teachers talk most of the time and only ask low-level literal questions, rather than provide active and interactive and rich language environments that could enhance language, literacy, academic, and cognitive development (U.S. Department of Education, 1991, 1992).

The example of Anne's first-grade class during reading demonstrates that this is not only a characteristic of classes in which students are learning English as a second language. Anne is one of the students I have been reading to for seven years. She and other students like her have been eager to talk about literature with me, or in class-rooms where their voices are honored such as in Paul's bilingual class, when she visited and joined the *Encounter* literature group. When I have observed these students in their text-centered classrooms, they have been remarkably silent when the teacher indicated that the text and the questions drawn from the teacher's guide were more important than their voices.

The next three chapters of this book show more about many of these ideas. They are case studies of three students over a six-year period, describing their back-grounds and home influences, language development, progress as students, and per-sonal responses to literature while listening and talking about literature with me. As you read them, pay particular attention to their individual voices and how they have been able to use them inside and outside the classroom. The idea of student voice is a fundamental issue in the acquisition of both a first and a second language and reading and understanding literature.

THINGS TO THINK ABOUT

1. Think about how your teachers taught with literature when you were in elemen-tary school. Which theoretical models do you think were behind their approaches? Why?

2. The term *whole language* is often controversial. Why do you think this is so?

3. Think about the lesson with *Anna Banana and Me*. How might you use this same story with a more response-centered approach?

4. Think about more response options for children to respond to literature in addi-tion to those listed in the chapter.

5. What do you think the role of literature should be in second-language education? Compare your ideas with the research on how literature is used and reading is taught, explained in this chapter.

THINGS TO DO

1. Examine a basal reading series that its publisher labels "literature-based"; look at both the student material (e.g., reader, workbook) and the teacher's guide. Which models of the reading process and approach to teaching with literature does it reflect?

2. Observe in a class with a majority of limited-English-proficient students during the time when the teacher is teaching with literature. Take notes and analyze them according to the teacher's approach. What do you think about it? How do you think you will teach with literature?

3. Observe in a bilingual class and do the same activity as in #2 above. Compare the two classes. Notice and record any differences in approaches.

4. Ask at least three teachers of limited-English-proficient students (1) what they think about "whole language" and (2) to what extent they use ideas behind whole-language instruction in their classroom. Jot down your own answers to these two questions. Analyze what you find. Think about your findings in terms of your own teaching.

5. Outline a lesson plan for teaching the story *Anna Banana and Me,* using it in a more response-centered way, compared with the text-centered way it was used as described in this chapter.

6. Read the children's book *Encounter.* Read the description of what happened in Paul's class when a literature group formed around the group and brainstorm some of your own ideas for using this book with a response-centered approach. Try some of them out with a group of limited-English-proficient children or use any good children's book and a response-centered teaching approach.

FURTHER READING

Cantoni-Harvey, G. (1987). *Content-area language instruction: Approaches and strategies.* Menlo Park, CA: Addison-Wesley.

Chamot, A. U., & O'Malley, J. M. (1986). *A cognitive academic language learning approach: An ESL content-based curriculum.* Rosslyn, VA: National Clearinghouse for Bilingual Education.

Crandall, J. (Ed.). (1987). *ESL through content-area instruction: Mathematics, science, social studies.* Englewood Cliffs, NJ: Prentice Hall Regents.
   These three books all address approaches to content area instruction for second-language learners.

Peregoy, S. F., & Owen, F. B. (1993). *Reading, writing, and learning in ESL: A resource book for K–8 teachers.* White Plains, NY: Longman.
   This book provides background on second-language learners but focuses on second-language acquisition and development and literacy instruction, as well as content area instruction, with specific methods and examples of students' work. It addresses the use of literature, including a brief discussion of Rosenblatt's transactional theory as it applies to second-language learners.

Perez, B., & Torres-Guzman, M. (1992). *Learning in two languages: An integrated Spanish/English biliteracy approach.* White Plains, NY: Longman.
   Many examples of students' work illustrate strategies for language and literacy instruction for second-language learners.

Richard-Amato, P. A. (1988). *Making it happen: Interaction in the second-language classroom from theory to practice.* White Plains, NY: Longman.

With an introduction of theories and practice related to second-language learning, the book focuses on the importance of interaction in second-language learning, illustrated with methods and specific activities. Included are selected readings on second-language acquisition theories.

REFERENCES

Ada, A. F. (1988). The Pajaro Valley experience: Working with Spanish-speaking parents to develop children's reading and writing skills in the home through the use of children's literature. In T. Skutnabb-Kangas & J. Cummins (Eds.), *Minority education: From shame to struggle* (pp. 223–238). Clevedon, UK: Multilingual Matters.

Altwerger, B., Edelsky, C., & Flores, B. M. (1987). Whole language: What's new? *Reading Teacher, 41,* 147–155.

Altwerger, B., & Flores, B. (1994). Theme cycles: Creating communities of learners. *Primary Voices, K–6, 2,* 2–6.

Au, K. H., & Mason, J. M. (1983). Cultural congruence in classroom participation structures: Achieving a balanced bill of rights. *Discourse Processes, 6,* 145–167.

Battle, J. (1993). Mexican-American bilingual kindergartners' collaborations in meaning making. In D. J. Leu & C. K. Kinzer (Eds.), *Examining central issues in literacy research, theory, and practice* (Forty-second yearbook of the National Reading Conference, pp. 163–170). Chicago: National Reading Conference.

Bruner, J. (1983). *Child talk: Learning to use language.* New York: Holt, Rinehart & Winston.

Bullock, A. B. (1975). *A language for life.* London: Her Majesty's Stationery Office.

Cox, C. (1996). *Teaching language arts: A student- and response-centered approach.* Needham Heights, MA: Allyn & Bacon.

Cox, C., & Zarrillo, J. (1993). *Teaching reading with children's literature.* Upper Saddle River, NJ: Merrill/Prentice Hall.

Cullinan, B. (Ed.). (1987). *Literature in the reading program.* Newark, DE: International Reading Association.

Cullinan, B. (Ed.). (1992). *Invitation to read: More children's literature in the reading program.* Newark, DE: International Reading Association.

Cummins, J. (1989). *Empowering minority students.* Sacramento: California Association for Bilingual Education.

Delgado-Gaitan, C. (1990). *Literacy for empowerment: The role of parents in children's education.* London: Falmer Press.

Diaz, S., Moll, L., & Mehan, H. (1986). Sociocultural resources in instruction: A context-specific approach. In *Beyond language: Social and cultural factors in schooling language-minority students* (pp. 197–230). Los Angeles: California State University, Evaluation, Dissemination, and Assessment Center.

Edelsky, C. (1986). *Writing in a bilingual program: Habla una vez.* Norwood, NJ: Ablex.

Edelsky, C., Altwerger, B., & Flores, B. (1991). *Whole language: What's the difference?* Portsmouth, NH: Heinemann.

Fitzgerald, J. (1995). English-as-a-second-language reading instruction in the United States: A research review. *JRB: A Journal of Literacy, 27*(2), 115–152.

Froese, V. (1994). Language across the curriculum. In A. Purves (Ed.), *Encyclopedia of English studies and language arts* (pp. 456–457). New York: Scholastic.

Goodman, K. S. (1986). *What's whole in whole language?* Portsmouth, NH: Heinemann.

Goodman, K. S., Shannon, P., Freeman, Y., & Murphy, S. (1988). *Report card on basal readers.* New York: Richard C. Owen.

Gough, P. B. (1976). One second of reading. In H. Singer & R. Ruddell (Eds.), *Theoretical models and processes of reading* (2nd ed., pp. 509–535). Newark, DE: International Reading Association.

Hakuta, K., & Gould, L. J. (1987). Synthesis of research on bilingual education. *Educational Leadership,* 38–45.

Herman, J. L., Aschbacher, P. R., & Winters, L. (1992). *A practical guide to alternative assessment.* Alexandria, VA: Association for Supervision and Curriculum Development.

Hudelson, C. (1987). The role of native language literacy in the education of language-minority children. *Language Arts, 64,* 827-841.

Johnson, K. E. (1992). The relationship between teachers' beliefs and practices during literacy instruction for non-native speakers of English. *Journal of Reading Behavior, 24,* 83–108.

Krashen, S. D. (1991, Spring). *Bilingual education: A focus on current research* (Focus Occasional Papers in Bilingual Education Number 3). Washington, DC: George Washington University, Center for Applied Linguistics.

Krashen, S. D. (1993). *The power of reading.* Englewood, CO: Libraries Unlimited.

Krashen, S. D., & Biber, D. (1988). *On course: Bilingual education's success in California.* Sacramento: California Association for Bilingual Education.

LaBerge, D., & Samuels, S. J. (1976). Toward a theory of automatic information processing in reading. In H. Singer & R. B. Ruddell (Eds.), *Theoretical models and processes of reading* (2nd ed., pp. 548–579). Newark, DE: International Reading Association.

Langer, J. A. (1992). *Literature instruction: A focus on student response.* Urbana, IL: National Council of Teachers of English.

Langer, J. A., Applebee, A. N., Mullis, I. V. S., & Foertsch, M. A. (1990). *Learning to read in our nation's schools: Instruction and achievement in 1988 at grades 4, 8, 12.* Princeton, NJ: Educational Testing Service.

Loban, W. (1979). Relationships between language and literacy. *Language Arts, 56,* 485–486.

Mace-Matluck, B. J., Hoover, W. A., & Calfee, R. C. (1984). *Final report: Teaching reading to bilingual children study: Vol. 8. Executive summary.* Austin, TX: Southwest Educational Development Laboratory.

Moorman, G. B., Blanton, W. E., & McLaughlin, T. (1994). The rhetoric of whole language. *Reading Research Quarterly, 29*(4), 309–329.

Morrow, L. M. (1992). Promoting voluntary reading. In J. Flood, J. M. Jensen, D. Lapp, & J. R. Squire (Eds.), *Handbook of research on teaching the English language arts* (pp. 697–704). New York: Macmillan.

Peterson, R., & Eeds, M. (1990). *Grand conversations: Literature groups in action.* New York: Scholastic.

Raphael, G. E., & Brock, C. H. (1993). Mei: Learning the literacy culture in an urban elementary school. In D. J. Leu & C. K. Kinzer (Eds.), *Examining central issues in literacy research, theory, and practice* (Forty-second yearbook of the National Reading Conference, pp. 179–188). Chicago: National Reading Conference.

Shannon, P. (1988). *Broken promises: Reading instruction in 20th-century America.* Granby, MA: Bergin & Garvey.

U. S. Department of Education, Office of the Secretary. (1992). *The condition of bilingual education in the nation: A report to the Congress and the president.* Washington, DC: Author.

Case Studies of Children

The case studies in this section of the book describe the language and literacy development, progress in school, and responses to literature of three children from kindergarten through fifth grade. These three children are participants in a longitudinal study I (Carole) have been conducting since 1989 (Cox, 1994). I have been reading and discussing books with them since they were in kindergarten. They are now in sixth grade.

The purpose of these case studies is to show children as unique individuals who come to school with differing backgrounds and home influences, languages and language development, experiences as students, and patterns of response to literature. Anne, a native English speaker, is described in Chapter 4. Juan, a native Spanish speaker and English learner, is described in Chapter 5. Eduardo, a bilingual student fluent in Spanish and English, is described in Chapter 6.

As you read the stories of these children, think about points of connection to the principles and practices explained in Chapters 1 through 3. Also think about them in terms of your own teaching, what might be learned by taking a closer look at a particular child, and how you might apply this knowledge in your classroom.

It is important for the teacher to know as much as possible about the students in his or her student- and response-centered classroom. Theory and research from the fields of reader-response criticism, first- and second-language acquisition, and social constructivism suggest that listening to children tell their ideas, interests, and life experiences is the first act of instruction. Briefly put, teachers teach children, not curriculum.

CHAPTER FOUR

The Native English Speaker:
Case Study of Anne

MEET ANNE

Anne has been an excellent student and has been identified as gifted and placed in a gifted program at a public school in pre-kindergarten. She enjoys art, has played the violin since age five, takes dance lessons, and has participated in drama programs and Girl Scouts. She is small, blonde, and outspoken. Someone watching her challenge an older child on the playground for breaking a school rule said: "She doesn't know how small she is, does she?"

Background and Home Influences
Literate family who are readers; books in the home
Many and regular reading experiences
Related story experiences: drama, music, song, dance, art

Language Development: Native English Speaker
English spoken at home
Adults, siblings, and friends listen to and talk with her
She communicates well with others; has a strong "voice"

Anne as a Student
High grades and scores on standardized tests
Quiet in school, compared with outspoken at home
Frustrated with lack of time to read and assigned writing

Anne's Response Process Style: Challenges the Text

Questions what puzzles her; shreds the story

Hypothesizes possibilities, associating her own experience

Has intense drive to create personally meaningful interpretation

Connections to Principles and Practices

Anne learned by doing—speaking and reading; example of social constructivist, communicative-based language acquisition at work at home (many opportunities to use language and engage in literacy experiences).

Anne is a successful student but a quiet "voice" inside school, compared with a strong "voice" outside: example of transmission model of learning (teacher directs and may talk more than students).

Anne challenges the text; example of transactional model of reading (active role of reader in creating literary understanding; primarily aesthetic stance toward literature).

Anne is angry and frustrated about lack of opportunities to read in school and to read for personal exploration; example of dissonance between a child who loves and enjoys reading in teacher- and text-centered classrooms.

BACKGROUND AND HOME INFLUENCES

Anne comes from a white, middle-class home. Her mother is a teacher; her father owns his own business. Both are avid readers. She has two brothers. One was thirteen when she was born; the other was two and a half. Many children's books are in the home. The family makes weekly trips to the library.

Reading is a family affair. When Anne was a baby, her mother read to both young children every day, several times a day. She now encourages Anne's father and older brother to read to her. Her father most often reads to them at bedtime, choosing classics like *Goodnight Moon* and *The Runaway Bunny* by Margaret Wise Brown. He also likes the interactive book *Pat the Bunny* and small board books with action rhymes like "Teddy Bear, teddy bear, turn around." Anne's older brother reads to her, too, when he takes care of her when the mother is busy. He has learned that she is easier to handle when he is reading to her. He is an active teenager and likes to act out the books. He often chooses *The Three Billy Goats Gruff* illustrated by Marcia Brown. He reads the book dramatically, using a different voice for each character. Anne's younger brother is usually involved in reading sessions with their older brother, and they both like to act out the story, with the big brother as the troll. He also likes to read Anne's favorite: *Mother Goose*. They act out these, too. Anne plays Miss Muffet, and one of her brothers is the spider. Or Anne is the cat with the fiddle, and one of them is the cow that jumped over the moon and the little dog that laughed to see such sport. One of them is always the dish that runs away with Anne, who is always the spoon.

Anne has also had exposure to stories through audiotapes of children's books and songs. She has watched *Sesame Street, Mr. Rogers Neighborhood,* and other public television shows for children. Anne's family and home have supported her language and emerging literacy development by providing a print-rich environment, models of literacy, and many opportunities to experience literature and stories in an active, engaging way.

LANGUAGE DEVELOPMENT: NATIVE ENGLISH SPEAKER

Everyone in Anne's family is a native English speaker. She spoke early and well. She was always verbally assertive, not afraid to talk to others or speak her mind. Her family encouraged her to do this. Her baby-sitter came to the home when her mother worked. The sitter took Anne out into the neighborhood, where she played with other children and interacted with their families. The sitter took her shopping and on errands, so Anne was frequently involved with people in the community. She talked a lot, did not wait to be spoken to, and had no trouble expressing an opinion to children or other adults or telling others what they should do. Her brothers describe her as having a "big mouth." Her father says, "There's no question about who's in charge here. It's Anne."

ANNE AS A STUDENT

Anne went to a private preschool half-days when she was two years old. She has had many experiences with books, as well as finger plays, drama, and art. When she was three years old, Anne was tested for the public preschool gifted program and qualified. She said she liked books and enjoyed looking at pictures while the psychologist tested her. He wrote, "Anne is a three-year-old girl who at present time is functioning, according to educational testing, 1 1/2 years above her chronological age in math and 2 1/2 years above in reading. She is a very friendly child who appears to enjoy educational tasks. She should profit greatly from being placed in a preschool class for the gifted."

She attended from eight o'clock to twelve o'clock each day. Her teacher read aloud frequently. Students dramatized stories by dressing up like characters and acting out the stories and made their own book versions of *Brown Bear Brown Bear, What Do You See?* by Bill Martin, Jr. They performed a class musical about Australia. Anne sang a solo about kangaroos. She had many varied experiences with books, stories, and their extensions. Her teacher described her as a child with "excellent concentration, sense of order, inner discipline."

Anne went to kindergarten half-days in the afternoon. Her kindergarten teacher provided daily time for sharing, reading aloud, and self-selected reading. Because Anne was beginning to read independently, the morning kindergarten teacher spent time reading one-on-one with her.

Anne's brother was an early, natural reader and read to her. Although she had many early, enjoyable experiences like this with literature at home and in preschool and kindergarten, she became frustrated with a teacher- and text-centered approach in later years.

Anne's teacher liked to sing. She used poems that could be put to a tune, such as Dennis Lee's "Alligator Pie." The students sang the poem, used hand motions to go with it, read other books about animals, and did a "musical" about animals. They made masks and costumes and presented the musical to the parents. She also provided many art, cooking, and hands-on experiences related to books.

Anne liked her teacher and the time she was given to read books with the morning teacher, and she self-selected books on her own. Her teacher describes her:

Cute little thing. Bright but quiet in a large group, but will talk your ear off in one-on-one situation. Lots of good ideas about books. Read her a story and she can pick out that little idea between the lines. Wonderful little girl. A thinker. You know those little wheels are turning, you know she's thinking when you're talking or reading a book. She's thinking of something great to say, or a story.

At the end of kindergarten, Anne was tested for the gifted program and qualified. The psychologist who tested her noted that she was "quick to answer questions but took time when necessary, was socially confident and at ease with adults, and had a delightful sense of humor."

Anne's first-grade teacher had great charisma. Anne loved to go to school. The school district had just adopted what were called "literary readers." These are basal readers that contain excerpts from children's books. The teachers used the accompanying teacher's guides and the "pupil response" booklets with prompts for students to write after reading. Although Anne still loved books and reading, she did not like these readers.

During reading-aloud sessions with me, she asked questions and talked throughout the reading of the book. By the third session at the end of the year, she asked to read to me herself. During a classroom observation of a literary reader lesson on the story *Anna Banana and Me* (described in Chapter 2), however, she was uncharacteristically quiet. If you remember, Anne's teacher took a text-centered approach, using questions from the teacher's guide and focusing on having students arrive at an agreed-upon meaning of the text and making sure everyone came to similar conclusions. Although Anne was very talkative in the one-on-one reading sessions with me, she did not readily answer the more efferent, text-based questions.

At the end of the year, Anne received an E (excellent progress) in reading on her report card. Her teacher wrote, "I am pleased with Anne's social and academic growth. She takes her job as a student very seriously and is held in high regard by her peers and her teacher."

Anne's second-grade teacher was very relaxed, and Anne was relaxed in school that year. She had become an avid, independent reader. During a classroom observation, I saw the teacher read two versions of *The Three Billy Goats Gruff*. The teacher had a sheet of chart paper with two columns titled "Alike" and "Different." The students were directed to write lists for both columns. The teacher explained that they must always have a specific reason for writing.

Anne's report card and standardized test scores at the end of this year showed she was succeeding academically according to her teacher, school, and district criteria. She received an E in reading. Her teacher noted, "She writes well and is an excellent reader." She received 99 percent in reading on the Metropolitan Achievement (MAT 6) Test.

In third grade, Anne read and talked enthusiastically all the way through our reading-aloud sessions but rarely responded during group discussions in class. She complained about writing and other assigned activities after reading and about assigned reading and book reports. This year, I began asking students what they were reading on their own and how they felt about reading. Anne said: "I like to read a lot. I'm reading *Scared Stiff* and *The Ghost in the Window* from the library at home. I'm more than halfway through it, and it hasn't mentioned anything about a ghost. It's supposed to be a ghost story. There's a ghost on the cover."

I asked her about reading in school and reading at home: "I don't like reading at school very much because I don't have very much time. Like when I'm at home, I can read all I want. I can't at school." Anne again received a grade of E (excellent progress) in reading.

Anne's fourth-grade teacher provided many content-rich activities. Anne thought her teacher was fun at the beginning of the year. But she soon began to struggle with the paper load. Book reports were assigned one after another. The teacher chose the books the students could read from each genre (e.g., mystery, biography). She assigned very structured projects to go with each report. For each of the three biographies the students were required to read from a limited selection of titles, they did one of three projects: (1) dress as the character, (2) make a paper doll, and (3) make a soda can doll. Anne generally enjoyed these things but did not enjoy the books she had to read.

Uncharacteristically, she rebelled against the structured written reports for all the assigned reading in the class. At the end of the year, the class read the paperback *The Great Wave* from the literary reader series, and the teacher gave them ten pages of questions photocopied from the pupil response booklet. Anne stalled on these and barely finished before the year was over. At one point, she asked me whether I thought she would graduate from fourth grade if she didn't do them. She told me she'd been kept after school and had had her name on the board frequently for not keeping up on this kind of work.

Her report card showed, however, that her teacher believed her to be an excellent student who understood the content taught and had exceptional reading skills. The school district switched to a new type of progress report that uses a 1 (low) to 6 (high) scale with a description of each level in all areas graded. On the Reading/Literature Assessment Scale, her teacher gave her a 6 (exceptional) and an E (excellent effort). The scale defines 6 as:

6 Exceptional Reader

An enthusiastic, independent, and reflective reader. Is capable of reading in all content areas and can read a wide range and variety of materials. Consistently produces work that demonstrates comprehension. Is able to make predictions and draw inferences without teacher support.

Despite her high evaluation, Anne was frustrated about reading and her experiences with literature and literature assignments in school. Here are some things she told me at the end of fourth grade about how she feels about reading at home, in school, and in general.

On reading at home:

I love to read at home. My favorite authors are Betsy Byars and Lois Lowry. I'm reading the *Anastasia* books. My favorite series books are *The Babysitter's Club* and *The American Girl* series.

On reading at school:

I hate reading in school because you have to read what they make you. Unless it's a good book, but even if it's a good book they read it to you or you have to read certain parts when you have to. The only time I like reading in school is when the teacher's reading aloud and we can read along, or when we can read for fun—which is never. We never have time to read.

You have to write down the stupid thing. (She sounds very frustrated and is practically crying.) I hate that. You gotta write down everything you do. I don't get how that is reading. And one time I told the truth and she put it wrong. She said, "What was your favorite part?" and I didn't have a favorite part. I said I just liked the whole thing and she counted it off. So I have to make up something, which is real dumb. And they do the hardest things and they get mad at you when you get behind or something. Like, "If you could interview Abel (*Abel's Island*, by William Steig), what questions would you ask him? (In an authoritarian voice.) You had to list twenty questions, and you couldn't ask yes-or-no questions or simple ones. Why not? 'Cause sometimes they're the important questions. Answering questions instead of reading is the dumbest thing in the whole entire world.

After her extended and even angry comments about what she didn't like about reading in school, I asked her what she would like to do in reading at school.

Read it! (emphatically, followed by a long pause here). Think about it. You don't have to talk to anybody. I like thinking. After I read a book, I think for a million years and then go back and read my favorite pages again. Sometimes I read through a book really fast, and then I go back and read my favorite parts again.

Finally, because she had so much to say about how reading was taught and what she didn't like about it, I asked how she would approach reading if she were the teacher. She didn't hesitate:

I'd just say, "Read this book. Go read whatever book you want, and if you want to come tell me about it, you can; or if you don't, just think or just go do something else like read it again or read another book." I'd make it so that you'd bring as many books as you want and just read, read, read, all day.

She is really warmed to the subject by this time and continued to tell me how she felt about reading in general. But more, I think about her feeling of powerlessness in school, especially with regard to not having the kind of experiences with literature she would like and really wanted.

On reading in general:

I love to read. It's my favoritest thing in the whole world. If there was no such things as books, I'd die (spoken dramatically). 'Cause it's not fair if nobody invented books. I'd be so mad. I'd invent a book. What if suddenly, that really mean guy . . . Adolf Hitler . . . what if someone like him came and took away all the books in the world? I'd be so mad that I'd say, "You're the stupidest, ugliest, meanest person in the whole entire world." I'd punch him in the nose. Didn't you do that once when you were little, you told me, (in a previous session) when someone teased your little brother? (Yes.) Did you get in trouble? (Not exactly; I was little and blonde and a girl. Nobody thought I'd do anything like that.) *Blonde?* What does that have to do with it? Little? Girl? I'm blonde, little, and a girl. If somebody as mean as Hitler took over, I'd beat him up.

My question about reading obviously touched a nerve with Anne, and I sensed that a lot of feelings she had kept quiet were exploding now. She was ready to punch Hitler in the nose if he took books away. She was only partly joking, and I don't think she really meant Hitler. I sensed real anger here. Remember, this is not a child who has not succeeded in school, but to the contrary: one who has been extremely successful, from standardized test scores to teacher performance evaluations. Her comments about reading, as well as those of other students in this study, mirror her feelings that reading is something she wants but can't have in school. Real reading takes place in the library or at home. Think about how this could influence decisions that teachers make about teaching with literature and language and literacy development for all children.

ANNE'S RESPONSE PROCESS STYLE: CHALLENGES THE TEXT

Anne's most frequent type of response in reading-aloud sessions with me is to aggressively question something she finds anomalous. To seek a resolution, she forms hypotheses, tests them against her own experience, and develops an explanation.

To understand Anne's response process style, picture a courtroom with a trial in session. At any point during testimony, an attorney may question a witness to clarify details, to prevent simplification of a complex question, or to expand partial information. Anne is the attorney. The text is the witness. She is relentless whenever she sees even a possibility to chip away at what appears to be generally accepted as the truth. Anne is most actively engaged with the text when she can challenge it through questions, uncover ambiguities, and probe for possible explanations.

Anne's response process style is to challenge the text. She pounces on any part that strikes her as odd. She wrestles it to the ground until she has developed some sort of satisfactory explanation for herself. She does not ask questions because she is confused and wants the teacher to explain things to her; rather, she asks questions because she is confused and trying to figure it out herself.

In kindergarten, for example, during my reading of *Make Way for Ducklings*, she stopped me toward the end of the story, when the mother duck, followed by her ducklings, waddles across the street and into the Boston Public Garden to make a home. Something was apparently bothering her.

Anne: Why is it public?
Carole: Public? That means anybody can go there.
A: Oh. Like a public school.
C: Yes.
A: Anyone who wants to can go there?
C: Yes.
A: No. No. Not robbers. Not people who don't know this school.
C: Not robbers?

A: Not just robbers, but people who are bad at this school. Guess what happened once?

C: What?

A: Lauren—and I forgot, someone else—but they were by, you know, the corner of the kindergarten gate. They said there was this boy, he came into the school and he had this knife and he killed an old man there.

C: What?

A: They saw him, and then after, um . . . It's a true story!

She was also one of the three students in kindergarten who asked to read words. It is important to note that these were the words that were hand-drawn by Robert McCloskey to show quacking and sound effects: "Quack! Honk! Weebk!" These were the only words any of the three asked to read.

In first grade, Anne talked throughout the reading of *Alexander and the Terrible, Horrible, No Good Very Bad Day*. She questioned many things. Alexander said over and over that he was going to Australia because he was having a bad day. Anne obviously didn't think this was a good idea. She had strong feelings about this. She didn't hesitate to talk directly to Alexander and tell him exactly what she thought:

> But why are you going to Australia? Why are you going there? It's boring! There are too many kangaroos. There are too many ostriches. Too many . . . Oh, God.

She enjoyed *Rosie's Walk* and took the book from me and read it aloud, one of only four students to read independently to me in first grade.

In second grade, Anne talked all the way through the reading of *Caps for Sale* and at the end said, "Can I read?" She pretended to put a cap on her head before she read. As she read, she flipped back and forth among the pages, comparing them. She slouched in the chair when I read, but sat up energetically while she read, touching the book and acting out her ideas. In this response, she again stopped the story to challenge a character's idea. The peddlar in the story has not been able to sell any of his caps. He is tired and decides to sit under a tree. This scenario did not sit well with Anne. This time, she put herself in the same situation. She began to read the story aloud and then stopped to challenge the peddlar's statement:

> "That's a nice place for a rest," thought he. *It is?* I would get ants on me. Because trees have ants on them. I wouldn't want to sit there. They hurt me. I would sit in the ocean. With my bathing suit on. I'd try to turn into a mermaid. I like lying in it with my life jacket on.

In third grade, Anne talked all the way through *Ira Sleeps Over* and read parts aloud herself. This part of her response to this book clearly showed that her characteristic response process style is to shred the text. In one part of the story, Ira is spending the night at his friend Reggie's house. They are telling ghost stories. Ira has been afraid to go to Reggie's house even though they are best friends and live next door to each other, because he sleeps with a teddy bear and is afraid that Reggie will laugh at him. Anne dealt with this issue but first challenged the idea that ghost stories are necessarily scary. She didn't think so.

What if it's a good ghost story? Ghosts don't have to be scary. I love ghost stories. (She makes ghost sounds and tells about a ghost book she's reading.) . . . Is he hard of hearing (when Ira asks him whether he sleeps with a teddy bear)? No. I don't think so. He just doesn't want to answer because he thinks they'll make fun of him. He's pretending to be asleep. I think I figured it out. He pretended to fall asleep because he didn't want to talk anymore about his teddy bear. And maybe he thought Ira wasn't going to get his teddy bear. I think that's dumb. What's wrong with a teddy bear? I like taking my teddy bear to my friend's house. You know what I think? He should do? I think he should—even though he's just saying that so his sitter won't make fun of him—he should every night practice sleeping without his teddy bear. So he'll get used to it.

In fourth grade, Anne talked throughout the reading of *A Chair for My Mother.* She had heard the book before, but this did not seem to diminish her enthusiasm. She followed her usual pattern of asking questions when something intrigues or puzzles her, something she thinks is amiss. She began immediately on page 1:

How old is she? I think she's my age. No, I think she's seven or eight. When does this take place? Her pants look like the 70s or 80s. They have bell bottoms, well, not exactly bell bottoms but it looks like the 70s.

In fifth grade, I was surprised that Anne almost tried to sit on my lap as I read to her. She seemed needy for the intimacy of a personal one-to-one reading session. I wondered whether she would still feel this way. Contrasted with what she said in fourth grade about never being able to read, it was not surprising that she wanted to slip back into an almost lap-reading mood. She asked questions all the way through my reading of *Song of the Swallows.* She frequently put herself into the story, comparing it with her own experiences and how they were alike and different.

Anne follows a pattern in her responses. She questions, challenges, or notes something that puzzles or intrigues her, something she is uncomfortable with and wants to "fix." She hypothesizes or speculates some possibilities, often associating her own experience to reinforce her concern or to support one of her hypotheses. Somewhere she explains why it could have occurred or what the outcome might be.

Sometimes it's a quick response; at other times she launches into an extended monologue or occasionally draws me in for information or verification. Not much of what I say seems to move her away from her drive to figure out whatever intrigued or bothered her to begin with. These are the times when she is most enjoying the reading and the story—when she makes it her own. She demands ownership of her reading. Her comments about reading in school, however, show that she is rarely able to exercise her passion for reading and her strong voice in response to literature, nor does she even have time or opportunities to read in school. There is a dissonance between Anne's experiences with literature inside and outside school, and she is increasingly dissatisfied and frustrated with it. She wants to read and believes she can't. She has strong feelings about her reading but believes she can't express them. Her metaphor for the teacher and reading in school is Hitler burning books.

A Thought
from Paul
Reading this case study of Anne, I've had some thoughts about implications of reader-response theory for all students, not just the language-minority students I have always taught. My original assumption was that marginalized children were the most silenced when it came to responding to anything that went on in school. I have believed that affluent, white, English-speaking students like Anne are readily perceived as having knowledge and experience to contribute to the discussion of a literary text and are encouraged to give voice to their thoughts in response to literature, whereas low-income bilingual students tend to be taught with the notion that they are at a deficit. And students who sense being perceived as deficient resist instruction. They know they are being devalued and respond accordingly. Most of the programs that I have seen designed for remedial as well as bilingual instruction control the words, the texts, and the thoughts that students have access to in school. Many of my students come from illiterate homes where no books are available to them. But after reading Carole's case study of Anne, it has become obvious that, even among the highly gifted, predominantly English-only classrooms, students are not given the opportunity to respond to literature out of their own experience.

THINGS TO THINK ABOUT

1. Think about the lessons with literature in Anne's first-grade class (described in more detail in Chapter 3) and second-grade class (described in this chapter). What learning theory and model of teaching with literature guide these lessons? (It is also the model guiding the literary readers series used in the school district.)

2. Compare reading experiences at home, in class, and with me for Anne. What are some of the similarities and differences?

3. How do you think Anne sees her role as a reader? The role of the adult?

4. How do you think Anne's teachers see her role as a reader? The role of the adult?

5. What ideas do you have about teaching with literature, and language and literacy development after reading this case study?

THINGS TO DO

1. Keep a journal of children's responses to literature and reading patterns. If you are teaching, do this with your own students. Keep a notebook with a page for each student, noting such things as books they read, reading behaviors, reading conferences with you, and responses during discussions.

2. If you are not teaching, observe in a classroom in which the students have time and opportunities to read. Take field notes of general activity in the room; note students reading and interacting with texts, with other students, and with the teacher as they respond to literature.

3. Start a case study. Choose up to three students in your own or someone else's class. Observe them in the classroom, interview parents (and teachers if you are not the classroom teacher), and tape-record reading and responding to literature

in a one-to-one session or in small groups. Collect student writing related to experiences with literature.

FURTHER READING

Read other case studies and narratives of students and teachers, such as the following:

Bissex, G. L. (1980). *Gnys at work: A child learns to read and write.* Cambridge, MA: Harvard University Press.

Dyson, A. H. (1994). *The social worlds of children learning to write in an urban primary school.* New York: Teachers College Press.

REFERENCE

Cox, C. (1994, April). *Young children's responses to literature: A longitudinal study.* Paper presented at the annual meeting of the American Educational Research Association, New Orleans.

CHAPTER FIVE

The English Learner:
Case Study of Juan

MEET JUAN

Juan spoke little English entering school in kindergarten when he told me, "I don't know that much because I speak Spanish." He made remarkable progress in English through first grade. He was not in a bilingual program, nor did he have any primary language support, and he has struggled in school. He loves soccer and riding horses when he visits his grandfather's ranch in Mexico. He greatly admires his father, who is dedicated to helping Juan succeed.

Background and Home Influences
Family ties strong, including extended family
Parents have limited education, less than high school
Importance placed on learning English and succeeding in school

Language Development: English as a Second Language
Spanish spoken at home
Placed in ESL pull-out class
Learned English quickly by end of first grade

Juan as a Student
Intellectual potential greater than school performance
Repeated first grade; special education pull-out class
Still receiving special services through fifth grade

Juan's Response Process Style: Makes Personal Connections

Links literature to his own experience

Most fluent when telling family stories

Enjoys, understands, and appreciates literature

Connections to Principles and Practices

Juan's father dedicated to his success but opposes bilingual education even though Spanish spoken primarily at home and limited literacy experiences in either language; example of gap between home and school language and culture.

Juan learned to speak English easily but struggles in English-only classrooms; example of limited bilingualism lacking primary language support, other factors notwithstanding.

Juan responds fluently and interested in reading, takes time in one-to-one sessions; less responsive in classes in which emphasis is on language versus communication.

Juan makes personal connections in response to literature; example of importance of linking reading to life in reader-response driven approaches and second-language approaches that emphasize prior experience.

BACKGROUND AND HOME INFLUENCES

Juan is a first-generation Mexican American. Juan's mother is an at-home mom, and Juan has three siblings: an older sister and two younger brothers. Spanish is the home language. Juan's father speaks English but slips into Spanish when he can't think of a word he wants or becomes philosophical.

Both parents attended school in the same Mexican village of about 5,000 people. His father went to school for six years, and his mother for seven, although she repeated years and didn't go every day. His mother said she doesn't remember anything from her school days, doesn't enjoy reading, and doesn't have time with four children. The father said he loved school and "read most books I have in my hand." The only books in their childhood homes were the ones they were given at school.

Juan's parents said he does not like to read enough to initiate reading events. The father tries to read to Juan every night but sometimes works late. They average reading three times a week. They read stories and the children's page in the newspaper on Wednesday. He said: "The reading Juan likes the best are comic books, sometimes history, like George Washington or somebody. Sometimes I read to him. I don't know if he picks it up or not."

Sometimes his older sister reads to him. She is the best English-language role model but loses patience when Juan reads to her and does not know all the words. Juan's father and sister apparently do not discuss Juan's ideas about a story or the meaning of the text. They focus instead on reading the words correctly and pronunciation.

Juan's father wanted to continue in school because his father wanted him to become a "big person—a doctor or a priest, a professional," but they didn't have money. He left school at age thirteen. Like many other Mexican Americans with ambition but without money, Juan's father emigrated to the United States at age fifteen. The family live in a non-Hispanic, middle-class area because the father's employer bought a house for the family to live in so that the children could go to a "good school." Juan's father said: "He (Juan) have to be somebody . . . a doctor . . . a lawyer . . ." To this, Juan said: "No—a mechanic so I can fix your truck. (His father laughs heartily.) I really want to be a policeman."

Juan's father has been unhappy with the bilingual program his daughter is in. But he wasn't happy when he found out she signed up for typing as an elective in middle school instead of Spanish. He said she will take Spanish in the future.

The extended family is an important influence in Juan's home. His father expressed dismay at the differences in the importance his non-Hispanic associates place on the extended family. Juan's family members from Mexico come to visit frequently, and Juan and his family return to Mexico frequently. They exchange letters regularly. Relatives who live locally take an active role in caring for the children in Juan's family.

LANGUAGE DEVELOPMENT: ENGLISH AS A SECOND LANGUAGE

Juan attends the same school as Anne. The school has a 14.7 percent limited-English-proficient (LEP) population. Juan is the only Hispanic student in his class. The opportunity to speak Spanish does not often arise at school. None of the teachers at his school speak Spanish. He is in a pull-out English as a second language (ESL) class held in the foyer of the auditorium.

Juan made remarkable progress in learning to speak English from kindergarten through first grade. The first time I read to him in kindergarten, he was very shy. The book was *The Snowy Day*. All he said was, "I don't know that much because I speak Spanish," which is a lot to say if you supposedly don't speak English. A year later at the end of first grade, he gave fourteen separate spoken responses to a book and was one of only four students out of thirty-eight to offer to read aloud to me.

At the end of first grade, a test of oral English placed him at the intermediate fluency level. His placement in ESL class, however, continued through fourth grade even though he had reached the M (mastery) level on the IDEA Proficiency Test (IPT; used in the district to evaluate oral proficiency in English for identification and redesignation of LEP students) two years earlier. The scores on this test ranged from A to F—the best score—until a student reaches the M level. This test is one of three components for redesignation as a fluent English speaker: (1) IPT score, (2) achievement test scores, and (3) teacher recommendation.

On the basis of his IPT score of M, Juan should have been redesignated as fluent-English-proficient (FEP) two years earlier, but he was not. Evidently, low achievement test scores and lack of teacher recommendation were prevailing factors. Interestingly enough, also at the end of fourth grade, Juan took the California Assessment System (CAS) 2 standardized test while most other students in the district took the Metropolitan Achievement Test (MAT) 6 to assess students' mastery of basic skills in reading, language, and mathematics.

Paul told me of two interesting consequences of Juan's lack of redesignation as FEP. One is that his standardized test scores could not be used in school or district averages because most other students took a different test. The second is that he was not eligible for obtaining other services unrelated to language because he was still classified as LEP. The question arises whether Juan's educational interests were best served or whether he was not reclassified to keep his anticipated lower test scores from the school average.

In fourth grade, Juan told me with some pride that he had a cousin who was bilingual Spanish/English, had learned French, and was on a scholarship at UCLA. I told him I had lived in France, and we talked about how a person learns to speak a language by using it with people. Later in this same discussion, he told me about a cousin who had been killed in a random drive-by shooting because the cousin was Latino—not a gang member, but a good student, baseball player, and prom king. Juan said his dad was concerned about things such as dress and being mistaken for a gang member and especially that Juan stay in school. Juan said: "When I grow up, I want to give him a Corvette and a house in Mexico. If you're bilingual, you can get a job helping doctors and they pay you a lot of money. Or, I could go to college and play soccer and get a lot of money."

JUAN AS A STUDENT

Juan's kindergarten teacher had a very student-centered approach. She mentioned self-esteem first when asked how she teaches. She wanted children to love to be at school, enjoy it, use their own ideas and think, and work independently. It was important to her that children discover things on their own through play and experimenting.

With literature, she liked children to think about what is happening in a story or what could happen—not just retelling an event or the name of a person, but how they can relate it to their own experiences. She suggested these kinds of aesthetic prompts to them: "If I tried to do that . . ., that story reminded me of . . ., maybe I could handle it that way," and so on. She liked lots of discussion during and after reading, for them to create their own story.

At the end of the school year, she thought Juan would have a hard time in school, not just because of language but because it was hard to get answers out of him. She suggested it might be immaturity and language but that it might also be some kind of learning problem. She said it was difficult to talk with him about a book, for example, because he didn't seem to know what was going on. At the end of kindergarten, Juan scored at the 1 percent level in language (English) on the Test of Basic Experience (TOBE) 2.

Juan's first-grade teacher did lots of literature-based activities. During one week, all the students made puppets of their own design of the characters from *Katy No-Pocket* and shared them with the whole class. Afterward, she reread *Katy No-Pocket* and they discussed the book along the way. She asked the students, "What do you think Katy is thinking?" She called on Juan, but he didn't answer. Other students hypothesized: If she has more babies, she'll have more pockets; the baby's excited; maybe the mother will let him have friends. His teacher said:

> Juan tried hard but frequently "shut down." He would not make eye contact when you talked to him. He was more comfortable after school. He would cry if pushed. He wants to be a leader. He was uncomfortable making choices. An effective approach with him is using consistent guidelines and positive reinforcement.

Juan tested at the average level for cognitive abilities. It was noted that there seemed to be a consistent discrepancy between his ability and his achievement in reading and writing. Juan was retained at the end of first grade, it was noted, primarily because of his limited English and low reading scores.

Juan repeated first grade with another teacher. He was put into the "lowest" reading group. His teacher used a highly structured phonics reading program, the Spaulding method. Here is a Spaulding lesson on writing letters she did one day with Juan's group. She called them "phonograms." She wrote the following letters on the chalkboard: d g y x z e o s v. Each child had a red pencil and copied the letters as they talked.

Juan: I did it wrong.
Teacher: What do you do when you do it wrong?
J: Correct it.
T: Raise your hand if you left a space and wrote "qu."

(Juan raises his hand but another child, Mark, doesn't.)

T: Mark, did you write it?
M: Yes.
T: You need to raise your hand so I know. Put your finger on the next phonogram. Read to me the next phonogram. Now write it down. You should have written this (J). What does this letter remind you of Juan?
J: My name.
T: Move to the next phonogram (P). What does it say?
J: PPP with mouth.

She remained in tight control of all classroom activities. Talking with other students was highly discouraged. She read aloud, and the students answered questions she asked that directed them back to the text for answers.

Art or writing in response to literature occurred only once a week and was very teacher-directed. For example, after reading a story to the whole class aloud about scary things in a tree, she directed students to draw their own creatures in a tree. She told them to work without telling or showing their neighbor what they were doing: "I'll show you what everyone's done."

Despite this direction, Juan whispered to his neighbor that he would draw a two-headed snake. He couldn't seem to get started, however. He whispered to his neighbor: "My uncle has a snake, and he puts it around his neck. Sometimes he puts it around my neck and lets me touch it." Then he started to draw but continued to tell his neighbors about his extensive snake experience. He went to the teacher to show her, and she came to his desk to write his name. He said: "I can write my own name. I have another name. I have four names. My mom's name, too." The teacher said suspiciously: "Is that so? I don't know about that fourth name." She obviously did not know about use of the mother's maiden name among Hispanics.

She used the same literary reader as the other first-grade teacher for reading lessons with the whole class. Because this was Juan's second year in first grade, he had already heard most of these stories. He seemed bored and frustrated by some of the repetition of books, and as a result he appeared uninterested in the work. His teacher thought it was a developmental problem or he's "lazy." Juan's father said he knew Juan could work more in reading but that Juan was learning to speak English so well that they didn't want to "push" him in reading and "confuse him." His mother said: "When he doesn't know a word, he asks me what it says. This year, I only tell him one time and he remembers. Last year, I had to tell him many times. Many times, he confuses the b and d." They thought his repeating a grade had been successful because "he seemed to be learning a little more every day." Unfortunately, the teacher did not share this view of his progress.

English language learners like Juan who enjoy talking about family and friends in connection with literature would benefit from many opportunities to share their experiences in the classroom.

In second grade, Juan's teacher did lots of cooperative group work in which students interact with each other. She encouraged discussion, when she talked with the whole class, and language exchange among students in groups. She incorporated many activities across modalities. By this point, Juan had spent two years in first grade and was receiving special education help an a pull-out and ESL classes. She commented:

> He's hard to describe. You have to look. He is a sensitive and deep person. He wants to be a perfectionist. He loves sports. That's all he wants to talk about. He says he wants to move back to Mexico like his Uncle and have a ranch. That's his goal. He is very intimidated to speak in front of the class. He doesn't readily participate in whole-class discussions but is a leader in small groups. His writing is simple but to the point. When he tells his story, he will embellish it greatly. He is more confident with his writing skills now. He will write some and then tell us the way he wants it. I have met his father three times. He is very loving and wants the best for Juan. He is not able to spend enough time with him to make a difference. A lot of his upbringing has been by his older sister. He puts her on a pedestal. He doesn't talk much about his mom. She has no English, really. I think maybe Juan may be embarrassed about that. He goes to ESL and RSP. His spoken and written language don't match. I think there may be perceptual problems. He took a big step in February. He started to go to the library when it stayed open after school to pick out a book he knew he could read. He picked sports books, and he would tell stories based on his reading. He did a biography report on Bob Griese, former quarterback for the Miami Dolphins. There is still a big gap between Juan's potential and his performance. He speaks well, and he does choose to read, especially about sports. He never chooses to write. They worked on that in RSP.

All second-grade students in his school took the MAT 6 test. He tested at 4 percent in reading, 19 percent in language, and 54 percent in mathematics. It was noted at this time that Juan did not read or write Spanish.

Juan's third-grade teacher said he seemed frustrated, and the RSP teachers said, "Something is missing; you can only teach him strategies." He was still in an ESL pull-out class.

When I asked him about school, he said that it was fun and that he was doing fine. About reading, he told me his dad was going to take him to the public library after school if his dad came home early and could still take him to soccer practice. I asked him about books he liked to read. He said:

> Sometimes I pick out sport books, sometimes make believe books, sometimes truth books. My favorite book was a sport book about Péle. . . . At home, I read by myself, but if I don't know a word, I ask my sister and she tells me. She's fifteen. My dad reads with me, too. Actually, I read to him—soccer books, regular books, all kinds. I read to my little brother. He's in kindergarten. I read to him, and then my dad signs his home reading chart. Once I read to him, then my dad signs mine, too, and then he signs my little brother's. I read "Cinderella," easy books.

He talked about his motivation for doing well in school:

> My dad says if I study I can go to Mexico for a whole summer by myself. I would stay with my grandpa, grandma, and other grandpa. On the ranch, a baby horse got

born. But it died. He was running and there were like little things on the bars so no one could go in there and there's only one way by a gate and you could have to walk a half a mile and he got in there.

When Juan was in fourth grade, an English language development (ELD) teacher came to Juan's class and worked with him. His teacher said he gained a lot of confidence and was more mature.

JUAN'S RESPONSE PROCESS STYLE: MAKES PERSONAL CONNECTIONS

Juan responded little in kindergarten. Even though the situation was very informal— we sat on the floor in the anteroom outside the classroom—Juan was nervous and ill at ease, even frightened, compared with the other fifty-six students. He seemed inhibited because of his limited English although he spoke well enough to say to me, "I don't know that much because I speak Spanish," when I read to him the first time (the book *The Snowy Day*). The only other thing he said was, "He's sleeping," about the little boy in the book. He said little the rest of the year—one comment about the size of the ducks in *Make Way for Ducklings* and to tell me he got *Miss Rumphius*, one of the stories I read, out of the library.

What a difference a year made. Juan's development in English through first grade was remarkable, and he showed a marked change in his behavior during our reading sessions. From saying little or nothing in kindergarten, he had a lot to say and seemed to enjoy talking with me about books.

He sat close, smiled, touched the book, and turned the pages back and forth to look again at parts of the story I had already read. Like Anne, he responded primarily aesthetically. He seemed most engaged with the text, however, when he could associate it with his own experience. After I read *Umbrella*, he talked about a friend.

Like my friend Jonas, he got an umbrella when it was a cold day and it went over a car. (He got an umbrella?) On the car. He was holding it like that. It was cold and it was kind of rainy. The wind blowed it all the way to the car right there. It was kind of funny and we was laughing. (Oh, really? It blew away from him?) Yeah, and he was saying, "It's not funny. It's not funny." (It wasn't to him?) It wasn't funny to him. No.

This was the longest sustained speech on a single topic that had occurred so far in our reading-aloud sessions. Notice that he didn't talk about the book; rather, the book triggered the talk about his friend.

At the end of the year when I read the single, long, simple sentence that is the text for the picture book *Rosie's Walk*, Juan commented about what was happening throughout the reading and asked a few questions. Afterward, he said very forcefully, "I want to read." It was as though he had waited during the reading, made a few comments he thought I wanted to hear, but primarily wanted to show me his new reading ability. He seemed to remember more than he was actually reading the words, focusing on the meaning of the story. He said *chicken* for *hen* and *gate* for *fence*. What's interesting is that while reading, he asked pointed questions and developed plausible hypotheses and explanations as a result and did not wait for me to ask him about the book as he had done before. He was more actively involved in the reading. This was not surprising because he was doing the reading and seemed to feel in charge of the situation. We were co-discussants, rather than teacher and student. He seemed pleased with himself when we finished. He asked me when I'd be coming again. He asked whether he could read to me again then.

Juan was one of only four of thirty students who asked to read to me at the end of first grade. He got many words wrong, but he tried hard and obviously understood the story by substituting words that made sense for ones he didn't know and seemed to enjoy himself—quite a change from the child who told me, "I don't know that much because I speak Spanish" only a year ago.

Three important things occurred, each coinciding with the reading of each book. The first time I read, he demonstrated his ability and confidence in speaking English, which had developed significantly over a year's time. He responded much like the majority of the other students, taking a predominantly aesthetic stance. The second time I read, he really opened up through making associations with the story and his personal life. His speech in English was fluent and extended. He had a lot to say. The third time, he asked to read aloud to me. During the reading, instead of asking me questions about things that puzzled him, he asked the questions but developed his own hypotheses and explanations. He was more confident about not only his English and reading but also his ideas. This was "meaning construction" in the best sense of the term, integrally tied in with language development, literacy, and personal response to literature.

In first grade the second time, Juan's response was predictable and similar to that of many students. *Caps for Sale* is a predictable pattern book. He answered the question posed in the text: "What do you think he saw?" Juan had little else to say in response to the book. This was typical of many of the other students who responded to this book.

Juan's richest—certainly most fluent—response was to the second book I read in second grade, *The Nicest Gift*. We talked and read for close to an hour. He acted it out through facial expressions, pantomiming, and voice characterizations. He was highly engaged in the story. I believe two things triggered the explosion of association-type responses Juan made. First, the book has words in Spanish, and second, he corrected my Spanish pronunciation:

Juan: Where is this?
Carole: L.A. Downtown.
J: This? (pointing to hills around city).
C: Hillsides. East L.A. His house is pink. (Reading . . . *cabaillto*.)
J: *Caballito* (he corrects my pronunciation).
C: Thank you. What does it mean?
J: Little horse.

His interest was piqued here. Juan's first language was suddenly important, and he knew more about it than I did. After this, he made one personal association after another with his own life and the lives of the Hispanic characters in the book.

J: Tamales? My mom makes 'em. My grandma at Mexico and she has a rancho and she has my horse and when my dad went to Mexico and took 'em and when there was a fiesta we were in 'em—me, my dad, my grandpa.
C: You ride?
J: Yeah (pretends the chair is a horse and shows me how to get on and ride on it).

After that, he never got out of the saddle but galloped through this book, telling me one story after another about his life. Sometimes one part of a picture or even one word—especially when he could correct my pronunciation—would set him off on an extended anecdote. He was having fun. I was amazed to see how much he had to say. I read. He talked. I listened. He talked some more. This was different from going from saying very little (". . . because I speak Spanish") to talking and reading in English. That could be expected from his year's experience in an English-only classroom. What was notable was how much more he had to say when he was interested, engaged, and could draw on his own life experience as a basis for his talking and responding. He also knew he was impressing me. And I was, indeed, impressed. He told me many things, especially about his family. For example:

> (I read ". . . calls out *como* . . ."). "That means "How are you?" My dad were gonna go to Christmas down there. (Mexico?) Yeah. But no fair. They're going and I'm not. (Not going to take you?) No. Plus, my uncle's getting married and my uncle wants me to give those little things that men put on, right here . . . (Boutonnieres?) Yeah. Mom said, "No, 'cause you'll miss school." But I said, "He wants me." She goes, "No. Stay here. With aunt or grandma." I'd rather stay with my grandma. My aunt just likes to go to the beach with my other uncle and get wet and I say that's boring, even cold. He shouldn't go to the beach when it's cold. My cousin is nice, though.

Juan most's characteristic response type is association. He most frequently shared family stories and stopped to talk about a part of the story when he could make an association with his own experience. He asked questions for information and suggested explanations for things in the story through dialogue with me. He searched for explanations and for understanding the story while he did so. The story *The Nicest Gift* was about a lost dog and a boy's search for him. Juan wove questions and hypotheses and explanations for the whereabouts of the dog throughout his family stories. At the end, he told me he liked the whole thing, especially the way the story went up and down and around, just like the pictures of the hillsides and city streets of Los Angeles—a rather sophisticated analogy, comparing the structure of the story to the style of the illustrations.

In second grade, before we sat down, Juan asked whether he could read to me. He told me his dad had said, "Please, could I?"—but not, Juan declared, with the tape recorder. As he read, he stopped and commented often. His reading became very halting at points. It seemed to me he had been "over phoniced." If he didn't know a word, he would say the first letter—and then look at me. Through my experience with Juan since kindergarten, it was obvious he understood and enjoyed stories but seemed to believe he should use other types of knowledge—for example, like letter names—when reading even though this technique rarely worked for him.

In first grade, he substituted words in *Rosie's Walk* that still made sense in the story and enabled him to keep reading. It seemed, however, that after a year in a class with a teacher using the Spaulding method and tightly controlling all classroom activities, he believed reading was a process of "sounding out," rather than of putting meaning and sounds together. He has also had RSP and ESL classes that also emphasized "the code" and that took a grammar-based rather than a communicative-based approach. He seemed much more tense talking about reading. He still enjoyed it when I read to him and interacted with me freely.

After he read and stopped several times, I asked whether he wanted me to read to him first and then he could read to me if he wanted. He was happy with this. His responses to the book I read, *Ira Sleeps Over*, were similar to those of many of the other students. Most comments were aesthetic: He hypothesized about story events, noted a part he liked, asked questions, and made associations. His efferent responses were typical, too: about story content and an explanation. He did not provide the detailed family stories as he had done the year before in response to *The Nicest Gift*.

This was the first year I asked students questions about reading: How do you feel about reading? What books do you read? What about reading at home? In school? Juan's answers were revealing.

> I'm trying to get my Super Nintendo. Study, my dad says. I tried to pass a test today. (Which?) Spelling. (How do you feel about reading?) Good. (What are you reading?) About flowers and how to take care of them. Three stories. (How do you feel about reading in school?) Sometimes I'm embarrassed. (Why?) 'Cause I don't know some of the words. But I'm trying to practice them at home. (How?) My dad usually helps me. (What?) He reads with me, and sometimes my mom even helps me. She knows a little English. (Do you have your own books at home?) A lot. A whole bookshelf full. Sometimes my sister and I read. I read to her, and then I read to my mom, and she reads to me and Dad. (Is your sister older?) She's fourteen. She's a good reader. (You said earlier you wanted to read to me.) Yeah. But without the mike. Why do you want to read to me? (I'm interested in what children think about stories). Mmmmm. (Did your dad ask if you could read?) Yeah. My dad asked if I could please read to you! (OK. Read to me!)

In third grade, Juan was glad to see me. He said nothing while I read *A Chair for My Mother* but responded at the end. He mentioned a few parts he liked and told how "bad he would feel if all my stuff would be gone." When I asked about school and reading, he told me a lot, especially about his family here and in Mexico and the ranch in Mexico.

It's important to note that Juan's pattern of making associations with his own life and telling family stories did not occur each time he read. He barely spoke at all in kindergarten. In first grade, he spoke much more, and his responses were varied. The most frequent type were questions during *Alexander* and associations during

Umbrella. The most significant thing is that he asked to read to me at the end of first grade. In second grade (or a repeat of first grade for him), he simply responded to the questions in the predictable pattern book *Caps for Sale* but exploded with responses to *The Nicest Gift*. The fact that the book had Spanish words—and Juan was in the driver's seat when he corrected my Spanish pronunciation—and that he could relate things the Hispanic family did in the book to his own Hispanic heritage seemed to be all he needed to talk for almost an hour in a rich and meaningful way about the story and his own experiences. Theory and research tells us over and over that this is exactly what children should be doing when they read: becoming actively engaged in the reading process and story, linking it to their own lives, and seeking meaning as they read.

I would be very hesitant to suggest that the key to helping second-language learners is to simply read them books about their own culture in English, with a few words in their native language sprinkled throughout. See, for example, in Chapter 7, what happened in Paul's class when he read the book *Island Boy*, the story of a family in Maine of obvious British heritage. The students related to it, but not because of language or culture. In Juan's case, however, an insightful teacher would do well to notice his interest in talking about this book and run—not walk—to the library to get other books about Hispanic families by Leo Politi, other authors, and any bilingual Spanish books, particularly about families.

It would be a mistake, however, to assume on the basis of Juan's response that all children who resemble him in terms of English language development and Hispanic culture will respond to this book in the same way. The next case study is a good example of a child of Hispanic heritage whose response process style is different from Juan's. They are two different children who share a common heritage.

In fourth grade, when I read *Song of the Swallows*, Juan was very confident and mature. We reminisced about the study. He was attentive to the text and pictures. We talked about San Juan Capistrano and how California had changed. He was interested in where it was, what it was like there, and so on. This discussion led him to talk about his family's life in California, covering things like immigration, family in two countries, a cousin who was shot in a drive-by shooting, the importance of not being mistaken for a gang member, and staying in school and going to college. It was a seamless discussion, beginning with the book but going through his future. He obviously understands and appreciates literature and art. Midway in the discussion of everything from not wearing baggy pants to the advantages of being bilingual, he said, "What we're doing is ELD (English language development) isn't it?"

| A Thought from Paul | Juan's case study calls to mind the image of a flawed performance with devastating consequences, like a novice violinist in front of an impatient audience. Even though Juan entered school without support in his primary language, he was expected to perform as a fully fluent native English speaker. When he failed, he was retained in first grade, pulled-out for ESL instruction (even after attaining mastery level on the IPT of oral English proficiency), placed in special education, and given a heavy dose of phonics instruction. Juan |

appears to be the product of a system that refused to recognize and validate his background knowledge, experience, and culture.

With the exception of additional help in English, none of the above treatments apply to Juan's educational needs. The treatments may, in fact, have a reverse effect on his education. One has to wonder why the school retained him for lack of English fluency. Even more damning is the question of why special education was chosen as the remedy for his struggle to read aloud in English. By fourth grade, he was in a dilemma: He has received no academic support or literacy development in his primary language, so the language he speaks at home, the language he thinks in, is negated at school; he continues to struggle with the mechanics of English, so he is therefore neither fully bilingual nor fully monolingual in English. Add to that the stigma of retention and special education placement, and you have a strong candidate for a future dropout. Failing to perform in English reading, he is fed phonics in the hope that he will pronounce words correctly in English.

Phonics is to reading what penmanship is to writing. It falls under the heading of performance and elocution. It is helpful in making the reader understood by others, just as penmanship makes one's writing more understandable to someone else. Phonics is merely correctly pronouncing letters and words; penmanship is correctly forming letters and words. But to confuse the application of phonics (pronouncing letters and words) with reading print (making meaningful connections) is a misunderstanding of the entire process of reading. It is like saying that having good handwriting fully equips one to write a poem, a story, or a book. Reading and writing, discovering and expressing meaning and understanding from a text, does not take place in the realm of correct pronunciation or accurate handwriting. Frank Smith (1978) derided phonics instruction as "barking at print" (p. 78). He went on to point out how knowing how to pronounce words correctly depends on understanding the context in which the word appears (e.g., We READ books daily or we READ books yesterday).

The haunting words of Juan, "I don't know that much because I speak Spanish," give evidence of an environment in which his knowledge, culture, and language are devalued. The significance of reader-response, particularly in a multicultural context, is the repositioning of knowledge from the text to the reader. Reader-response looks to the reader to express his or her own insights in response to the text. Reader-response treats Juan more as an author than as a performer. He is an authority on his own life, family, feelings, and ideas. As he reads and hears stories read by Carole, he creates his own story and thus constructs his own understanding.

Juan brings to reading a wealth of experience. He makes sense of his reading as he is given the opportunity to connect the words to his life. Connecting the text to life takes place in dialogue with others about the multilayered meanings of story, the public and personal understandings of the text. It is not a question of performance, like a trained seal "barking at print." It is a question of authorship, of touching one's experience to a juicy story.

THINGS TO THINK ABOUT

Think about Juan's experience as a non-English-speaking child entering kindergarten and a developing English learner in terms of what current second-language acquisition theory suggests is good second-language education practice:

1. How would you evaluate the schooling of this language-minority child?

2. Compare the approaches of Juan's teacher in first grade, in first grade the second time, and in second grade. What models do they each reflect of learning, second-language acquisition, and teaching with literature?

3. What would you do about Juan's English language and literacy development if Juan were a student in your class?

4. What are ways you and Juan's father might join forces in Juan's education?

THINGS TO DO

1. Observe in several types of classrooms/programs that serve language-minority students: English-only classroom, classroom with primary language support (e.g., bilingual aides, flexible scheduling, peer tutoring), ESL pull-out class, and a bilingual classroom. Keep notes of what kind of language and literacy instruction is provided. Compare them with each other and the theoretical models of teaching with literature and second-language education described in Chapters 2 and 3.

2. Observe and participate in at least three different bilingual classrooms. Compare what you see in each according to the theoretical approach driving second-language education in each one.

3. Interview two teachers of language-minority students, one English only and one bilingual. Ask about their thoughts on the best approach for teaching English as a second language and for teaching with literature. What models of learning and language acquisition do they reflect?

4. Interview at least three bilingual teachers. Ask the same questions as in #3. What models of learning and language acquisition do they reflect?

5. Observe in two different language bilingual classrooms (e.g., Spanish/English, Korean/English). What differences do you notice?

6. Read the collaborative teacher narrative of language and literacy development in a bilingual classroom:

Hayes, C. W., Bahruth, R., & Kessler, C. (1991). *Literacy con carino: A story of migrant children's success.* Portsmouth, NH: Heinemann.

FURTHER READING

Fu, Danling. (1995). *My trouble is my English: Asian students and the American dream*. Portsmouth, NH: Boynton/Cook.

   This book is a collection of case studies of four immigrants from Laos learning English and coping with school, written by a woman who is herself an immigrant from China.

REFERENCE

Smith, F. (1978). *Reading without nonsense*. New York: Teachers College Press.

CHAPTER SIX

The Bilingual Speaker:
Case Study of Eduardo

MEET EDUARDO

Eduardo is fluent and literate in both English and Spanish, a reflection of his early years in a bilingual and bicultural Mexican American-El Salvadoran American home. Although his teachers recognize his creativity, he is deemed "immature," repeats second grade, and begins to do well academically. He is very imaginative, and his response to a book often begins with the speech tag, "Know what?"—meaning I want to tell you a new story of my own.

Background and Home Influences
Mother has limited education and English
Mother provides encouragement and some books for reading
Great expectations for Eduardo; wonder at his potential

Language Development: Fluent Bilingual in English and Spanish
English his first language (his natural father's)
Mother and stepfather native Spanish speakers
Eduardo most proficient English user; loves to talk

Eduardo as a Student
Deemed immature by teachers; repeats second grade
Begins to succeed, and his creative ability valued
Notable storytelling ability, curiosity, and imagination

Eduardo's Response Process Style: Tells His Own Stories

Hypothesizes; text is springboard for own stories

Uses much metaphorical and symbolic language

Freely breaks through the boundaries of the text

Connections to Principles and Practice

Eduardo easily becomes a fluent speaker of the two languages spoken at home—English and Spanish; example of communicative-based language acquisition occurring naturally in the home.

Eduardo is highly verbal in his English-only classroom but immature—most successful in an interactive classroom; example of a student approach benefitting a highly creative but nonconforming child.

Eduardo has unfulfilled potential for literacy development; example of gap between school literacy expectations and limited literacy experiences at home.

Eduardo breaks through the boundaries of the text in responding to literature; example of highly idiosyncratic personal transactions between reader and text.

BACKGROUND AND HOME INFLUENCES

Eduardo lives with his El Salvadoran mother and maternal grandmother and his stepfather. All of them speak Spanish at home. From birth through the preschool years, his English-speaking Mexican American father lived in the home. Eduardo has one younger brother. Although it appears that Eduardo spoke English as his first language, his mother and grandmother have provided him with his first culture, El Salvadoran.

Eduardo's mother grew up on a ranch and completed six years in a rural school in El Salvador. She says she enjoyed school. She describes it as "academia de señoritas" where the students learned sewing and embroidering, as well as basic skills. Her own mother, who lives with her, learned to read when her daughter was eleven years old. Her own father—Eduardo's grandfather—was illiterate. It was difficult to obtain books or magazines where they lived.

Although Eduardo's mother says she spoke English to him in his early years, she did not read to him. He would not have understood Spanish, and she does not read English easily. Now he initiates reading events with her, but he is the reader. She says she guides him and helps him sound out words she does not know herself. Eduardo began reading independently about the middle of first grade (about the same time he asked to read to me during our sessions at school).

His mother works long hours cleaning homes and usually can only spend time with him on weekends. She says he does read by himself in his room and only comes to her when he needs help. When she does read to him, he corrects her English pronunciation. She says, "En inglés, he doesn't want any accent at all. So I say read it for me, and he does." She says he likes to read, and she buys him books when he asks for them at Kmart and the grocery store and at the school book fair. She says he also likes to read in the library when it is open after school.

Eduardo's mother believes he is a special boy even though she is concerned that he doesn't listen to his teachers and often wants to do things his own way. I asked her to describe Eduardo to me:

> He like to work, he talks when he grow up he's going to work. A lot of people say he's so smart you know, we had a friend, she's from America and she says Eduardo has this, you know, like grow up, and I say I don't know I say, but then she say it's OK for him, he talk like grownup people, and I say, "Oh!" He say when he grow up he going to have money, he going to work so hard, and sometimes he say he want it be a policeman and things like that, yeah, he thinks. I think he thinks too much, I don't know why. When he don't go to school, when I stayed home with him and we sat down with him, he talk too much. If you stay with him all day, all day, he talks you know. I don't know. I think he's . . . he thinks too much and I think I'm excited with him. I think he's a special boy, he tries hard (she gets teary-eyed).

LANGUAGE DEVELOPMENT: FLUENT BILINGUAL IN ENGLISH AND SPANISH

Eduardo's Home Language Survey filled out by his mother and returned to school in kindergarten says that he is a native English speaker, that English is the language spoken most frequently at home, that the adults in the home speak English to him, and that English is the language spoken most often by adults at home. This may not be entirely the case, however. Eduardo's mother can communicate in English, but during interviews she requested the questions be in Spanish. She states that she only spoke English when she was with her first husband—Eduardo's father. After ten years in the United States, she is still more comfortable with and prefers to speak Spanish.

Eduardo's natural father was an English-speaking Mexican American born in the United States. He lived in the home until Eduardo was four. During this time, Eduardo's mother attempted to speak in her limited English to her son, rather than in Spanish. Her current husband speaks Spanish. Eduardo now finds himself living in a Spanish-speaking household in which he is the most proficient speaker of English. He loves to talk and used metaphors and similes even in kindergarten. He has a poet's voice, and he uses it. If you will listen, he will speak.

EDUARDO AS A STUDENT

Eduardo attended a full-time preschool day care facility for several years because his mother worked out of the home all day.

In describing her approach, Eduardo's kindergarten teacher said she tries to meet the needs of children as much as possible. She takes a text-centered approach to teaching with literature. She asks the class what the book is about and then to join in on repetitive phrases. She asks for lots of recall and prediction. She uses a basal reading series to "teach skills of inferences, recall, word recognition, beginning and ending consonant sounds, decoding, context clues, and phonics." She said she wants to turn children on to reading. Here's how she described Eduardo:

> This little boy is something (laughing). He is bright but very immature. He's allowed to do what he wants to do at home, so he doesn't "have time" to do what you're asking him to do. There's a lot going on in his brain, and sometimes he's right on top of it and he almost amazes you. And the next day, he'll sit in front of you and fall asleep.
>
> He's got it up there. It will all fall in place for him in a few years when he's older and can really focus in. Some English and Spanish is spoken at home, and Grandmother speaks Spanish most of the time. Eduardo is "Let me hurry and get this done and let me get on with other important things like play Legos." I've had to say, "How do you feel about this? Take your crayon like this and do better." He'll say, "OK." We've spent lots of time on learning to complete a task and getting it done. He works independently but not all the time. He tries. He's often tired in the mornings. Sometimes he comes in in the morning with the most beautiful eyes and says, "I need to tell you something," all determined. I have to listen and I also have to stop.

Eduardo enjoyed stories in first grade. His teacher (the same one Juan had when he repeated first grade) took a very teacher- and text-centered view of literacy development. She used the Spaulding phonics method extensively, along with a basal reader series and literature. When she used literature, the students did very teacher-directed art or writing follow-up activities.

Eduardo's teacher read *The Giving Tree* by Shel Silverstein one day. She wrote the title on the chalkboard and asked all the students to read it and to show that they had by putting their thumbs up. She said, "Some didn't show me with your thumb that you read it. What does it say, Eduardo?" He read, *"The Giving Tree."*

The teacher read the book. The students were on the floor around her. They were very attentive and quiet. Eduardo had his chin on his hand, intensely absorbed in the story. She asked, "Why do you think the page says the tree was happy after it gave away its trunk?" Eduardo said: "Do you think the tree was happy? No. 'Cause the boy cut off his trunk and branches. Why did he take so much?"

After the reading, she told the class, "Today you're going to write the story in your own words for the beginning, the middle, and the end. Fold a paper in three columns—1, 2, 3, just as we do in spelling: 1 for the first part, 2 for the second part, 3 for the end." She showed an example from last year and told the class she did this every year. She told them, "Many things happened in the middle, but only one thing at the beginning and the end. You can use more sentences in the middle. Use at least one sentence. On spelling, she said, "Do your best." She directed them to go to their seats and explained "base lines," or where to write on the page.

Eduardo was at his seat, already writing. The teacher knelt at his desk and reexplained the assignment to him. She carefully monitored him. Later, his hand went up and he pounded the desk with a pencil. No one came. His paper flew off the desk. The teacher came over, and he handed the paper to her. She said, "Read it back." He did, and she said, "OK."

His teacher described him:

> He's immature and wants things when he wants them. He says, "But I want to talk." He responds well to positive reinforcement for a short time. He is loving but also doesn't behave at home. Academically, there is definitely something there. He has progressed a lot. He came in here not knowing most of the sounds of the alphabet. It's a problem to keep him on-task. In this last month, I've seen lots of growth. He can sound out some words, but he's still at the place where he doesn't always know it's a word.
>
> He is reading in a pre-primer. He is the highest in the lowest group and not aware that he's the highest. He hasn't understood that he has a place in the group. He helps other people when he's on-task. He's low in math. He sometimes forgets simple operations.
>
> He doesn't participate in group discussions, but rather sits back and has to have something to play with. He can't zero in on things because of his immaturity. He's made inadequate progress this year. He is fluent in both English and Spanish. His mom can speak English but has a cleft palate and is hard to understand. His stepfather speaks limited English. I haven't seen them too much. He works well with the aide. My student teacher fell in love with him.
>
> It's hard to tell about his understanding of literature. I concentrated on Spaulding with him this year. I put him in Scott, Foresman's (a publisher) *Taking Off!* In two weeks, his attitude was, "I'm reading." He doesn't read in a group, but with VIPS (Volunteer in Public Schools: parents who work with children on a regular basis). He does great with them. He interacts constantly. He wants to tell you he's reading.
>
> He must first understand something at the literal level. He has to picture it, and then he takes off. He talked about the tenth row of seats in our class. We don't have a tenth row. He said he pictured it in his mind and then got up and walked to where he pictured it. A story read, ". . . only a merry-go-round horse." He read it, ". . . only a chair-rest." All the students did self-portraits, and he showed himself doing karate. He showed his leg multiple times to show movement. He doesn't do things like anyone else in the room.

When Eduardo was in second grade the first time, his teacher had a very student-centered approach with an emphasis on actively engaging students. She incorporated activities across modalities, used cooperative groups, and encouraged language exchange.

Eduardo demonstrated that he was a creative, divergent thinker in this class. During even fairly mundane lessons, he brought his own unique view to bear.

The teacher showed cards with a such phrases as "My room" and asked students to make it a complete sentence. One student said, "My room is dirty." Eduardo said, "My room has dirt and sometimes on my walls I have balloons. They pop. My hair is spiked, and I can pop a balloon with it." It takes very little to set Eduardo off telling a story.

When they were supposed to write their ideas down, however, he struggled. Whereas his ideas and oral expression were fluent and fluid compared with those of

Natural storytellers like Eduardo should be encouraged to share their uniquely personal responses to literature through talking, drawing, and writing.

other students in his class, his writing skills were much less developed. It didn't seem to bother him, however, and he worked hard at writing.

Although Eduardo seemed to flourish in this class, he was retained to repeat second grade with this same teacher. His test scores on the MAT 6 test were 42 percent in reading, 46 percent in language, and 54 percent in mathematics. His teacher indicated he was retained primarily because of his immaturity, rather than his lack of writing ability or reading problems. He attended summer school at his home school.

When Eduardo was in second grade the second time, his teacher continued to recognize Eduardo's strengths and special qualities. She observed the following about him during his second year in her class:

> He's a smart cookie. He's very literate in both languages. He's serious. His writing has progressed. He writes great stories. He is a great storyteller and creator of narrative. He loves science. He tells stories about nature and the outdoors. He is a thoughtful participant in groups and listens to others. He's very aware and sensitive and watches the reactions of others when reading. When he sees things are not going well, he interjects humor.
>
> His mother speaks limited English and has hired a tutor for him. Eduardo brings the tutor lists of things he doesn't understand so that they can talk them over. His

mother sees the spark in Eduardo and wants to nurture it. She gets him magazines and takes him places.

It would be great if you could cap him in a bottle and open him up to the rest of the class. He's eager to do everything. He has gone from the bottom to the top in performance and has grown up a lot this year. He has almost outgrown his mother. She sees him slipping away, and she's sad. He's a peach.

He likes to read. He loves *Zoo* books and easy chapter books: the *Boxcar Children* series, mysteries like *Nate the Great*, Marjorie Sharmat stories. He will choose to read on his own, and he will really read. He lives in the library on days that it's open after school. He will sit in the rocking chair in the library and bring library books to me to read.

At the end of second grade the second time, Eduardo's scores on the MAT 6 were 76 percent in reading, 88 percent in language, and 83 percent in mathematics—a tremendous leap from his scores at the end of second grade the first time.

Eduardo's third grade teacher took a fairly traditional approach. Students were less active than in her class the previous two years. It was not unusual to see the teacher at her desk and students doing worksheets at their desks. They came to her if they had a question. Eduardo told me that school was fine, however, and that he enjoyed reading and writing. He volunteered information about books he was reading and his reading habits.

He said that, at home, he read the dictionary and liked books like "a legend story, a fake one, and it tells you about the sailors and something." He said he read to himself at home and drew—monsters, aliens, people. He read *The Stinky Cheeseman* and got excited, asking me whether I'd read it to any children. He told me he read it to his little brother, and other books like *Snoopy* and "little books, Disney books."

His test scores on the MAT 6 declined in three of the four areas since the year before. His score on the spelling section went from 88 percent to 93 percent. His scores in reading, however, went from 76 percent to 55 percent, language went from 88 percent to 75 percent, and mathematics went from 83 percent to 40 percent. These may not be a true reflection of his performance. He may have had a bad testing day.

In fourth grade, Eduardo was more focused but still so creative and visionary. He told me about his reading—*The Adventures of Ratman* by Ellen Weiss—and that he likes adventures books "where you go different places, see other things you've never seen before like dragons, magical things, and animals." He also talked about becoming a scientist and helping people and maybe discovering a new species of animals or becoming a doctor and going around the world looking for plants that could help people because "the horror of letting people die makes me feel real sad. Is there a cure for AIDS yet? . . . The more you help people, the more better the world is." He said he wanted to go to college and believed "there could be something spiritual looking over me." He could channel his ideas and articulate the stream-of-consciousness series of images he has always been able to generate.

EDUARDO'S RESPONSE PROCESS STYLE: TELLS HIS OWN STORIES

Eduardo is a storyteller—a natural with a powerful imagination. Picture him in front of a fire, telling stories as the smoke drifts up, perhaps even making up a story about something he pictures in the smoke. A book or story or even a word or two is enough to set Eduardo's imagination to work. One thought or idea or image triggers another. On the surface, they may not seem related, at least according to an adult understanding of narrative. But when listening to Eduardo, I found myself straining to follow and understand his type of narrative, not because of what he said but the way he said it—enthusiastically, authoritatively, as if it ought to be perfectly obvious that the story made sense, had a logical flow, and was perfectly understandable if only I was astute enough to follow it.

His most frequent response type is hypothesizing: speculating, predicting, retrospecting, anticipating, generating story options, and breaking through the boundaries of the text—although this was closely followed by associations: relating his hypotheses to his own experiences. Whereas Anne likes to shred the story and Juan uses it as a reason to tell about his family, Eduardo jumps on it like a trampoline to springboard to other images, tales, or worlds. He is the most creative of the three.

In kindergarten, for example, when the little boy in *The Snowy Day* makes a snow angel, Eduardo keyed in on the idea of angels in general, rather than the snow angel in the story. This excerpt showed how his ideas bounce one off the other and finally lead to a hypothesis about stars.

> Oh, angels. I like angels. Do you know what an angel is? (What?) It's an angel that got wings. And do they got this something on their head. Yeah. I know. You know what um I saw the one that um—once I went to Disneyland and I went under the water, then I saw a mermaid. Yeah, the one where all of the fish was not real. I saw a shark and they weren't real. Not the mermaids. And then the man said you could hear them talk. And I saw gold there. It wasn't real, I know that. So I know. You know I saw a star. It looked like Bambi. And then a long time ago, you know what's gonna happen? They won't be real. I mean the star's not real. From a long time ago, they were real, but not now, they're not real.

In response to *Make Way for Ducklings*, Eduardo moved the story forward in time and speculated what it would be like if it took place today:

> If he didn't have a police car, he could go on the police helicopter. And then he could bring down a paper that says, "Come quick, there's a family of ducks." And it fell down and then with a rock moving down it fell on a rock so they hurt it and then they send a note. And then they made another paper, a sign that they'll get there soon.

In response to *Miss Rumphius*, he hypothesized a creation myth that could explain how Miss Rumphius was born and grew old:

We were in a brown egg. My mom made me, but she didn't make me because she was in the brown egg. Everybody was in the brown egg. And then they turned . . . and I saw this movie, and we turned the brown egg and everything was fine. We were all yellow. And that she was turning into a baby, and then they turn into them. Yes, I saw a movie of it. And they said they used to come home, and the baby turn into a boy. Yes. What when I'm talking it goes right in there. Know what? Um. Here her hair is not white. So if she, if her hair's not white, her hair's going to turn white. And she was old now, huh? Know what? Know what? Um. That's not fair. She was at there. No. I try. She was there. Why did she turn into an old lady? (Why do you think?) The God sent her to turn into an old lady sometime.

His hypotheses, like Anne's questions and Juan's family associations, often lead him to develop his own explanations for things. He had an interesting speech tag leading into this. He often said, "Know what?" and then hypothesized and developed an explanation. I think he meant, "Do you want to know what I'm thinking?" It's obvious that what he wanted was simply somebody to listen to him. And at that time, he was most actively engaged with the text and using language.

Compared with his behavior in kindergarten, Eduardo talked a lot about the story, but his responses were restrained the first time I read in first grade. The book was *Alexander,* and he did not tell the extended stories he did before. His responses were more like those of other students. Several times, he simply noted a part that interested him. But he still questioned and hypothesized throughout. He also started to read it to me, like both Juan and Anne. It seems significant that out of thirty-eight students in this study in first grade, only four volunteered to read and two of those were the only two Hispanic students.

Eduardo was less restrained while I read *Umbrella* and renewed his free spirit. Throughout the reading, he talked about a magic umbrella:

On the front, she's saying, "This must be a magic umbrella. She thinks it's magic. . . . It fly wherever she wanted. I know where dragonflies are. In the park. She didn't want to leave the umbrella. She thought it was magic.

Here again, Eduardo used the text as a starting point to tell his own stories. This was when he was truly engaged in reading. He seemed to be brimming with other stories that were triggered by the one in the book and that were much more compelling to him because they were his own. Then he volunteered to read to me again. "Want me to read this story to you? I know how. Let's try." While he read, he continued to ask questions and develop hypotheses and then explanations for what was happening. He told me, "I knew that because I heard you." His understanding of the story was deepened. He laughed at the end and said, "How'd I do?"

Eduardo's response pattern and that of the others suggests that teachers should rethink the traditional way of teaching reading through stories, with the teacher introducing it and the students reading aloud or silently to themselves. When I read aloud to these students and they were allowed to respond freely—and go as far afield as Eduardo liked to—they were ready to build on that engagement and pleasure in the story and to use it as a basis to read on their own. They had already heard it and analyzed it. Now they had a chance to experience it and enjoy it, instead of the other way around: read the story, answer efferent questions, and write or do an art activity. Let's think about reversing this order and letting the efferent emerge from the aesthetic, which is the natural way these students responded.

In second grade the first time, Eduardo made fewer comments than in kindergarten or first grade, but he was more focused on the story itself than before. He pointed at many things in the text with his finger.

Something different occurred in Eduardo's response to the first book I read in second grade, *Caps for Sale*. He asked many questions about words: "Where's sale, for sale? Where does it say cents?" He did this throughout the reading. He continued his hypothesizing, extending the story, and making up his own version:

> The caps can't talk. He thinks the caps are going to get mad at him, when the caps can't do nothing to him. . . . My favorite page was when . . . this one because they look like they're flying. And the monkeys . . . oh, I know. I know why they did it because when he would do something then they would copy him.

Here he goes from what appears to be a tangent about personified caps that can get mad and fly to a succinct and plausible explanation of the peddler's actions. It is Eduardo's way. He listens, catches a piece of the story and puts his own spin on it, and then comes to a reasonable explanation or goes beyond that to a generalization, what a teacher wants students to do when they read. Again, order is important. He needed to play around with the story first before he nailed it, like cats playing with a mouse or bird before they kill it. He needed time and the freedom to do that.

After he basically explained that the monkeys had the hats because they copied the peddler, he rewrote the story, focusing on the problem the peddler had selling caps in the first place. He "fixed" the peddler's problem:

> He should have done it with a, like a car, then he could show everybody and go other places. Like that, so he could make it better. Try to go other places, not just around the town. Because um . . . then people might see him and they might buy them. (That's a good idea.) Yeah, but he didn't try that. He thought that going around the town he would make it, huh? Make money.

He appeared very satisfied with himself at this point, and he should have been. He had fun with this story. He listened to it, asked about words he wanted to read, pictured flying caps that got mad, developed plausible explanations for characters' actions, and then hypothesized a whole new ending for the story that would resolve the main character's problem of selling caps. Next, he said the words that should warm the cockles of any primary teacher's heart: "I want to read the story to you." He did, asking for a word or a word meaning in a very relaxed, natural way. He read haltingly, one word at a time, but his mood was upbeat, positive. He asked for many words. He stopped when he wanted to clarify meaning or to talk about something of interest to him. He read the entire book to me.

Finally, he saw some information about the author-illustrator Esphyr Slobodkina. The blurb on the back cover said the book had won an award. He told me about another book he was reading at home with his mom and offered to bring it to show me. This was an extremely satisfying reading episode with Eduardo.

In response to *The Nicest Gift*, Eduardo stopped me at the same point in the story as Juan did, the part where I read the word in Spanish ". . . *caballito* means little horse." Whereas Juan corrected my pronunciation, Eduardo simply said, "I know that," and, "I know Spanish, too." He read a little, asked more questions, told me it was "great," and offered a simple explanation at the end: "Blanco was scared and ran far away." He did not provide the rich associations for family and culture that Juan did, simply because he is not the same person as Juan.

It is important to remember that language and culture are two of the many things that make people different. This idea points up the highly idiosyncratic nature of the response process, and teachers should be careful not to assume that all Spanish-speaking Hispanic students will respond similarly to a book like *The Nicest Gift* anymore than all girls or all boys or all oldest children in a family will respond the same way. What is important is to listen to what each child has to say, keeping in mind the general tendencies of children at that age but not forgetting what a unique individual each one of them is.

In second grade the second time, Eduardo was subdued when I read *Ira Sleeps Over*. He listened attentively, asked one question, and then asked to read the book to me, which he did. He was proud of his reading.

In third grade, Eduardo talked throughout my reading of the book. He was more mature and focused this year but still imaginative and insightful. He could talk about reading. When I praised him, he told me he read to his two-year-old brother in English.

In response to *A Chair for My Mother*, Eduardo's predominant response type again was hypothesizing. He guessed that it was a big fire and wondered how it started in the house and speculated that it might have been cooking carrots and they exploded and started the fire. This is classic Eduardo, imagining another whole scenario. Although no exploding carrots are shown in any picture, a potted snake plant is shown in an orange pot on the stove, and the border around the edge of the page is a jagged white and orange shape that looks something like the shape of a carrot. This is speculation on my part. What is not speculation is that it takes very little to trigger Eduardo's fertile imagination and to set him spinning another story in his mind.

In fourth grade, Eduardo shared what he had been learning about the missions in response to *Song of the Swallows* and what he'd heard about the swallows returning to Capistrano on the news. He still wove his own stories throughout the reading, speculating about what types of formations different types of birds made in flight, that young Juan was going to be the gardener someday like old Julian, and that he imagined that Father Serra would be like his imaginary friend. After reading, he told at length about his dreams of becoming a scientist or doctor and going all around the world looking for plants to help people or perhaps discovering a new species of animal because, "no one's ever seen all of the world, have they?" Eduardo may not either, but he roams all sorts of possible worlds in his mind as he responds to literature.

Eduardo reminds me of the words of the composer and guitar virtuoso Carlos Santana, who in describing his own son said, "His imagination is so loud that sometimes it is hard to get through to him, but that is the way it should be with imagination" (NPR Interview, July 4, 1996). Reading is truly an imaginative and shared experience. Eduardo envisions his own world when he reads and eagerly shares "you know what?" with someone willing to listen. His unique responses to stories are at times wild and in rough form like the first draft melodies a composer generates in the process of creating a complete work. Yet even in their rough form, his thoughts about a story invite others to join him along a creative path to interpretation.

His imaginings are beyond the control of the teacher. Getting through to Eduardo appeared to be a concern of his teachers. It is easy to see how such an idiosyncratic thinker could pose a problem for a classroom teacher trying to impose a uniform, text-centered approach to reading. Seeking a single correct answer to closed questions would create tension and struggle for an individual like Eduardo.

Conventional instruction treats reading as a kind of clerical task in which each word or story element is recorded and accounted for; yet reading is more than a mechanical task. With some programs, running records are checked off as each word is pronounced correctly. With literary theory, New Critical formalism asks the reader to match story elements to a set structure. Once each item is accounted for, the story is considered finished, the ledger sheet balanced. But stories are more organic in nature.

Reader-response approaches, however, begin with open-ended questions and invitations to dialogue about the text. Reading becomes a shared task of exchanging and refining interpretations. John Dewey (1961) talked about a "pooling of ideas" to create understanding and to solve problems. Even something so far afield as Eduardo's "creation myth" for Miss Rumphius is fair game in a reader-response environment. This is not to say that anything goes or that every response, no matter how unsettling, is to be celebrated. Quite the contrary, responding to literature in the classroom takes place in a collaborative setting. Participants are called to justify their musings, compare their ideas with the text, and push each other to expand their thinking. Pooling Eduardo's imagination with a group of students could only enhance the richness of the discussion. I also suspect that his uninhibited imagination could release inhibitions of other classmates to express their imaginations creatively.

One good story plants dozens of other stories in the fertile soil of a creative mind. Eduardo's images of a Miss Rumphius's birth or the lopped-off branches of a Giving Tree caused others to pause and reconceive a new conception of the story in seedling form. And when the seedling is cultivated by teachers and classmates, it grows to bear the fruit of a new and creative story, poem, or even song.

THINGS TO THINK ABOUT

1. Plan a reading program for Eduardo. What books, experiences, and form of evaluation would you use?

2. How is Eduardo different from or like Juan and Anne in terms of their personal response process styles?

3. Compare Eduardo with both Juan and Anne in terms of background and home influences, language development, and success as a student. What ideas does this comparison give you about teaching language-minority students? All students?

4. In what ways could you support Eduardo's writing development through response-centered, literature-based teaching?

THINGS TO DO

1. Read and tape-record one child's responses to some of the books I read to Eduardo. Transcribe these responses and discuss and analyze them in terms of the child's response process style. How do they compare with Eduardo's? Anne's? Juan's? How would you characterize the child you read to?

2. What types of language and literacy experiences would you plan for this child?

3. List literature response options for children like Eduardo who consistently break through the boundaries of the text. How would you also check for their understanding of the text?

4. List books you think Eduardo might enjoy.

5. Brainstorm ways to collaborate with Eduardo's mother and to forge meaningful home-school connections with her on his behalf.

FURTHER READING

Gallas, K. (1994). *The languages of learning: How children talk, write, dance, draw, and sing their understanding of the world.* New York: Teachers College Press. This is another excellent case study that celebrates children's creativity.

REFERENCE

Dewey, J. (1961). Democracy and education. In *Philosophy of education: Problems of men* (pp. 16–32). Paterson, NJ: Littlefield, Adams.

Literature and Language Crossroads in a Bilingual Classroom

In this final section, I (Paul) give a classroom teacher's perspective of the crossroads of response-centered instruction with literature and language. Reflecting on my own practice in a bilingual third-grade classroom, I attempt to give a picture of what reader-response looks like in action and discuss the "how-to" questions vital to putting theory into practice.

In Chapter 7, I take an in-depth look at a morning in my classroom from the moment I walk in the door at the beginning of the day until cleanup time right before lunch. This chapter is intended to illustrate how reader-response requires a shift in the role of the teacher from the primary transmitter of knowledge to a co-learner in a student-centered setting. Creating a reader-response learning environment calls for the teacher to be open to the lead of the students. Following the path to understanding of one student in particular, Jackie, demonstrates how reader-response opens unlimited possibilities for instruction, creative expression, and language development.

In Chapter 8, I discuss the various components of response-centered instruction, including preparation and planning for the literature cycle—a way I have developed for organizing a class to use literature. I review language and literacy development options available to the teacher, resources, materials, and tools acquisition and application. (Notice the appendix on computers and software.) Also spelled out in detail is the process of the literature cycle based on choosing and using quality literature, fostering self-direction with students, and responding to the ripple effect generated by aesthetic readings of a text. I answer important management questions about forming literature-response groups, conducting response forums, presenting student work, and evaluating. The dynamo of the cycle is the response forum, in which the teacher models the use of open-ended questions, tugs at metaphors, and employs a technique I call "color mapping" for collaborative writing.

The crossroads of literature instruction and language development intersect in the milieu of reader-response. As students creatively respond to literature, they connect their lives to a story. It is the contention of this book that the more students connect the story to their lives, the more receptive they will be to language development. This is particularly evident in culturally diverse learning environments where students bring to the classroom prior knowledge and experience that may or may not be shared by the teacher and others. Significant language development takes place when the teacher listens for a student's responses to literature and they collaborate to create meaningful instruction that matches the needs of the student.

CHAPTER SEVEN

Reader-Response in a Bilingual Classroom

What paths do readers follow as they read? Readers trek to faraway lands or unfamiliar islands. Sometimes they explore ancestral homes in their reading. As they read, they hoe their own rows and create stories in their minds. The experience is primarily aesthetic (Rosenblatt, 1986). Readers create images, feel sensations, share their own stories, and express their interpretations of the stories verbally and nonverbally through conversation, writing, music, and visual and performing arts.

In the classroom, the teacher initially establishes the environment for reader-response. If the teacher's stance is predominantly *efferent*, the students will follow by reading for informational purposes so that they can give correct answers on a test or some other form of assessment. But if the teacher is predominantly interested in connecting the text to the students' lives, *aesthetic* reading comes to the forefront. In reader-response, the students' aesthetic experience is the ground of prior knowledge (Krashen, 1985), which connects the multiple worlds of children (Dyson, 1990) to their reading. The primary vehicle for bridging the written word across their worlds is dialogue (Freire, 1970). The conversations among students and with their teacher open places for instruction (Tharp & Gallimore, 1989) to integrate learning across the curriculum, but the literature is art and is understood within the realm of the aesthetic (Rosenblatt, 1986). Exploring aesthetic readings of children's literature is an inclusive process that invites diverse understandings and divergent thinking. Reader-response calls individuals from all cultures to share their experiences and to join in the journey.

Jackie: I love my picture. (She holds up a watercolor painting of a lone *vaquero* standing in the shade of a huge saguaro cactus.)
Paul: What do you love about it?
J: The fields . . . the man standing all alone.

P: Do you want to write a poem about it?

J: (Nods head yes.)

P: When you create a poem, you paint a picture with words.

Jackie's painting was a response to a number of books she had read and shared in a literature-response group. She followed her own path to interpretation (Rosenblatt, 1986): reading, composing metaphors, painting images with watercolor, and painting pictures with words. Her path began with a story from Puerto Rico. It took her to a book about an island off the coast of Maine, to another book about the saguaro cactus of the deserts of Arizona, and to a painting of a huge saguaro in Oaxaca, Mexico.

One late spring morning, I found myself caught up with Jackie's literature-response group in a single sitting for more than an hour and a half. Later, I was astonished to realize that it took place in a classroom of thirty students with curious minds and busy hands without pandemonium breaking out. The other students saw my engagement with one group as an hour and a half of uninterrupted work time for

Jackie and Paul discuss the poem she wrote about her picture of a saguaro cactus as she followed her own path to interpretation of literature.

their own literature-based projects. This begs the question: What kind of instruction captures the imaginations of a group of young students and their teacher for such a long period of time?

In this chapter, I follow Jackie through a morning in my classroom to paint a picture of what captured both our imaginations. The experience was recorded in the form of field notes by Carole Cox as observer. She sat on the outskirts of the group and took copious notes of our conversations and her observations. Her husband, Stuart Spates, also came into the classroom to videotape the proceedings and to take still photographs of the activity in the classroom. Later, I pored over her field notes and added my comments about what I experienced at the time. We would get together and discuss what we were seeing on video and compare our experience with the various theories circulating in schools. Noam Chomsky's (1979) theory of language acquisition and Stephen Krashen's (1985) input hypothesis told part of the story of what was going on with the bilingual students. The students appeared to be the most actively engaged in language development when the story of their lives was touched by literature and the expressions of their interpretations resonated aesthetically. My own emergent understanding of reader-response theory contributed significantly to my understanding of what was happening in my classroom. It began to change the way I listened to my students' side comments, digressions, and personal narratives as we discussed a story. In those meanderings, paths to interpretation began to open. In the following pages, I retrace the steps that led the students and me from island hopping to desert trekking. I discuss how the day was structured for reader-response and self-direction; look at classroom setup, organization, and management for whole- and small-group instruction; and discuss issues of planning for the next day: responding to needs and solving problems. In the following chapter, I detail a critical path of how to create a response-centered classroom.

DESCRIPTION OF THE SITE

Edison Elementary School is situated in downtown Long Beach, California, in a low-income neighborhood populated predominantly by Hispanic, Southeast Asian, and African American families. Eighty-five percent of the students are Latino. My entire third-grade class was comprised of native Spanish speakers identified as limited English proficient (LEP). The students ranged in academic ability from gifted to requiring special educational assistance from the resource specialist teacher. Parental support ranged from parents volunteering regularly to assist in school to full-time working parents with latch-key children.

Even though each student came from a low-income family, parents generally held high expectations for their child's academic success. Jackie's father, for example, like all my students' parents, spoke Spanish at home and knew some English at a functional level. He summed up his dreams for Jackie this way:

> I did not get to go to school past the second grade. I had to work hard in the fields
> and suffer a lot without much to show for it. I don't want Jackie to have to suffer

the way I have. She must do well in school to get a job that pays well so that she can have a better life. (spoken at a parent/teacher conference)

Whether a reciprocal relationship exists between schooling and obtaining a good job is not the issue here. Jackie understood that going to school was her job, and she attended to it seriously and conscientiously. School was not a burden for her. She enjoyed her friends, journaling, reading, and other subject areas. She was the kind of student who, on first observation, was easy to overlook. Her quiet demeanor belied the vibrant imagination she brought to school. But given the opportunity to follow her own paths to interpretation in a literature-response group, Jackie expressed her ideas about her reading in the form of art and poetry. She explored a wide range of literature, and as a product of her exploration, she developed language and literacy.

A MORNING IN PAUL'S CLASS

Classroom Setup

On this spring morning, Jackie and a number of her classmates greeted me at 7:45 as I entered the school's main entrance, and they followed me into the classroom. Some of the students dropped off their backpacks and went outside to play until the bell rang; many stayed in the room to socialize or get some extra time on one of the class computers. (With only two computers for thirty students, time at the keyboard was at a premium.) Next to each computer was a calendar of who would have first priority to use the computer. If the students listed on the calendars did not need to use the computers, they could trade days with other students. The primary software was word processing for the production of books, newsletters, and poetry. Before I set my books down, the computers were already booted up and the students were settling in to the new day (see Figure 7.1 for the schedule).

On a dry-erase marker board at the front of the classroom, I outlined the day's activities, which included a meeting with me and Jackie's literature-response group, "La Isla." I also used the marker board as a reminder to students to hand in their permission slips for a walking field trip to the public library the next day. I listed the students who had yet to hand in their permission slips, with the intention of erasing

8:30	Opening and role/Individual math
8:45	Teacher reads aloud a chapter from *James and the Giant Peach*, by Roald Dahl
9:20	Student whole-class interview
9:45	Journals and pleasure reading
10:10	Recess
10:25	Literature response groups
12:00	Lunch

FIGURE 7.1 A morning in Paul's class

their names as they returned them. In a wooden box below the message board, the students deposited their homework folders with work from the previous night. My aide's first task of the morning was to check the homework and to mark the monthly homework chart for those who had done their work.

On the other side of the room, several students organized the behavior chart for the day. It consisted of poster board with thirty-one small library pockets (one for each of my thirty students and one for me to monitor classroom behavior). Each library pocket contained three 3-inch by 5-inch colored paper rectangles: one green, one yellow, and one red. A green paper showing in a pocket meant good classroom behavior, a yellow paper showing meant marginal classroom behavior, and a red paper showing meant inappropriate classroom behavior. Below the behavior chart was a grid with each student's name and mine as well. Two students put a stamp next to the name of each student who had "maintained green" the previous day. They noted students who had gained ten stamps and gave their names to my aide. She prepared certificates with a gift pencil as a reward for ten stamps on the chart. Earlier in the year, the students had voted to include me on the behavior chart so that the behavior monitoring could be a shared experience.

Jackie and her friend Daisy prepared the individual math folders for the class to work on during roll call. These were simply short, self-correcting math exercises to prepare students for an upcoming standardized test format. Each student had a folder with an exercise sheet according to the level he or she was working on. The girls placed the appropriate sheet in each folder and set it on the student's desk so that as they sat down, each student knew immediately what to do.

The classroom setup routine freed up my time to respond to parents or special needs that arose first thing in the morning. My students were a tremendous resource and help in organizing the room for instruction, and I used that help extensively. Although not all students in the room were busy working, many were just socializing. I liked the fact that they felt that the classroom was a comfortable place to be.

Whole-Group Instruction, Individual Space, and Small-Group Work

Whole-Group Instruction

At 8:30, the day officially began with the entire class. I personally found it easiest to begin with the whole group. This approach allowed me to deal with classroom business such as announcements, role call, previewing the day, reading aloud, journals, and class interviews. While I took role, the students worked on their individual math folders. After they completed their work, they switched folders with a partner to check their work. Once the work was corrected, Jackie and Daisy collected the folders to prepare for the next day.

Reading aloud. At 8:45, I sat down in a chair at the front of the room with the Spanish version of *James and the Giant Peach* by Roald Dahl (1982). As the class moved over to listen to the story, Abel and David wanted to show off some of their work based on the book *Island of the Blue Dolphins* by Scott O'Dell (1960). They were interested in the marine life in the story, especially references to whales and dolphins. Abel held up a mobile of the various whales he had read about. I recommended that Abel use those whale designs to create illustrations for a book about the whales he was researching. David called out, "Mr. B.-B., did you know that sperm whales can stay under water for almost an hour?" I said, "That's probably why they've got such big noses. Let's listen to the chapter about James with all his creature friends inside the giant peach being attacked by sharks as they float in the ocean."

We did not have enough copies of *James and the Giant Peach* for a class set, but several students had checked the book out from the library to read along and read ahead of the class. As I read, I tried to explain how the sharks could not bite off large chunks of the peach because of the shape of their snouts. David stood up, went to the chalkboard, grabbed a piece of chalk, and began to draw. He said, "Mr. B.-B., this is how you draw a shark. Its nose sticks out this way, and his mouth is back here. The peach is so big it can't bite a hole in it."

Collaborative interview. At 9:30, as a follow-up to the reading, we had a guest student visit our room—Gordon, a fourth grader who had recently visited the local marine life museum. The class interviewed him by using collaborative interviewing. Collaborative interviews are used in my classroom as a whole-group language development activity. It follows a seven-step process, explained below:

1. Students one-by-one ask questions of the interviewee.
2. The teacher transcribes the answer, but with a twist. The student who formed the question tells the teacher what to write. (The reason for this is twofold: When students tell the teacher what to write, it engages them in active listening and places the responsibility of accurately paraphrasing the answer in third person, thus eliminating confusion in the transcription.)
3. Students take notes as the interview is conducted.
4. At the end of the interview, the responses are organized by using the color mapping technique explained in Chapter 8. Similar answers are marked with the same color, sentences are numbered in order within each color group, and color groups are numbered in order.
5. The students color-map their notes as modeled by the teacher.
6. For homework, the students write up their color-mapped interview notes in paragraph form.
7. The chart is also rewritten by the teacher and illustrated by student drawings.

For the interview, Gordon chose who asked him questions, with one rule: If you start with a girl, then follow with a boy, then a girl, then a boy, and so on. As I transcribed the interview on a large sheet of chart paper, the person who asked the question told me what to write as the response. The students asked Gordon about his favorite marine animals. Gordon had several books that his family had purchased, and he also shared a homemade book about whales. The students had lots of questions about the museum, the whales, and how he made his book. (See Figure 7.2 for

---

Science Content

▲ Anatomy of marine animals
▲ Sperm whales' ability to dive for over an hour
▲ Shark's snout
▲ Marine museum

Instructional Note

▲ Spontaneous moment
▲ David free to demonstrate newfound knowledge
▲ Gordon student guest expert (sharing marine life experience)
▲ Interview to uncover knowledge using dialogue

FIGURE 7.2 Science tied to literature

an outline of how science was tied to literature in this lesson; see also Figure 7.3 for strategies for the monolingual teacher in this type of interview.)

Individual Space

I like to give the students time to reflect and write on an individual basis after a whole-group experience. It not only changes the pace of the instruction but also provides a space to think. Interactive journal writing is ideal for creating such a space. Students also need time to read for pleasure on their own. I have found that the two activities complement each other when scheduled side by side.

Interactive journal writing. Following the interview at 9:45, I asked the students to return to their desks and to write in their journals. Writing in journals interactively in my classroom means that a written dialogue goes on daily between the students and the teacher and among the students as well. The students and the teacher write a personal reflective piece in the journals. Once a written piece is completed, it is taken to a respondent. The respondent reads the journal entry with its author

---

▲ Model writing with the transcription on chart paper.
▲ Faithfully transcribe the student's words.
▲ Think aloud with students about how to phrase sentences.
▲ Check for understanding by asking the interviewer to paraphrase the answer.
▲ Check with the interviewee to ensure fidelity to what was originally stated.
▲ Make special note of key words that convey essential meaning of the topic.
▲ Ask the students to tell you how to spell key words.
▲ Draw a picture to illustrate a word whenever necessary to increase understanding.

FIGURE 7.3 Interview strategies for the monolingual teacher

Paul talks with a student while writing in her interactive journal, and another student joins the conversation.

and then writes a reflective response in dialogue form. I say "dialogue form" to emphasize that the respondent is not there to correct or edit someone's else's journal entry. The written response is simply a conversation in print that models standard conventions of writing. (See Figure 7.4 for interactive journaling strategies for monolingual teachers.)

I found it difficult to adequately respond to each journal every day by myself, so I organized the class to assist in journal writing. With thirty students in the room, I divided the class into five groups with six students in each group. On Mondays, Group 1 helped respond to other students' journals; on Tuesdays, Group 2 responded, and so forth. This way, I was no longer alone as the sole respondent to

- Use a bilingual aide to dialogue and respond with non-English speakers.
- Write authentic responses, commenting on the story behind the drawing.
- Share about your own similar experiences.
- Read the entry with the student.
- Label pictures in the drawing for the student.
- Feel free to ask students to write about another topic if entries appear redundant.

FIGURE 7.4 Interactive journaling strategies for monolingual teachers

the class. With my aide, the six students, and myself, the eight of us responded to the rest of the twenty-four students. In other words, by changing the management of the journals, I moved from a thirty to one ratio to a three to one ratio of writers to respondents. This freed me to spend quality time reading journal entries of a few students at a time, to talk with them about what they had written, and to write an authentic response without feeling the rush to quickly dash off something in all thirty journals. Occasionally, students used the journaling time to write about their pleasure reading. (See Figure 7.5 for a sample of Jackie's journal writing.)

MAY 26 1993

The black stallion I like the part wen they reis because alex let is hands go from the string i could not belive that he let his hands go in the air I like horses i even like riding them i Never ride a horse

Jackie,
    That part was pretty amazing letting go of the reins like that. I hope you get a chance soon to ride because it's lots of fun I like it!
                    ♡ miss Sara

FIGURE 7.5 Copy of Jackie's journal

Reading for pleasure. As students finished their writing, they knew it was time to spend in reading for pleasure. The students selected books from the in-class library, their own books from home, and books borrowed from the school and public libraries. (See Figure 7.6 for stocking the classroom library.) The purpose of this activity was to cultivate a personal love for reading. Cultivating a love for reading requires that students have the power to select their own books and to pursue their own interests. The interactive journal writing and pleasure reading took us to recess time. After recess, we were ready to begin small-group work.

The first segment of the morning concentrated first on whole-group instruction and then on creating individual space. Throughout the course of this first segment of the morning, the students were involved in listening, speaking, writing, and reading activities. After recess, during the literature cycle time, I met with Jackie's litera-ture-response group to discuss their reading in a response forum. This was the most exciting time of the day, when students engaged their imaginations and the literature functioned like a pebble thrown into a pond and creating a ripple effect (Cox & Zarrillo, 1993) of wave after wave of ideas and creative endeavors.

Small-Group Work

At 10:25, the students reentered the room, ready to work in literature-response groups. Literature-response groups were formed around literary works the students selected. The current literature cycle had five groups. Each literature-response group took on the name of the primary book their group was reading: *Encounter* (Yolen, 1992), about Christopher Columbus's arrival and takeover of what is now Puerto Rico from the perspective of a Taino Indian; *Columbus* (D'Aulair & D'Aulair, 1955), a book with a much more conventional reading of the "discovery" of the New World; *Los Delfines*, from a Spanish version of the book *Island of the Blue Dolphins* (O'Dell, 1960); the *Doll House* group, reading *The Doll House Murders* (Wright, 1983); and *La Isla*, taken from a story written on the island of Puerto Rico, "La Gaviota Roja" (Belpré, 1987).

Each literature-response group was developing a Literature Plan that involved in-depth reading of the literature, research, extended reading, student-generated

---

Literacy begins with a juicy story. Consider the following when stocking your class-room library:
- Select quality stories with vivid illustrations.
- Avoid purchasing sets of readers controlled for vocabulary and predictability.
- Buy literature books in groups of six to ten copies so that they can be shared.
- Buy several class sets of captivating chapter books to read aloud with the class.
- Conduct a class "Book Shower" so that families and members of the community can purchase books for the school.
- Coordinate book purchases with other teachers at your grade level to increase the selection available for the students.

FIGURE 7.6 Stocking the Classroom Library

writing projects, poetry or music composition, creative idea(s) project(s), and a class presentation. During the literature cycle, the groups met with me or my aide to discuss the reading and to chart out their Literature Plans in response forums.

The charts were hung by alligator clips tied to fishing line attached to the ceiling. This arrangement made charts visible and easily moved or stored. The students looked to the charts for directions as to what they needed to work on. If it was a writing project, the initial cluster of ideas was written out on the chart. If it was an art project, the materials needed and procedural steps were listed on the chart as well. Writing on the charts was a shared responsibility of the teacher and the students. Pens were readily available for students to note their ideas and directions there on the chart. (See Figure 7.7 for integrating content area instruction.)

At the start of the work session, each member of the small groups already knew what he or she had to do from the previous day's projects. The students working together on reading, writing, and creative projects gave evidence of wave after wave of ripple effects splashing around the classroom. The *Encounter* group was developing a play about the encounter between the Taino Indians and Christopher Columbus. Several of the students were reworking a draft of the script while others were creating props and costumes. The *Columbus* group was interested in the various flags of the period, noting that Christopher Columbus had planted a flag as a symbolic claiming of new territory. They were busy researching the flags that various European countries had designed in the fifteenth century. Members of the *Los Delfines* group were pursuing their marine life interest with Gordon, our classroom guest, who was demonstrating to some of the group how he made his own whale book. Others were rereading the story to each other or making whale and dolphin mobiles with wire hangers, string, and stuffed paper whales. The *Doll House* group was struggling with a longer novel in English. They had to work harder at their book, so they sat in pairs, reading a chapter to each other with the help of my aide. Two

- In a response-centered learning environment, content area emerges according to each story.
- History and science may emerge at the same time among the various literature-response groups.
- The process is not linear, with every student studying the same concept at the same time.
- Regular, direct instruction in content areas continues at different times during the day.
- *Integration* of content area instruction is the application of previously learned concepts of mathematics, social studies, science, or the arts to a new context.
- Keep reference materials (encyclopedias, field guides, maps, and dictionaries) available for easy access.
- Cultivate using textbooks in two ways: (1) as a traditional text for instruction and (2) as a source of reference for emergent integration of content.

FIGURE 7.7 Integrating content area instruction

of the group members were seated at a computer, writing spooky poems based on the book. And the *La Isla* group took seats next to me to discuss their story in a response forum. (See Figure 7.8 for ideas for composing poetry and song with English learners.)

Jackie's group, *La Isla*, had been reading "La Gaviota Roja" by Pura Belpré (1987), a story about a boy from the island of Puerto Rico who finds a rare, red seagull with an injured wing and seeks to nurse it back to health. In addition to Jackie, the members of the group were Baudelio, Carmen, Jeanette, and Vicente. We began the response forum by tacking the Literature Plan chart to the chalkboard behind me. The group sat in a small circle so that each person was facing each other for dialogue. I began by asking the students what they were currently writing about. They showed me drafts of their writing about seagulls. Their papers already had editorial marks in red pencil from peer editing. After each student wrote a first draft, he or she took it to another member of the class, who edited the work in red pencil. The editor then wrote his or her name at the bottom of the page so that I know who edited the draft. I review each draft and make my own comments and suggestions in pen. I show the work to the author, the editor, and the group to highlight common errors or what to look for when editing someone else's work. One of their collaborative writing projects was a song about Puerto Rico and a bird. The group had practically written the song before coming to the group but were having trouble with the chorus section of the song. We worked on it some with little success, until Adrianna, from the *Doll House* group, overhearing our struggle, stepped up and provided a countermelody with words that fit for an appropriate chorus (see Figure 7.9).

A Journey Begins

With the writing reviewed, we set out on a long literary journey in an open-ended way. I started our travels by saying in our response forum: "Tell me about the story. . . . Talk to me. . . ." Instead of starting at the beginning of the story, Jackie and Baudelio talked about the point in "La Gaviota Roja" when the boy took a taxi ride, with the injured bird in a box on his lap, around the island of Puerto Rico from Ponce in the south to the capital city, San Juan, in the north. I pulled down a map of Puerto Rico, and we retraced the route the taxi followed. Vicente wanted the group to make its own map of the island, so we grabbed a large sheet of butcher paper and a pencil for drawing a four-foot map of the island. While the group talked about how to make the map, Jackie's friend Daisy walked up to our group, carrying a book in her hands as if she were holding a golden ring on a pillow. The book that Daisy gave to Jackie was

---

- Remember that all students are composers.
- Count the syllables per line in a familiar song and substitute phrases with the same number of syllables.
- Rhyming is fun but not essential for poetry or song.
- Use phrases that paint a picture: metaphors and similes.
- Play with the language.

FIGURE 7.8 Composing poetry and song with English learners

1. En Puerto Rico hay muchos ricos igual que tú y yo.	1. In Puerto Rico are many rich people just like you and me.
En Puerto Rico hay muchos pericos que me gustarían mirar.	In Puerto Rico are many parakeets that I like to see.
Aunque me piquen en mi pobre nariz, todavía los puedo amar.	Even though they peck me on my poor nose, I still love them so.
2. En Puerto Rico hay muchos ricos igual que tú y yo.	2. In Puerto Rico are many rich people just like you and me.
En Puerto Rico hay una cotorra que no decía "Cataño." La cotorra regresó y Yuba la amaba.	In Puerto Rico is a parrot that refused to say "Cataño."* The parrot returned home and Yuba still loved it.
3. En Puerto Rico hay muchos ricos igual que tú y yo.	3. In Puerto Rico are many rich people just like you and me.
Si tú me quieras todavía igual que los pericos, no te hagas tontita y vente aquí conmigo.	If you still love me like the parakeets, don't be foolish and come along with me.
A San Juan de Puerto Rico.	To San Juan of Puerto Rico.

*Cataño is the name of a town near the city of San Juan.

FIGURE 7.9 Lyrics to "En Puerto Rico" in Spanish and English translation

Island Boy (Cooney, 1988). Even though the book was in English, Daisy knew she had contributed something special to the group, so she stayed on the outskirts of the circle to see what we would do with the book.

From Puerto Rico to Tibbetts Island. *Island Boy* followed a family living on an island off the coast of Maine through several generations. None of the students had ever been to Maine or had lived on a island; however, the story of this family, and particularly the "Island Boy," connected with many of their experiences. As I read the book aloud, many small, seemingly insignificant parts of the story caught our attention. The group first noticed that Tibbetts Island was much smaller than Puerto Rico and that it was inhabited by only one family. They were fascinated with how a family of six boys and six girls worked out sleeping arrangements in a small home. They also noticed the wide variety of seabirds mentioned in the book. No one in the group knew what a cormorant was, so I asked Jeanette to bring over a copy of a field guide to bird watching in the United States. We compared the varieties of gulls, terns, cormorants, eiders, and sea pigeons, noting their colors and sizes. The students were surprised to see how much Little Mattias, the youngest member of the family, changed as he aged. It took a moment to realize what had happened to Old Mattias, the grandfather, how he was lost at sea, at the end of the book. (See Figure 7.10 for how reader-response, language acquisition, and content area instruction intersect.)

Response forum discussion. The following is an excerpt of the conversation conducted in Jackie's literature response group with the book *Island Boy* (Cooney, 1988). I selected this section, not because it is a flawless example of student-teacher interaction, but because of the richness and variety of the dialogue. As I read over the transcript, I saw occasions where I missed opportunities to follow the students' paths to interpretation; I also saw significant connections. Interspersed with the dialogue are my reflections and commentary about what I was thinking during the discussion. The comments are at times instructional, and at others times reflections of my own self-critique. The purpose of the following section is to listen over my shoulder and to think aloud with me as a group of students responds to the reading of a wonderful story.

Teacher: What happened to [Old Mattias]? Talk with your neighbor.

(Asking students to talk with their neighbors is a safe way to start discussion. Students can try out their ideas on a friend before risking sharing in front of the group. For English learners, it also provides a run-through of what to say so that they can make sure they have the words to describe what is on their minds.)

Vicente: He went away in a small boat.
Jackie: He died (pointing to a picture of the funeral).

(Baudelio was wide-eyed. Jeanette and Carmen were surprised and leaned forward to see the book.)

- Response-centered teaching with quality literature creates multiple learning environments.
- Students acquired language as they compared Puerto Rico with Tibbetts Island, classified birds, and contrasted their home life with the home life of a family off the coast of Maine.
- Avenues of learning intersect and enrich each other in a response-centered setting.

FIGURE 7.10 The intersection of reader-response, language acquisition, and content area instruction

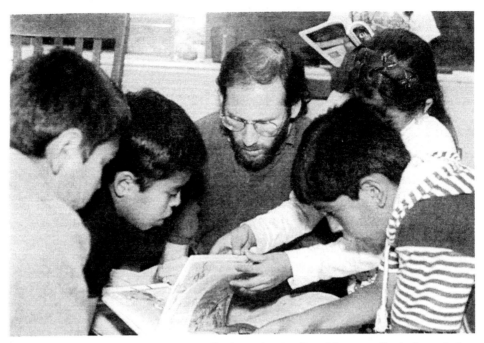

Students are actively engaged as they flip through a book and focus on illustrations during a typical response forum with Paul.

Vicente: He got lost in the storm.
Teacher: Do you know what a funeral is?
Students: (Nodding their heads yes)

(Asking, "Do you know what a funeral is?" I was checking for their understanding of the word funeral. I was confident that they knew what a funeral was in Spanish, but I wanted to know that the students did not miss it in English. I was interested in pursuing the issues of life and death and their rituals brought up in the story; but as you see, the students had other ideas.)

Baudelio: (Taking the book in his hand to show the page of the funeral, he pointed to the boat docked in the foreground of the picture.) They found his boat.

(Long pause)

Teacher: What did you think about the story?

(The discussion appeared to stall, so I used an open-ended question to get it going again. The question put the direction of the discussion back into the students' court. Leaving the direction of the discussion with the students shifted my role from transmitter of information to responder to the text.)

Carmen: Why wouldn't they let Little Mattias work?
Teacher: Do you have big brothers and sisters?
Carmen: Not me.

Vicente: I have a little brother. He follows me everywhere.
Teacher: Is he always interested in what you do?
Vicente: Yeah.
Jackie: My little sister is Norma.
Teacher: Do you call her "Little Norma," "Normalita"?
Jackie: "Gorda" (Spanish for "chubby").
Baudelio: I've seen her. She's fat.
Jeanette: When I was a baby, they called me "Gordita."

(Looking back at my response to Carmen's question, "Why wouldn't they let Little Mattias work?" I think it would have been better for me to repeat her question for the entire group to answer, saying, "That is a good question. Why wouldn't they let Mattias work?" As is evident by Carmen's response, my question took the discussion away from her thinking. My response to Carmen was to put her in touch with her own "lived-through experience" (Rosenblatt, 1986) as she tried to figure out the story. She was inquiring about Little Mattias as a toddler. My question was intended to bring the entire group into answering her question; however, it led to a digression. Not to worry, as they say. Dialogue rarely follows a systematic path from a to b, particularly with young children. Rather than pull the group through a single line of thinking about the story, I poke and prod from many angles until the group latches on to an idea of substance. If one line of thinking appears to lead nowhere, I or, ideally, one of the students simply changes the direction of the conversation.)

Teacher: Where were you children born?
Jackie: Here.
Vicente: In a park . . . Drake Park (the local neighborhood park).

(Everyone laughs)

Vicente: No, here.
Baudelio: Harbor City Hospital.

(Carmen pulls down a map of Mexico from the map set on the chalkboard and points to where she was born.)

Carmen: My house was here, Guerrero. A little girl was playing with a plastic bag there and she died.
Teacher: Your cousin?
Carmen: My friend.
Teacher: Did she live in your home?
Carmen: She was my neighbor. My dad told me that he can never get lost at home because everybody knows him. Like in the story. Everybody knew Mattias.

(The above segment is a digression that I initiated to get the students more in touch with their own lives as they engaged the story of Mattias, the island boy. I found it fascinating that even with my question seemingly out from left field, the students brought it back to engage the book. I was not sure where the discussion was leading at this point. I continued to listen for the group to latch on to a thought. After Carmen's comment came a lull in the conversation. Many teachers begin to panic when confronted with silence, but I see silence as a time to breathe and think.)

Baudelio: (Takes the book and shows the final page, with all the people coming to the funeral and a final picture of Little Mattias standing under the red astrakhan tree where Old Mattias was buried.)

(Long pause)

(One technique of guiding group discussion is to use wait-time to let the group reflect on an idea or an image. During the discussion, the book was passed around from student to student. Here, Baudelio selected a point of interest, but Jackie jumped in to touch base with her favorite part. Notice how Baudelio got to answer my question later in the discussion by nonverbally hanging on to the book, open to his favorite page. Asking about a favorite part of the story is a simple, open-ended question that allows readers to share where they connected most powerfully with a story. Notice how the book and the students' lives intertwined as they talked about their favorite parts.)

Teacher: Baudelio, do you have a favorite part?

Jackie: (Breaking in) The pillow fight. One time, my sister and I were having a pillow fight, and my little brother came in and threw his bottle at me, and the milk spilled all over the bed.

Teacher: I have two older brothers. We'd get into pillow fights from our bunk beds. One time, I fell off and almost broke my arm.

Baudelio: I did that to my brother.

Vicente: I liked the part when they slid down the hill in the snow.

Carmen: Once I went to the snow with my family. We slid down the hill and hit a tree and it fell over. Then we made . . . (points to the snowballs in the book).

Baudelio: Snowballs!

Carmen: We had a big snow fight. I was all wet. And my mother said, "Why are you all wet?" My dad said, "Because you kids were throwing snow." Then I sat in my bed and got it all wet with snowballs.

Teacher: Yuck!

(Baudelio held on to the book tenaciously and continued to project the picture of Little Mattias under the tree. During the above discussion, I kept asking myself, "What is Baudelio trying to tell the group?" In thinking about the book, the image of the tree growing up through the seasons, cycling from blossoms to bearing fruit to losing its foliage to budding again, seemed to parallel life on Tibbetts Island. In fact, at that moment I realized that Barbara Cooney used the tree as a metaphor for the family as it cycled through several generations. Old Mattias is even buried at the foot of the tree. The theme of trees jumped out at me. I recalled my favorite trees as a child and as an adult. As I thought about Little Mattias standing under his tree, I wondered whether anyone in the group had a strong attachment to a special tree.)

(Baudelio continued to show the picture of Little Mattias standing below the tree.)

Teacher: Baudelio, do you have a favorite tree?

Baudelio: Apple tree.

Vicente: A little orange tree about a block from here.

Carmen: Fruit tree.

Baudelio: I took a little wood and made a tree house to climb in.

Teacher: I loved climbing trees; I was the world's greatest tree climber when I was a boy living in Hawaii.

Jackie: At Ocean Park, by my house, I was climbing a big tree and got sticky sap all over me.

Teacher: What did you do about it?

Baudelio: Make glue?

(Laughter)

Jackie: I like the big cactus because it reminds me of home.

Teacher: It sounds like this group needs to make trees.

Baudelio: Make a tree house . . .

From Tibbetts Island to the saguaro cactus of Arizona. Trees indeed became a unifying metaphor for this group. The metaphor of a tree gave this group a way to understand the seasons of the family in Barbara Cooney's book *Island Boy.* Just as Old Mattias and his grandson Little Mattias sat under a special tree, we all had a favorite tree. As we discussed how to make a tree, I was caught up by my own lived-through experience of being an island boy living in Hawaii as a child. As we worked on our projects, I chatted away about when I was a boy and how much I had loved climbing trees. I had lived near a row of palm trees that were bowed by the wind at such an angle that I could run halfway up a tree without even having to hold on with my hands. We talked at length about our favorite trees: where they were planted, what they looked like, making tree houses, climbing the branches, sitting in its shade, or eating its fruit. We experienced the effect of ideas rippling out of the response forum's discussion.

Jackie loved the saguaro cactus, which is common to northern Mexico and the Southwest United States. The saguaro cactus reminded her of her family's home in Sonora. She went to the class library and found the book *Cactus Hotel,* by Brenda Z. Guiberson (1991), illustrated by Megan Lloyd. (This beautifully illustrated book traces the life cycle of a saguaro cactus as it pops up in the shade of a paloverde tree in the Arizona desert.) She began to develop her own personal Literature Plan, which included making a papier-mâché cactus, creating a book about the life of a cactus plant, cataloging the various animals that live in the community of the tree, writing poetry, and re-creating a famous painting with watercolor. (See Figure 7.11 for how discovering an icon from reader-response affects language arts and content area instruction.)

Jackie looked through the book *Mexico: Splendors of Thirty Centuries* (O'Neill, 1990), published by the Metropolitan Museum of Art, and found the painting *The Candelabrum of Oaxaca* (p. 535) by José María Velasco: a lone *vaquero* (Mexican cowboy) standing in the shade of a magnificent cactus.

Later that week, Jackie reproduced that painting in watercolors for herself. Her watercolor painting reflected the magnitude of the saguaro, and her poetry sang of the companionship the saguaro provided and included the paloverde from the book *Cactus Hotel.* She went on to write about the gila woodpecker, which lives off the saguaro's seeds and fruit and makes its home in the cactus (see Figure 7.12).

> ▲ Responding to literature, students adopt *icons*: unique characters, plants, animals, or inanimate objects that serve as meaningful connections between the story and their own lives.
> ▲ Like signposts, icons hold a reference point around which much of Jackie's learning is directed.
> ▲ An icon is a personal choice embedded in the individual's cultural background and experience.
> ▲ Jackie's icon was the saguaro cactus plant because of its tie to her family's home in Sonora.
> ▲ The saguaro cactus icon opened ways to aesthetically develop language arts, social studies concepts, and science.
> ▲ Language arts: poetry and prose about the cactus
> ▲ Social studies: studying Mexico's art and plants
> ▲ Science: exploring the life cycle of the saguaro cactus

FIGURE 7.11 Discovering icons affects language arts and content area instruction

It amazed me that, the following year in the fourth grade, under a different teacher, Jackie continued her personal investigation of the saguaros. When I visited her room, she showed me another book she created about the various saguaro cacti and the other animals living in the *Cactus Hotel*.

11:55. Before I knew it, lunchtime had arrived, and it was time to clean up. Throughout the discussion of *Island Boy*, I kept my eye on the rest of the class, who kept actively engaged in their own projects. It would be impossible to have this kind of open-ended, creative experience in a traditional classroom setting. Spending more than an hour with one small group is possible only if the rest of the students are clear about their tasks and are very much self-directed. Fostering self-direction demands that the teacher trust the creative insights of the students to develop a plan of action that will hold their interest and challenge them intellectually. Having a teacher's aide who knows to look for groups that need special assistance is a tremendous help. My aide was tuned in to the needs of the groups so that she could provide an idea or a push in a creative direction. *Island Boy* was a special experience, and we as a group got carried away by Barbara Cooney's literature. The class was accustomed to occasionally getting carried away by a good story, so they knew to just keep working on their projects. When lunchtime came around, many of the small groups had gotten carried away by the stories they were reading and responding to and did not want to stop working. (See Figure 7.13 for how response-centered teaching engages the teacher's imagination, too.)

Planning for the Next Day: Responding to Needs, Solving Problems

Before sending the class out to lunch, I took five minutes to meet with the group liaisons. They briefly reported to me about their groups' progress. This reporting included sharing their need for materials for producing the presentations. I do not

El Saguaro y el Paloverde

El saguaro está grande,
más grande que los otros.
Tiene las ramas grandes,
más grande que las del
paloverde.

El hombre mediano recoje
las hojas del paloverde
con el rastrillo,
porque no le gusta que
estén las hojas junto al saguaro.

El Pájaro Carpintero

Los animales van al
saguaro para tomar el nectar
de las flores. Un ratón viejo
se come la fruta que cae
del saguaro. La fruta tiene
dos mil semillas.
    El pájaro carpintero tiene
el pico grande. Tiene
la frente roja como
la flor del saguaro. Come
las semillas del las flores de saguaro.
El pájaro carpintero hace su nido
en el saguaro para protegerse
de sus enemigos. Las espinas
del saguaro no le pican
al pájaro carpintero.

The Saguaro and the Paloverde

The saguaro is big,
bigger than the other cactus.
Its branches are big,
bigger than those of
paloverde.

The medium-size man rakes
the leaves of the paloverde
with a rake
because he does not want
its leaves to touch the saguaro.

The Gila Woodpecker

The animals go to the
saguaro to drink the nectar
of its flowers. An old rat eats
the fruit that falls from
the saguaro. The fruit has
two thousand seeds.
    The gila woodpecker has
a large beak. It has
a red forehead just like
the flower of the saguaro. It eats
the seeds of saguaro flowers.
The woodpecker makes a nest
in the saguaro for protection
from its enemies. The needles
of the saguaro do not pierce
the gila woodpecker.

FIGURE 7.12 A poem and an essay about the saguaro cactus by Jackie Hernandez, in Spanish and English translation

- Teachers respond creatively to their own reading.
- When a story touches one of your lived-through experiences, you are imaginatively engaged in reader-response.
- Sharing the connection between the reader and the text is a pleasurable experience for the teacher and the students.
- Time flies when you're having fun!

FIGURE 7.13 Engaging the teacher's imagination

see the teacher as the sole provider for the classroom. When questions of needed materials arise, my first response is to put it back on the group, asking: "What are you going to do about it? How can you get what you need?" If it's an item the school readily provides, such as colored paper or paints, I ask the liaison to write me a note as a reminder to get the item from the storeroom. If the item requires special effort, however, we spend a moment thinking of the resources available to us, such as asking another teacher, writing a request of the principal, or asking parents via letters to provide the needed items. Putting the responsibility back on the students brings them into the planning process.

Often the response group liaisons report on problems the groups are experiencing. The problems are as diverse as not liking the book they selected and wanting to switch and personal difficulties with one or more members of the group. In the case of the story selection problem, I request that we have a response forum together the next day to articulate what is wrong with the book. If the complaints are valid, I encourage the students to write to the publisher, expressing their views and suggestions on how to improve the story. Then they are free to switch books. With interpersonal problems, I ask the offended party to write down his or her complaint on a piece of paper and to give it to a classroom judge. The judge reads the complaint to the entire class after lunchtime, during student court, so that the class can discuss the problem and devise their own solutions.

Retracing Jackie's Path to Interpretation

The path that Jackie took with her reading was not lockstep. She did not proceed in a preplanned route mapped out by a teacher's guide far removed from Jackie's life and thought. Looking at a map to chart her reading, you would conclude that she had an open plane ticket, rather than a set itinerary. She began by reading a story about a boy on the island of Puerto Rico who saved the life of a rare red seagull. The next stop was Tibbetts Island, off the coast of Maine, where a family's life cycle paralleled that of a red astrakhan tree. Her interest in trees took her back to her family's original home in Sonora, Mexico, and to the desert plains of Arizona to read about a saguaro cactus that was a hotel for a myriad of insects and other animals. Jackie did not go off flying by herself; she was accompanied by a small circle of friends who shared her interests. As teacher, I established the learning environment that trusted her to pursue her interests.

Keys to Following Jackie's Path to Interpretation

The key to captivating the students' and teacher's imaginations is bringing quality literature into a response forum that provides for rich transactional learning. What I continue to discover as a teacher is that responding to student transactions can be just as captivating for me as it is for my students. Even though no one in the classroom, including the teacher, had ever been to an island off the coast of Maine, Barbara Cooney's story touched the lives of each of us. Additionally, both the students and the teacher were engaged in sharing their lived-through experiences as they heard the stories. In a culturally diverse classroom setting, a response forum affirms what each student brings to the table. Each of us is a resource of rich experience and personal knowledge of our own world. The process of exploring the literature is a shared experience. (See Figure 7.14 for a summary of keys to following Jackie's path to interpretation in a literature-response group.)

Bringing your own life to the text shifts your teacher-student relationship. Paulo Freire (1970) identified the shift in the relationship as *dialogical*, one of students-teacher and teacher-students. As teacher, I listen to learn from my students about how they read a text; as students, together they share with me each other's lives and insights. And I also have room to muse and share my understandings of the reading or how the book touches my life. I am still knowledgeable as the teacher and educational leader of the classroom, but I do not presume to know what my students are thinking until they tell me what is on their minds. This strategy makes teaching a shared process of exploring the paths to interpretation that the students generate. And once the teacher and students begin to discover their paths to interpretation, they can begin to respond to the text in meaningful ways that work to develop the students' language and literacy.

For Jackie, the morning in my classroom was filled with opportunities for developing language arts. She was actively engaged in listening, speaking, reading, and writing. The product of the literature cycle was a wide range of language arts activities generated by her own interests. As she pursued her path, she produced oral and written language and nonverbal expressions of art. Jackie composed prose, poetry, and song. She authored her own language and literacy development.

CONCLUSION: AUTHORS, ARTISTS, AND EXPLORERS

Louise Rosenblatt posited the idea of following the students' "paths to interpretation" of literature, looking for their aesthetic responses to literature as an art form. Following Jackie's path was an experience in interpreting literature, writing prose

---

- ▲ Have quality literature on hand, in abundance, in the classroom.
- ▲ Look for ways that a story touches lived-through experiences.
- ▲ Affirm the rich experience and personal knowledge that each person brings to the classroom.
- ▲ Shift the teacher-student relation from lecture to dialogue.
- ▲ Use open-ended questions to open dialogue: "What was your favorite part of the story?"
- ▲ Pay attention to the aesthetic reading of a text: "How do you feel about . . . ? What do you imagine when . . . ? What does this story remind you of?"
- ▲ Listen for cultural metaphors in response to reading.
- ▲ Take time to wait for a response (deeper responses come more slowly than superficial ones).
- ▲ Tie responses to language development and content area learning.

FIGURE 7.14 Keys to following Jackie's path to interpretation

and poetry, painting, and bookmaking. She made excellent decisions about the direction of her study and how to express her ideas. She engaged her mind in the books and acquired essential skills for literacy development. Following her path to interpretation, then, was not a mindless pushing her out of the nest to fly on her own. She was guided to explore her interests within the context of literature conferences, process writing, and editing and was held accountable for her work with a final class presentation. The literature cycle, beginning with a story and following class musings to culminate in a class presentation, did not limit her to reading a single story. The six-week cycle was a way of framing an expedition to explore children's literature. The limitations were the parameters of the students' and teacher's imaginations.

All students bring ideas, imagination, and prior experiences to the table. Their minds are continuously active and curious. They are knowledgeable, and their knowledge is partial, just as the teacher's knowledge is partial. But the coming together around a story in a response forum connects that knowledge and is, as Howard Gardner (1991) quipped, "a time when my creative sluices [are] opened and the juices allowed to flow" (p. 56).

The paths of creativity are not straight. They wind around, double back, and sometimes take the reader beyond initial plans and itineraries. I did not set out to ask Jackie to explore the worlds of Maine's Tibbetts Island and Arizona's saguaro cactus. We started in Puerto Rico. Some students stayed in Puerto Rico, continuing to write and compose about the story of Ramon and the red seagull; others stayed on Tibbetts Island, mapping its story; but Jackie needed to move on. Whether in Puerto Rico, Tibbetts Island, or Arizona, the students engaged in significant experiences of reading and writing, of expressing themselves and giving voice to the wanderings of their minds.

Developing literacy with quality children's literature in a response-centered environment treats readers as authors. The students' ideas are substantive and authoritative in response-centered instruction. Rosenblatt (1978, 1986) calls aesthetic responses to literature a "poem" in which the reader generates a unique and personal understanding of his or her own reading. Reading is an act of authorship, a creative experience of reliving the story, of recreating the text anew. Jackie and her classmates came to realize that their reading was their open ticket to explore new and old territory. They grew to understand that following their own paths to interpretation was a task in becoming authors and artists and explorers to develop their emergent literacy.

A Thought from Carole

The literature group discussion of *Island Boy* by Barbara Cooney that Paul described in this chapter was memorable for me, if nothing else than it lasted an hour and a half—a long time for a group of third graders. During that time, Paul and the students in the group were totally absorbed in reading it, and the rest of the students were equally engaged in working on self-directed literature group projects of their own. The discussion focused primarily on the students' as well as Paul's more personal, aesthetic responses to the book, an excellent example of reader-response theory in action and Rosenblatt's notion of literature as a means of personal exploration. By drawing on their prior knowledge and links with their own life experiences, these students also used their second language of English in a natural, context-embedded, instructional framework advocated by second-language theorists such as Cummins and Krashen.

Both Paul and I commented afterward how we regretted that we hadn't had my husband on call to videotape it. But because it began spontaneously when Daisy brought the book to Paul, we couldn't have known what would happen. I did take extensive field notes, however, which revealed several significant things to me now that I reflect on what happened that day:

1. *The book was magic.* Although not particularly related to the backgrounds or cultures of Paul's students (it takes place on a island in Maine in the nineteenth century and is about people of obvious British ancestry), it is a great book, very literary, beautifully illustrated, and touched something in everyone, creating a magic spell that lasted an hour and a half. The book worked on many levels (e.g., death). Paul noted that several words needed explaining but that they were "good words."

2. *The discussion was like a "lap reading."* Several students frequently came up and touched the book; traced their fingers over illustrations, looking for something; counted something; or asked to look longer at an illustration. They talked with each other and with Paul. This is the kind of interaction that happens when a parent reads to one child or to more than one in a family bedtime situation.

3. *Lots of "clues" to understanding English were used.* Paul pointed frequently to the rich and detailed illustrations; Paul and the students frequently turned back to previous pages to check for understanding and to make links with what they'd already read; Paul gestured a lot and made faces to make the book understandable to his students (e.g., "Ma's fierce eye" he demonstrated by making a fierce eye himself; he drew a barrel stove on the chalkboard and showed how it worked).

4. *The students were engaged.* They asked many questions, referred back to things they had already read, and made comments linking the story to their own lives. Some sat spellbound a lot longer than I had seen them ever sit in one place before. Wide eyes were the rule. Carmen was by no means fluent in English. The only thing she had ever said to me was on the day I brought Easter eggs to the class. She came up to me shyly as I was leaving and said hesitantly, "Have a nice . . . on rabbit day." I noted that she was, however, very engaged in this discussion, which was all in English. Paul concurred that it was an unusually sustained discourse in English for Carmen.

5. *Aesthetic questions led to linking the story to students' prior knowledge.* Paul asked questions about where students were born, their families, their favorite trees, and so on.

6. *Students were given time to respond.* Paul waited a long time each time for responses to emerge, rather than rushed for a quick answer to a question.

7. *The teacher shared his own experiences.* Paul was a co-discussant, modeling for the students as well as just wanting to share his experiences of climbing trees as a child and his own family stories.

8. *The mood was that of a fireside chat.* All students seemed relaxed responding in English, and all responded. They sat on the floor and in chairs around Paul. It was intimate, warm, and cozy. Baudelio, often a very tentative student who receives special resource help, was very relaxed and the most "checked in" I had ever seem him. He sat close to Paul, smiled, and responded to other students as well, not the usual pattern for him.

These observations are offered, not as a recipe guaranteed to succeed every time, but as a description of the parts of one really great meal that could happen again, if not in exactly the same way.

THINGS TO THINK ABOUT

1. Look back at the transcript of Paul's discussion with students about the book *Island Boy*. What questions would you have asked?

2. If you were Jackie, where would the book *Island Boy* take you? Would you imagine a saguaro cactus in the desert of the Southwest? Or is your favorite tree in another part of the world?

3. Think about integrating language arts with content area instruction. When would language arts dictate mathematics, science, or social studies instruction?

4. Create a mathematics, science, or social studies unit that draws on children's literature.

5. Think about the issue of trust in teaching. In what ways did Paul demonstrate trust toward his students?

THINGS TO DO

1. Practice conducting a collaborative story interview with one member of the class. Use chart paper to record responses. Color-map the responses on the chart paper by marking similar ideas with the same color, and then number the order of the responses within each color group. Finish by writing up the interview in ordered form.

2. Maintain an interactive journal among your classmates. Between lectures and discussions, take five minutes to write down thoughts and ideas. Exchange journals with another student or the instructor to write a response.

3. Conduct a response forum in small groups in your class. Read a book such as *Island Boy* to the entire group. Ask one member of the group to role-play the teacher and to practice using open-ended questions, listening for metaphors, and noting how the story touches actual lived-through experiences of the group members.

4. Share a favorite children's book with the class. After reading it, brainstorm creative ways to express responses to the story.

FURTHER READING

Boyd-Batstone, P. (1995). *The great kapok tree musical* [Tape and teacher's guide]. Order by mail $15.00 (tape/guide) + $3.00 (shipping) c/o Paul Boyd-Batstone, 2890 Cedar Avenue, Long Beach, CA 90806.

Cherry, L. (1990). *The great kapok tree*. San Diego, CA: Harcourt Brace.

Douglass, M. (1989). *Learning to read: The quest for meaning*. New York: Teachers College Press.

Johnson, P. (1990). *A book of one's own: Developing literacy through making books*. Portsmouth, NH: Heinemann.

Krashen, S. (1996). *Every person a reader: An alternative to the California Task Force Report on Reading*. Culver City, CA: Language Education Associates. To order, call (310) 568-9338 or fax (310) 568-9040.

O'Hara, M. (1990). *Tesoro de poesia juvenil/A treasure of poetry for young people*. Ventura, CA: Alegria Hispana Publications. To order, call (805) 642-3969.

REFERENCES

Belpré, P. (1987). La gaviota roja. In *Campanitas de oro* (pp. 121–135). New York: Macmillan.

Chomsky, N. (1979). *Language and the problems of knowledge: The Managua lectures*. Cambridge: MIT Press.

Cooney, B. (1988). *Island boy*. New York: Viking Kestrel.

Cox, C., & Zarrillo, J. (1993). *Teaching reading with children's literature*. Upper Saddle River, NJ: Merrill/Prentice Hall.

Dahl, R. (1982). *James y el melocotón gigante*. Madrid: Alfaguara.

D'Aulair, I., & D'Aulair, E. P. (1955). *Columbus*. Garden City, NY: Doubleday.

Dyson, A. H. (1990). Weaving possibilities: Rethinking metaphors for early literacy development. *Reading Teacher, 44*(3), 202–213.

Freire, P. (1970). *The pedagogy of the oppressed*. New York: Contiuum.

Gardner, H. (1991). *To open minds*. New York: Basic Books.

Guiberson, B. Z. (1991). *Cactus hotel*. New York: Henry Holt.

Krashen, S. (1985). *Inquiries and insights: Second-language teaching, immersion, and bilingual education literacy*. Hayward, CA: Alemany Press.

O'Dell, S. (1960). *Island of the blue dolphins*. Boston: Houghton Mifflin.

O'Neill, J. P. (Ed.). (1990). *Mexico: Splendors of thirty centuries*. Boston: Bullfinch Press.

Rosenblatt, L. (1978). *The reader, the text, and the poem: The transactional theory of the literary work*. Carbondale: Southern Illinois University Press.

Rosenblatt, L. (1986). The aesthetic transaction. *Journal of Aesthetic Education, 20*(4), 122–128.

Tharp, R., & Gallimore, R. (1989). *Rousing minds to life*. New York: Cambridge University Press.

Wright, B. R. (1983). *The doll house murders*. New York: Holiday House.

Yolen, J. (1992). *Encounter*. New York: Harcourt Brace.

CHAPTER EIGHT

Components of Response-Centered Instruction

The Fearsome Crowned Eagle
by Jackie Hernandez
The crowned eagle weighs about 9 pounds and is a
bout 3 feet long. It gets its name from the big crest of
feathers on its head. Village chiefs once used the feathers
in their head dresses. Crowned eagles have to be fast to
catch monkeys in the trees.
If i would be a eagle i would be happi because i
will flie. I wuld have blaK talons. I will dill my prey with
my talons. I will haf feathers bown, blaK, white. I will haf
feathers and orange beeK. I would eet Rats, Birds, SnaKes.
They will Kill their prey whith hug talons.

Jackie, a third grader whose native language is Spanish, drafted "The Fearsome Crowned Eagle" (see Figures 8.1 and 8.2) in English as a response to her reading about the animals in tropical rain forests. The writing above was turned into a book, which she illustrated, bound, and donated to the school library for other students to check out. The student-made book was not the only product of her work; she also developed her language and literacy (Krashen, 1985). The numerous experiences of listening, speaking, reading, and writing, as well as drawing, painting, and word processing, all contributed to developing her Spanish and English language and literacy as languages of learning (Gallas, 1994). Her work was part of a literature cycle of reading, conversing with others in a response forum, and working in collaboration with classmates in a literature-response group.

The entire experience took place in a response-centered classroom environment structured for students to read quality literature, discuss ideas with students and teacher, and respond creatively to her thinking. Jackie's responses emerged out of her own experience (Dewey & Bently, 1949) and out of the multiple worlds she inhabits as a child growing and learning in two languages (Dyson, 1990). Response-centered instruction demands that the teacher be prepared to guide the students in their learning through dialogue, to act on their aesthetic responses (Rosenblatt, 1986), to develop their language and literacy, and to organize the presentation of their work for other students and parents. In broad terms, the components of response-centered instruction are threefold: (1) preparation and planning

Jackie is writing a cluster about "The Fearsome Crowned Eagle" in response to her reading about animals in tropical rain forests.

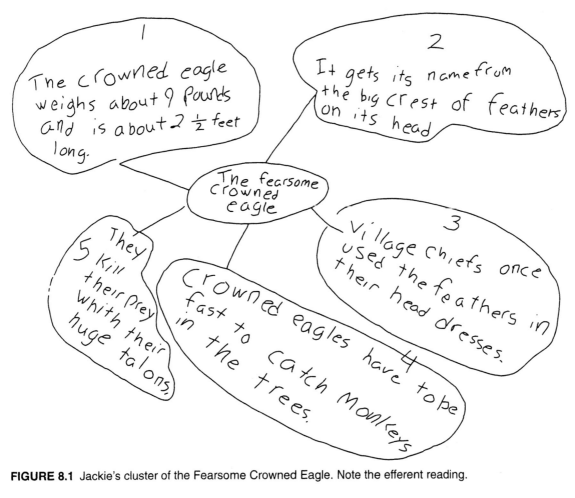

FIGURE 8.1 Jackie's cluster of the Fearsome Crowned Eagle. Note the efferent reading.

for the literature cycle, (2) response forums with literature-response groups, and (3) class presentations and evaluation. Included under these broad categories are practical concerns of the classroom teacher, such as determining what literacy options the teacher must have at-the-ready to develop primary and second language and literacy; identifying what essential materials must be on hand; judging what computer software is useful for student authors; choosing and using quality literature; conducting initial literature conferences; using open-ended questions strategically; tugging at metaphors; generating writing with collaborative color maps; conducting subsequent literature conferences; coordinating group presentations; evaluating student work; and establishing calendars and schedules.

Jackie and her classmates engaged their minds in a wide range of experiences with reading, writing, and creative projects. They explored their imaginations and expressed their ideas about their reading. As their teacher, I did not take a back seat in the process. I played multiple roles in the classroom: co-researcher, editor, project consultant, and at times mediator of disputes. My role as teacher is fluid, so I

FIGURE 8.2 Jackie's second cluster of the Fearsome Crowned Eagle. Note the aesthetic reading.

can move off-center and share these roles as researcher, editor, consultant, and mediator with my students. Conventional classrooms, characterized by teachers following scripted guides, cannot allow for this kind of flexibility and power sharing. Response-centered classrooms make teachers and students authors of their own scripts for language and literacy development as they enter into a literature cycle of choosing their reading, generating ideas and creating imaginative projects in a response forum, writing to express themselves, and finally making a presentation to classmates and parents.

PREPARATION AND PLANNING FOR THE LITERATURE CYCLE

The literature cycle begins when students select their reading and form literature-response groups around books. Then they engage in dialogue with the teacher in a response forum. Finally, they present their work to other students and parents. A *literature cycle* is nothing more than a period of time for exploring quality literature. As a rule of thumb, I think in terms of six weeks for a single cycle. (I discuss this in depth below.) The *literature-response groups* differ from conventional reading groups because they are formed by the students around a literary work of interest. Students self-select the stories or books they want to read and find others with the same interests to form a literature-response group. Within the literature-response group, the students do not all do the same activities. The various language and literacy development options they employ are dictated by their own responses to the literature, rather than by a preformulated set of tasks spelled out at the back of a basal or literary reader. A *response forum* is a meeting of the teacher and the students of a literature-response group at which the members discuss the reading and plan what to do in response to that reading.

Preparation and planning include carrying a set of literacy options, knowing the sources of language and literacy, and stocking the classroom with materials and tools readily available to students. The next section is a practical how-to section for pulling together the components of response-centered instruction.

Language and Literacy Development Options

Studying literature is like a journey. When preparing to go on a lengthy expedition, the wise traveler plans extensively ahead of time. Packing the proper items for the trip is an essential part of planning. Part of the planning process is to map the route and destination of the journey, knowing full well that detours and side trips occur spontaneously. A route mapped on paper can appear entirely different once on the road. Therefore, experienced travelers keep in mind travel options. Knowing the plan and being skilled in each option does not dictate which decision the traveler will make; rather, it is the terrain of the story and the interests of the fellow travelers.

As a teacher in a response-centered classroom and fellow traveler with my students, I carry as many as a dozen language and literacy development options in my head when entering a response forum with my students. In anticipation of the students' varied responses to reading, I can reasonably expect that they will want to do one of the following activities: rewrite the story in their own words, write an essay or reflective piece, make a script for a drama or media production, compare the story with another, report the events as if in a newspaper, compose a poem or song, research historical or scientific background information, conduct an interview with an expert about a certain aspect of the story, or create a Big Book format of the story or part of it. Although the list is virtually endless, I keep a variety of language and literacy development options at my fingertips for ready application.

A simple suggestion from me—or even better, from a student—can send a group of students to work on expressing their thoughts and ideas. Having this collection of options under my belt and the room properly equipped with writing materials and tools, I can confidently enter into a response forum discussion knowing that the students will come out of a literature conference engaged in appropriate tasks for literacy development.

Language and Literacy Development Options in Detail

The following language and literacy development options are not a complete list of possibilities, but are enough for students to express their thoughts about their reading. The key is that language and literacy options be at-the-ready in the teacher's mind so that little time is used to figure out what to do with an enthusiastic group of students.

Language Arts Options

1. *Rewrite the story in your own words:* Put yourself in the story, change the setting or time period, switch the characters of the story from animals to people (or vice versa), switch the roles of the "good guys" and the "bad guys," or change the outcome of the story. With primary students, this may be done as a language experience chart story. It may also be written collaboratively by using the color mapping technique explained below.

2. *Write an essay:* Critique the quality of the story, argue whether or not the author was successful, or suggest how the story could be improved. Young children have opinions about their stories and can express them orally. Even students at early stages of language development can respond to what they liked or did not like about the story, mediated by the illustrations in the book or via their own drawings of what was read to them.

3. *Write a reflective piece:* Describe your impressions of the story, elaborate on your feelings while reading a favorite part, relate the story to a similar personal experience, or put yourself into the story and explain how you would react. Everyone has a favorite part of a story. This is the point of connection between the lived-through experience of the reader and the text.

4. *Make a script for a drama or media production:* Use a two-column sheet of paper to describe character actions on the right and spoken words on the left. List props and costumes. Organize the responsibilities of each member of the production team. Design posters and programs for the production. Plan out the story board for videotaping. Write a letter to parents, inviting them to the showing of the production.

5. *Compare the story with another:* Identify similarities and differences of other stories by the same author, chart a Venn diagram listing the unique features of two stories and how they are the same, or compare stories from the same time period or geographical region or of authors of different ethnicities writing about the same theme. When using Venn diagrams to compare two stories, I have found that using two overlapping rectangles is much easier for writing purposes than two overlapping circles. On the left, list unique features of a story or book; on the right, list the unique features of the comparison book; and in the middle, write in the features common to both books. In writing a three-paragraph essay, the first paragraph would comprise the right section, the second paragraph would comprise the left section, and the third paragraph would comprise the middle section summarizing common features.

6. *Report an event of the story as if it were in a newspaper:* Set up a template on the computer for newspaper-style writing. Concentrate on reporting the who, what, when, where, and how of the event. Stress writing for detail and description so that the reader can imagine the scene. Make multiple copies of the newspaper for other members of the class, other classrooms, and students' families.

7. *Compose a poem:* Create your own cinquain poem, using a simple framework. Describe a single scene in the story, using the five senses. Write about the story,

using a single unifying metaphor (e.g., a burning house, charred possessions, billowing flames). Retell the story in a limerick fashion, maintaining meter and rhyme.

8. *Compose a song:* Borrow a tune from a familiar song, number the syllables in each phrase of the song, think up your own phrases with the same number of syllables, and plug them into the melody of the song.

Content Area Options: Social Studies, Science, and Mathematics

9. *Research the historical background of the story:* Compile what encyclopedias and nonfiction books have to say about the setting and time period of the story. Answer how significant historical events influenced the author's writing.

10. *Research the scientific background of the story:* If the story involves animals, describe the animal as a biologist would—identify its habitat, feeding habits, predator or prey behaviors, and species. If the story includes information about the planets, the students might be inclined to research and report on the solar system. Trees or forests and their conservation might be their choice to study.

11. *Interview an expert:* Anyone can be an expert: a parent, a student, another teacher, an administrator, a special guest. If the story takes place, say, in Puerto Rico, persons who have lived there are resident experts. Students can write down interview questions ahead of time and then, during the interview, take notes. After the interview, they can write up their notes in the form of a report or illustrated book.

12. *Generate a Big Book:* Any aspect of a story can be re-created in large format with illustrations and text. Big Books can be created by using large sheets of butcher paper bound together with masking tape. More elaborate bindings can be used, depending on what is available at each school site. Students can dictate the sentences to the teacher, who writes them on the pages of the Big Book. In turn, each student can illustrate his or her given page. After all the pages are illustrated, all the students can contribute to decorating the cover and back page.

13. *Reconstruct the story on a calendar to account for the passage of time in the story:* For shorter time periods, re-create the story on a weekly or daily planner format.

14. *Write a version of the story that includes a detailed account of the expenses:* Make a budget for the characters. Include travel expenses, meals, clothing, and postage. The possibilities are endless.

15. *Design sets and props for plays, accurately drawing the plans to scale before measuring and cutting out the materials.*

16. *Conduct an inquiry using an opinion survey:*
    1. Form a research question (What is your favorite pet?)
    2. Hypothesize the outcome.
       a. Establish the range of choices to five or six pets plus "other" for an open choice.

    b. Estimate which pet will be the class favorite.
3. Collect the data.
    a. Devise a way to record responses.
    b. Start asking the question.
4. Organize the data.
    a. Use a table.
    b. Represent the data on a graph.
5. Write down observations.
    a. Record in sentence form what the graph tells you.
    b. Note any interesting information.
6. Interpret the data.
    a. Calculate the percentages for each pet. Use this formula (# of votes in a category/Total # of responses) x 100 = _____ %
    b. Compare your results with your original hypothesis. Were you on the mark? How far off was the hypothesis? Why?
7. Report the findings to the class in writing.

Language and Literacy Sources

In a response-centered classroom, the teacher looks beyond the literary reader for sources of language and literacy development. The sources of language and literacy development can be drawn from written texts, as well as from visual performing arts media. Joined with the literacy options detailed above, the response-centered teacher has access to a tremendous number of possibilities (see Table 8.1).

Materials and Tools for a Literature Cycle

Just as the teacher must be equipped with a full set of language and literacy development options and sources, the classroom must be equipped with the materials and tools necessary for active learning. Materials and tools must be readily available so that students can follow their creative impulses. If the teacher has to go through an elaborate ritual of preparation, he or she cannot be very responsive to the students.

Acquiring Materials

Acquiring classroom materials used to be one of the more problematic issues I faced as a teacher until began to look at the students as one of my greatest resources. In the past, I would scrounge or spend my own money to get what the students needed. But when I began to put the responsibility back on the students, the acquiring of materials became an opportunity for developing literacy and self-direction.

    As an example, when a group of students wanted to put on a puppet show for the class and I did not have a puppet theater in the classroom, we sat down together and tried to figure out what to do. We talked about how the teacher across the hall had a beautiful puppet theater but was unwilling to lend it to another classroom. One student suggested building a puppet theater, but I suggested that we didn't have enough time before the performance date. Then Ernesto, one student in the group, suggested that the principal might be able to help out. So I recommended

TABLE 8.1 Language arts for English learners

Language and Literacy Sources	Supports	Possible Student Products
Songs	Story ladders	Anecdotes
Guest speakers	Story maps	Questionnaires
Video/Films/Laser disks	Venn diagrams, T-graphs	Labels, advertisements
Drama	Brainstorming	Rules/Directions
Concerts	Sorting/Listing	Greeting cards
Spoken recordings	Categorizing	Personal letters
Experiments	Outlining	Personal experiences
Photographs	Clustering	Cartoon captions
Posters	Charting	Poems
Bumper stickers	Word webbing	Reports
Drawings	Summarizing	Recipes
Literature	Journals, diaries, logs	Family histories
Newspapers	Notes	
Magazines		
Comics		
Articles		
Plays		
Essays		
Diaries		

Draft copy from the *Language Arts Framework for California*, February 1995.

that the group draft a letter to the principal, requesting his help in obtaining a puppet theater.

The principal sent a memo back to the students, saying he would be delighted to help. He knew of another teacher with a puppet theater who was willing to let us borrow it. He would ask the custodian to move it, but he needed more information as to when and where the performance would take place. The students responded to the principal by writing another letter with the date, time, and location of the show.

The show time drew close, and no puppet theater appeared. The students, a bit dismayed, came to me for help. My only advice was to send off a quick note to the principal, asking him to follow through on his promise to provide the theater. Needless to say, I was concerned at this point. The principal, however, immediately came to the room and began apologizing to me. I said that he needed to talk with the students as a group, and not to me. Then he gathered the group together and explained the oversight, apologized, and promised to provide the theater as soon as possible.

Within five minutes, the custodian arrived carrying a magnificent puppet theater on a dolly. But before the students began their production, we took a moment to reflect on how to move the system by the strategic use of correspondence to the

The principal is apologizing to Paul's students for not following through on their written request for a puppet theater, an example of how written communication can work for them.

right person and holding that person, even the principal, accountable for his or her promises. We obtained a puppet theater, but the students also learned the power of written communication and how it can work for them to meet their needs.

Acquiring materials is not always that elaborate. Nevertheless, the students are capable of obtaining what they need. Even if we need a ream of writing paper, a school-supplied item, I ask the students to write letters of request to the office. If we need cloth or some non-school-supplied item, I ask the students to think about where to get it and from whom to request it. It may mean writing to parents, businesses, or community agencies; what it really means is that the students are learning how literacy works for them and how to get what they need.

Materials and Tools

The following is a list of materials and tools to keep on hand for ready student access:

1. *Writing materials:* Pencils, erasers, scratch paper, red pencils (for peer editing), lined newsprint for initial draft writing, white lined paper for final drafts, ball-point pens, chart paper (for collaborative writing).

2. *Word processing and authoring tools software: Bilingual Writing Center, Children's Writing Center, Hyperstudio, KidPix, PrintShop Deluxe, Storybook Weaver* (see the appendix).

3. *Drawing materials:* Colored pencils, pens, felt-tip markers, crayons, drawing paper, construction paper, chalk pastels.

4. *Painting materials:* Tempera, acrylic, and watercolor paints; class sets of large-, medium-, and fine-tipped brushes; watercolor paper; easel paper; butcher paper for murals; sponges; drop cloths.

5. *Clay and pottery materials:* Modeling clay, water trays, wax paper, cellophane, rolling pins, objects for texturing and scrolling designs.

6. *Papier-mâché materials:* Wheat paste, large mixing bucket, instant papier-mâché, water trays, masking tape, wire mesh, toilet paper rolls.

7. *Mask-, hat-, and puppet-making materials:* Scissors, glue, hole punch, paper plates, ribbon, yarn, construction paper, felt cloth, socks, buttons, sewing needles, thread, tongue depressors.

Two students make a papier-mâché model of *The Great Kapok Tree* in preparation for a musical play based on the book.

8. *Big Book and binding materials:* Large sheets of chart paper, hard tagboard, masking tape, stapler.

9. *Costume and prop box items:* Hats, glasses frames, old suit jackets, ties, shawls, aprons, printed and white sheets, coveralls, dresses, shoes, silk flowers, scarves, nylon stockings, old shoes and boots.

10. *Correspondence materials:* Colorful stationery, school letterhead, pencils, pens, envelopes.

THE LITERATURE CYCLE

Choosing and Using Literature

Choosing and using literature implies that the students have available to them a vast array of engaging books. It is vital that the books capture the students' imaginations. Self-selection is key to the beginning of a literature group because it acknowledges the student as an active participant in the learning. Furthermore, students given the opportunity to choose their own reading for literature develop an intrinsic motivation toward their schoolwork. Allowing students to self-select their own reading is an act of trust that builds a response-centered learning environment. It speaks to the students that their choices can be very good ones for themselves and that their ideas are valuable as well.

In the past, I took all the initiative in forming groups according to ability levels and the stories as sequenced in the literary readers. I planned the projects and activities the students were required to do. But I also spent an inordinate amount of time managing behaviors of students expressing resistance to my own "neat" ideas that the students rejected. They forced me to rethink the underlying assumptions of my transmission mode of teaching. They showed me that their ideas and interests were advancing the goals of language and academic content development. As I began to look to the students' interests in their reading, I found myself questioning the arbitrariness of my criteria for grouping. And as the students demonstrated that I could trust their judgment, I progressively turned over much of the decision process to them.

Fostering Self-Direction in the Literature Cycle

For most teachers, the thought of elementary students selecting their own books to read spells confusion and chaos. Trying to manage more than three reading groups is nightmarish for teachers in conventional classrooms. The last thing teachers want to give up is classroom control. In conventional classrooms, students are rewarded for compliance, rather than for self-direction and intrinsic motivation. Generally, students are trained to wait for the teacher's direction before proceeding. A process of unlearning must take place before students can accept the responsibility of self-direction. This responsibility can be easily fostered in such a way as to lessen the stress of the teacher as well. Each round of a literature cycle I incrementally relinquish more control to the students (see Table 8.2). If I need to step in and take back control, I do.

TABLE 8.2 The literature cycle

Round	Duration	Teacher Role	Student Role
One	3–4 Weeks	▲ Select one book with multiple copies for each student to read. ▲ Assign students to three literature-response groups. ▲ Conduct response forums for each group, using open-ended questions about the book.	▲ All read the same book. ▲ Produce two process writing pieces, a group poem, and a painting based on the book. ▲ Present finished work to classmates.
Two	3–4 Weeks	▲ Select three books for students to choose to read. ▲ Negotiate the groups so that the numbers are manageable in each group. ▲ Conduct response forums with each group. ▲ Organize rotation for presentation.	▲ Choose to read one of three books. ▲ Select related books for additional reading. ▲ Form groups according to selection. ▲ Produce two to three process writing pieces, poetry, and an open-ended creative project. ▲ Present to classmates.
Three	6 Weeks	▲ Limit to four to six groups ▲ Establish a classroom criterion for forming groups (e.g., ratio of boys and girls) ▲ Conduct response forums. ▲ Coordinate presentations.	▲ Vote on what books are to be read. ▲ Choose additional reading. ▲ Negotiate the formation of groups around the books they selected. ▲ Present work to classmates and parents.
Four	6 Weeks	▲ Maximum six groups. ▲ Maintain grouping criteria. ▲ Conduct response forums. ▲ Coordinate presentations.	▲ Students nominate and vote on books. ▲ Select related reading. ▲ Negotiate literature response groups. ▲ Produce four process writing pieces, two poems or songs, and two or three creative projects. ▲ Present work to classmates and parents.
Five and beyond	6 Weeks	▲ Turn over self-selection and grouping to students. ▲ Consult with students in the response forum. ▲ Assist in coordinating the presentations.	▲ Self-select books. ▲ Negotiate groups around common interest in books. (Individuals may choose not to be part of a group and work by themselves.) ▲ Produce their own literature plan with a minimum of three written pieces, two poems of songs, and a creative project. (This may appear to be requiring less than the previous round, but projects tend to be more involved and lengthier at this point.) ▲ Present work in the school auditorium for parents and other classes.

The Ripple Effect

The transformation of the classroom for a literature cycle grew out of a change in my own thinking about the metaphor of classroom instruction. Rather than treat the classroom as if it were an assembly line for dumping ideas into empty receptacles, I prefer the metaphor of the *ripple effect*, coined by Carole Cox (1988). With the ripple effect, when someone reads a wonderful story, it is like the action of a pebble thrown into the reflective pond of the mind and heart. The story creates waves of lived-through experiences, ideas, and sensations that circle out and connect with other experiences, thoughts, and feelings.

Each one of us, students and teacher alike, comes to the classroom with a deep well of experiences, ideas, and feelings that are continually swirling about. At times when we are supposed to be sitting quietly and listening, our minds are dreaming or making associations. The expectation in a response-centered classroom is that each one has experiences, thoughts, and feelings to contribute to his or her reading. We can respond to what each one contributes to a discussion and find a way to express it creatively. As we come together around a work of literature, we look for the ripple effect of waves of experiences, ideas, and feelings.

In the literature cycle, no one is empty-handed. The teacher and the students bring something to the response forum. The teacher's expertise in language and literature and the students' responses to the literature combine to produce writing, creative ideas, poetry and music, and imaginative presentations of their work. The teacher brings a knowledge of available resources for literacy development, strategies of working with students to maximize their understanding of the text, questions for stimulating dialogue and thinking, preparation to respond to the direction a group of students decides to pursue, and the ability to form connections among other groups working on similar themes. The teacher facilitates the process of the literature cycle by skillfully accessing the content of the literature and the readers' responses to the story. The students bring substance to the response forum with their unique contribution of lived-through experiences, insights, ideas, feelings, and imaginations. The response forum is the pot in which the knowledge of both teacher and students cooks up the raw stuff of aesthetic responses to make a presentation of writing, creative ideas, poetry, and song (see Figure 8.6).

Transforming the classroom for a literature cycle means reorganizing grouping for maximizing listening and responding. The groups function more as forums for creative expression. The development of language and literacy in a literature cycle is a creative time of sharing our reading, our writing, and our imagining. The organization of the classroom involves literature-response groups, response forums with the teacher, and a literature cycle that takes approximately six weeks.

Forming Literature-Response Groups

There is no hard and fast rule about forming literature-response groups. Rather than form groups by an arbitrary decision, such as "balancing" ability levels, I prefer to ask students to form their own literature-response groups around books they want to read together. I do ask that each group reflect the ratio of boys to girls that is in the classroom. For example, if eighteen boys and twelve girls are a class of thirty students, the ratio of boys to girls is three to two. Allowing for a range of groups, I then ask that a group of five or six students have a minimum of three boys and two girls. Although groups may range in size from four to eight students, in some cases I encourage highly motivated individuals to work by themselves. If ten to twelve students are interested in the same book, I ask them to split to form a group of five or six students. Aside from that constraint, the students are free to form their groups around a captivating story.

The process of choosing literature and forming literature-response groups usually takes a class period, or about one hour of sometimes serious negotiating. During that hour, the students have access to every book in the classroom. I explain that they are to look for a book with multiple copies so that each member has one to read. As students browse through the books, I move through the classroom and make suggestions, give advice, and answer questions about the books.

A Group Liaison

Once a group takes form, its members decide on one member to be a group liaison. The group liaison is the one who voices problems and concerns from the group to the teacher and from the teacher back to the group. The liaison also assists the teacher with handing out materials and takes a lead role in disseminating messages back to the group.

Shared Reading

With the book selected and the liaison decided on, the students begin to read. They may read as a whole group taking turns or in pairs. If the pair is comprised of two skilled readers, they take turns leap-frogging through the text. If, however, one student struggles more with reading, he or she is to read with a more proficient reader; but instead of leap-frogging through the story, the more proficient reader reads a sentence or two and the less proficient reader follows by reading the same sentence or two that has just been read. I ask any paraprofessionals or parent volunteers in the classroom to sit with a group or with an individual student needing special attention and to read the story aloud with dramatic emphasis. Then the students follow by rereading the story in pairs. Each student is also asked to read the story at home with an adult, and each is given a form to sign as proof of having read for homework (see Figure 8.3).

Literature Folder

In addition to a copy of the book or story for reading, the students are given a literature folder to hold their written work and a reading journal. The folder is simply made of two sheets of twelve- by eighteen-inch construction paper. One sheet is folded lengthwise, laid over the other sheet, stapled at the ends, and folded down the middle to form pockets to hold the students' written work (see Figure 8.4).

Glued to the front of the folder is a half sheet of paper that I call a "progress record sheet." It contains a list of the expected written and creative projects each

Home Reading Log				
Name _____			Classroom _____	
Day	Date	Title of book and pages read	# of minutes read	Signature of adult
Mon				
Tue				
Wed				
Thu				
Fri				
Sat				
Sun				

FIGURE 8.3 Home Reading Log

member is required to complete, a box for date of completion, and a box for the grade (see Figure 8.5). The Progress Record Sheet keeps both the teacher and the student informed at a glance as to the progress of the group and of the individual student so that all parties are clear about what has to be accomplished. In this way, students are able to develop their work on their own with minimal consultation.

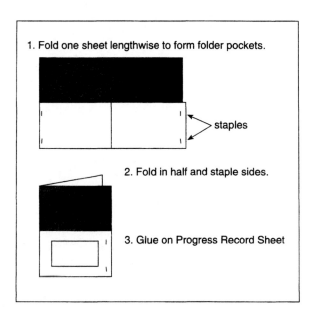

FIGURE 8.4 Directions for making the literature folder

Progress Record Sheet			

Name _____

Literature Studies Book Title _____

By _____

A. Writing

Title		Done	Grade
1.			
2.			
3.			
4.			

B. Poetry/music

1.			
2.			

C. Creative Ideas

1.			
2.			

D. Presentation
Describe Responsibilities

1.			

FIGURE 8.5 Cover sheet for literature folder

Reading Journal

A reading journal, a small composition notebook for note taking and reflecting on their reading, provides each student with a space for written reflection after reading a section or chapter in his or her book. Many teachers have the students divide the page into two columns, one side for taking notes of events and characters, the other side for more reflective comments and insights into the reading. The note-taking side of the page can be seen, in reader-response terms, as the more efferent, or informational, reading of a text. The other side of the page is much more personal and reflective, which can be seen as evidence of a more aesthetic reading of the text. I also ask that the students bring their reading journals to response forums for note taking during the group discussion.

Response Forum

The response forum, as defined above, is a time to meet with a small group and discuss a piece of literature. The focus of the discussion is the students' responses to the literature, rather than their answers to predetermined questions about the story. A forum is where all have an equal voice in the discussion. It is also a safe arena to try out new ideas and tentative thoughts to see how they fly. While other groups are reading, note taking, and decorating their folders, I immediately begin to conduct a response forum with a literature-response group to get the students started on their Literature Plan.

Literature Plan

For each group, I hang large back-to-back sheets of chart paper from the ceiling of the classroom by fishing line and alligator clips. The front sheet is labeled with the title and author of the book or story the group has selected. Below the title and the author is a schematic that maps out what the group will work on as they engage the story (see Figure 8.6). The literature-response group is expected to produce a minimum of three process-writing pieces of various genres, compose songs and/or poetry, and produce a creative project or two. In addition, group members keep track of their various resources on the chart and use the chart for planning the class presentation of all their work. On the back of the Literature Plan, they map out collaborative writing. (At the kindergarten/first-grade level, students are not involved in collaborative writing as such. Their work centers on producing language experience charts where they dictate to the teacher and practice reading the chart story as a group or as individuals. In their group work time, they illustrate the chart story or cut out the sentences to glue in a Big Book format with illustrations.)

First Response Forum

The goal of the first response forum (small-group meeting with the teacher) is threefold: (1) to reread the story or a portion of the story, (2) to connect with the group liaison, and (3) to engage the story in such a way as to provide direction for the first writing project. Once those tasks are completed, the group is on its own for the next day to work on writing. An initial forum lasts about twenty to thirty minutes. It is my goal to meet with half of the groups within the first ninety minutes of the literature cycle.

It is my experience that students who are less confident in their ability to compose may avoid writing unless nudged to start with collaborative writing. Collaborative writing encompasses listening, speaking, reading, and writing in a single activity. As a rule of thumb, I insist that we begin with a collaborative writing assignment so that the fundamentals of language and literacy are addressed from the outset.

Subsequent response forums tend to be more open to the direction of the group's interest and less structured by time constraints. A group might choose to compose a poem or a song, prefer to generate another writing assignment, or come up with an idea for a creative project. The order in which the students flesh out the dimensions of the Literature Plan is not a major concern.

Conducting a Response Forum

Three aspects of reader response are at the forefront of my mind when I am in a response forum with a group of students. First, I use open-ended questions to allow students to share their experiences, thoughts, and feelings related to a work of lit-

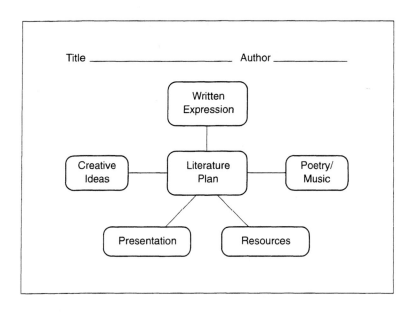

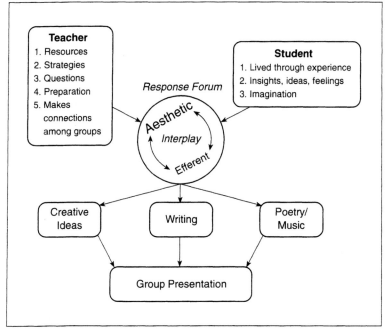

FIGURE 8.6 Literature plan cluster chart (top) and response forum flow chart (bottom)

erature. Second, I listen for students to express metaphors, which function as windows into the aesthetic workings of their minds. Third, I guide collaborative writing by clustering students' words on chart paper and by organizing their thoughts with a color and number system that I call "color mapping."

Open-Ended Questions

Responsive teaching requires inquiry into what students are thinking about their reading. The teacher's questions can either function as an open invitation to dialogue or act as a kind of check for correct answers. Open-ended questions invite the students to share their thoughts. Closed questions have a predetermined answer in mind. Closed questions are useful for students at the early stages of language development for expressing themselves in single words and short phrases in their second language. With beginning English learners, open-ended questions are much more fruitful in the primary language, but this does not preclude their use. Reader-response looks for the reader to share his or her insights, as tentative as they may be. The practice of opening self-expression is a valuable use of instructional time. Maintaining a diet of closed questions shuts the door to students' thinking and self-expression.

On occasion, my questions have been very closed, and at times embarrassingly silly. One student, Daniela, taught me a vital lesson about my questions and their hidden assumptions. I had never considered Daniela to be one of my brightest students. But Daniela taught me how an appropriate open-ended question can make a world of difference in affirming the unique intelligence of each student.

One day in February, I tried to initiate a discussion for an English language development lesson about George Washington. I asked, "Who was Martha Washington's husband?"—a poorly thought-out question, at best. Why that silly question occurred to me, I'll never know. Even more perplexing, what did I expect to accomplish by asking such a question? Was I hoping to trick the students? Was I looking to display my own knowledge? Hardly! Or was I looking to expose what I considered to be their lack of knowledge? Possibly.

Daniela immediately raised her hand and blurted out, "Martin Luther King!"

Hearing her answer to my question made me think that she was not going to catch on. Even so, Daniela's answer, apparently coming from left field, made me begin observing her more closely to figure out what was going on in her mind. I noticed that, during classroom discussions, she would often look up at the ceiling, her head would bob from side to side, and her mouth would move as if she were whispering a song to herself. I thought to myself, there she goes again, daydreaming and not paying attention to the lesson. But then I wondered whether something else was going on inside her head.

Finally, the day came when I asked a much more intelligent question. We were studying whales (*ballenas*, in Spanish). In their Spanish reading, the students found that whales communicated with each other through song and body movement. The whales slap their fins and their tails on the surface of the water to announce danger; they raise their heads out of the water and move them back and forth when in distress. In the middle of the discussion, I looked at Daniela; sure enough, she was looking at the ceiling, wagging her head, and mouthing some words to herself. I asked her a very simple and open-ended question, "Daniela, what are you thinking?"

This time, she spouted, *"¡Baila la ballena!"* (Dance the whale!).

Another student suggested that it sounded like "La Bamba," the famous Mexican dance song. Before I knew it, the group had reproduced the lesson about whales, *ballenas*, as a song to the tune of "La Bamba." The song is as follows:

La Ballena

Baila la ballena, baila la ballena, baila la ballena . . .
Para bailar la ballena, para bailar la ballena
se necesita una ballena grande,
una ballena grande y otra chiquita.
Ay arriba, ay arriba iré . . .
Yo no soy marinero, yo no soy marinero,
Soy capitán, soy capitán.
Por tí seré por tí seré

Para comunicar un mensaje
a las ballenitas
hay que mover la cabecita
y mover la colita.

Bamba, bamba . . .

[English Translation]

Dance the whale, dance the whale, dance the whale . . .
To dance the whale, to dance the whale
you first need a great big whale,
a great big whale and a small one, too.
Kick it up, kick it up I'll go . . .
I'm not just a sailor, I'm not just a sailor,
I'm a captain, I'm a captain.
For you I'll be, for you I'll be.

In order to send a message
to the dear whales,
you must move your head
and move your tails.

Bamba, bamba . . .

I realized that day that Daniela had a gift. She was very talented at putting words together in creative, poetic ways. Thinking back to when I asked my closed question about Martha Washington, I realized that she was responding to the question on a more aesthetic level. She was playing with the words. As she looked up at the ceiling and wagged her head, she mouthed the words back and forth: Martin/Martha. In a word, Daniela was a poet. She was an unrecognized poet. I did not recognize her gift; I could not see it until I began to listen openly for her aesthetic response.

Louise Rosenblatt's (1986) theory of reader-response speaks to this very situation. Reader-response theory recognizes that all readers bring something to their reading, that each person reads a text or situation according to the lens of his or her own experience. It is the teacher's responsibility to find that "live wire" in the students and to connect instruction to it via the student's knowledge and experience.

In terms of Daniela, her live wire was tapped when I, as the teacher, became open to her way of thinking. When she took an active role in the lesson about whales, her learning increased and the entire class benefited from her creative contribution. In other words, a transaction took place as she participated in mutually defining the lesson on whales. It took the simple act of asking an open-ended question to listen for and respond to her wordplay and metaphor.

The way teachers use questions is an issue of thinking, knowledge, and power. The extent to which students are heard and responded to indicates how thinking, knowledge, and power are shared in the classroom. It is an issue of thinking because it concerns inquiry into the ideas of all students; of knowledge—of *whose* knowledge is invited into the classroom setting and *whose* knowledge is silenced at school; and of power—of *who* has the power to affect the instruction in the classroom. Designing questions to look for preprogrammed responses, on the one hand, assumes that only the instructor has the insight and power to establish the parameters of knowledge. Asking and responding to open-ended questions, on the other hand, creates an ambience of openness to the collective wisdom of the students in a classroom of shared thinking, knowledge, and power.

I have often used the simple phrase "talk to me" to initiate a discussion about the story we are reading. Occasionally, a brief open-ended question such as, "What do you think about this character?" is all that is needed for a group of students to open their minds and imaginations. Once the students open up, I start to listen for metaphors. Metaphors unify thinking and express deep insights. When a student displays metaphorical thinking, I know he or she has connected with the text like a live wire.

Metaphors

Ingmar Bergman (1960) described filmmaking in much the same way that transactional learning takes place in the classroom:

> A film for me begins with something very vague—a chance remark or a bit of conversation, a hazy but agreeable event unrelated to any particular situation . . . These are split-second impressions that disappear as quickly as they come, yet leave behind a mood—like pleasant dreams. It is a mental state, not an actual story, but one abounding in fertile associations and images. Most of all, it is a *brightly colored thread sticking out of the dark sack of the unconscious.* If I begin to wind up this thread, and do it carefully, a complete film will emerge. (p. 11)

Rich metaphors like a "brightly colored thread" lead to the workings of the mind and heart. Tugging at that brightly colored thread—my students' metaphorical thinking—makes teaching an enlightening experience. In a transitional bilingual classroom, even though students are quite fluent in English, the use of Spanish is not discouraged, especially when it helps provide the students and the teacher with multiple ways to tug at rich cultural metaphors. Metaphors emerge in English or in Spanish spontaneously and pop out unexpectedly. When those brightly colored threads pop out, they signal an opportunity to tug at something deep in the minds and hearts of students.

The spontaneous nature of metaphors is illustrated by an interaction I had with a student. Before school one day, I was conducting my supervising duties on the playground. The night before, a storm had poured buckets of water on the city of Long Beach, leaving it washed clean. The morning was brilliant as the sun broke through the clouds. And like a flash flood without warning, metaphors spilled out and filled our conversations.

A Salvadoran boy named Santos, standing near me, squinted as he looked up at the sky and said, "*El sol está enojado hoydia*" (The sun is angry today).

Surprised at this statement, I asked, "*¿Por qué dices que está enojado el sol?*" (Why do you say that the sun is angry?).

"*Porque,*" responded the boy, "*me está pegando como un gigante*" (Because it is pounding me like a giant).

This brief conversation gave me pause. As I looked up at the bright sky, I, too, was pelted in the eyes by the sun's intense fury. Santos, in a rather matter-of-fact way, described the morning with the vivid sense of imagery of a poet. I thought of all the times I unsuccessfully tried to teach lessons on personification, similes, and metaphors. And here, in a seemingly mundane conversation, a child was deftly applying personification to "an angry sun" and the simile "like a giant pounding" his club down on earth. I wondered whether my students talked like this very often. I discovered that I was not tuned in to their use of metaphor even though metaphorical thinking was present in their daily conversations.

Sharon L. Pugh (1992) affirmed that metaphorical thinking is not only a higher-order thought process but also pervasive, powerful, and generally ignored:

> Through metaphorical thinking, divergent meanings become unified into the underlying patterns that constitute our conceptual understanding of reality. Indeed, metaphor is so much a part of our thinking and learning processes that we usually do not think about the essential role it plays. (p. 3)

Metaphorical thinking provides an open window into the way one sees the world. Tuning in to what students say metaphorically gives insight into their understanding and background knowledge. Scant education takes place with decontextualized instruction or learning situations that are foreign; however, building on students' prior knowledge is essential to effective instruction with English learners (Krashen, 1985). Building instruction around the metaphorical thinking of English learners is a way of "tugging at" the cultural and personal understanding a bilingual student brings to schooling.

Not only does metaphorical thinking provide insight, but its affirmation and development in the classroom also make for more powerful speaking and writing. I once heard a radio commentator call for a new business in Washington, DC, that markets the creation of metaphors. The sound of their power resonates throughout our nation's capitol with phrases like "iron curtain," "a thousand points of light,"

"Operation Desert Storm," and "contract with America." There is power in creating images that paint emotionally packed pictures in people's minds. Evocative and persuasive language skillfully applies metaphors to poetry and prose alike. Affirming and developing metaphorical thinking, speaking, and writing in the classroom adds power to the students' ability to express themselves. Therefore, I tug at my students' metaphors. And as metaphors appear in our classroom discussions, I structure the focus of instruction around them.

One example of this took place during a discussion of Lynne Cherry's (1990) fabulous book on the Brazilian rain forests, *The Great Kapok Tree*. I was conducting a response forum in Spanish with a small group of students. In the book, a tree sloth tries to persuade a man not to cut down the kapok tree. In our previous conference, I had asked the group to find out what they could about tree sloths. Now they were sharing what they had researched: how the sloth sleeps eighteen hours a day, how a newborn clings to its mother with its claws for the first six months of its life; and how it then goes to live by itself in the canopy of the rain forest. Then, out of the blue, Adrianna looked at the illustration of the tree sloth and said, "*Tiene la cabeza de coco.*" (It has the head of a coconut).

Delighted with this entrée into her way of seeing, I asked, "*¿Qué más tiene?*" (What else does it have?).

She immediately responded with, "*Tiene la nariz de chocolate.*" And she provided her own English translation, saying, "It has a nose like a chocolate bar."

I continued to encourage this line of thinking with, "*¿Y algo más?*" (And anything else?).

At this point, the entire group jumped in with all kinds of similes about the tree sloth, comparing its eyes to coffee beans, its smile to a banana, its body to a melon. This led the group to compose an original song about the newly created fruit sloth:

La Perezosa de Fruta

La perezosa de fruta, la perezosa de fruta.
Tiene la cabeza de coco
Que nunca se puede abrir.

La perezosa de fruta, la perezosa de fruta
tiene el cuerpo de sandía
igual que un melón.

La perezosa de fruta, la perezosa de fruta
tiene la nariz de chocolate
que me gustaría comer.

(Coro)

La perezosa de fruta
tiene el cuerpo de fruta
todo el cuerpo de fruta
de la selva tropical.
Cha, cha, cha.

[English Translation]

The fruit sloth, the fruit sloth.
It has the head of a coconut
that can never, ever be opened.

The fruit sloth, the fruit sloth
has the body of a watermelon
just like a ripe melon.

The fruit sloth, the fruit sloth
has a chocolate nose
that I would love to eat.

(Chorus)

The fruit sloth
has a body of fruit
the entire body of fruit
from the tropical rain forest.
Cha, cha, cha.

The group did not stop there, however. They continued composing, in English, a song about the life and habitat of the tree sloth:

The Sloth

The sloth moves very slow
slowly moves the sloth.
The little baby sloth
holds its mother with its claws.

The sloth moves very slow,
slowly moves the sloth.
When it is six months old,
it finds a way to live alone.

The sloth moves very slow,
slowly moves the sloth.
High in the canopy
it moves from tree to tree.

(Chorus)

The sloth moves very slow,
slowly moves the sloth,
as slow as it can be,
as slow as it can go.

The students did not stop at writing songs about the sloth in Spanish and English. The following day, each one brought in a kind of fruit or edible item to create an actual fruit sloth. It had a coconut head, coffee bean eyes, a chocolate candy bar nose, a banana for a mouth, a large papaya body, cucumber arms, and green chili peppers for claws. That afternoon, the entire class sang their praises of the sloth, and then we all shared in eating our metaphorical sloth and celebrating the students' ingenuity.

The centerpiece of the whole event was a work of art, a children's literature selection. The students experienced a delightful mix of reading, responding, researching, writing, sharing, creating, and making music. Their imaginations completed the circuit of Rosenblatt's live wire between a reader and a text. The meeting of their minds around an engaging story made for a juicier curriculum. It was an organic experience of teaching and learning, a two-way path to interpretation.

Color Mapping for Collaborative Writing

Metaphors, ideas, feelings, and thoughts tumble out of students' mouths randomly. They do not think in outline form. Even for native English speakers, the task of getting ordered thoughts on paper can at times be daunting, and for English learners, even more so. One of the most important jobs for a teacher is to model strategies for getting this jumble of language organized on paper.

In talking with professional writers, I have learned that many conceive of writing in two phases: (1) getting ideas on paper and (2) organizing the ideas into a pub-

La perezosa de fruta was made by Paul's students after writing a song using fruit metaphors for a tree sloth in response to reading Lynne Cherry's book *The Great Kapok Tree.*

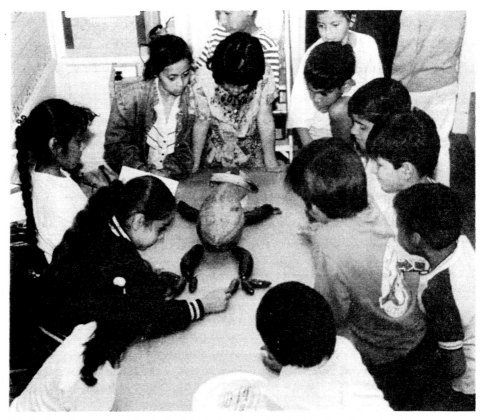

Students gather around the fruit sloth before they have a class party and eat it.

lishable form. Getting ideas on paper is paramount. Without the substance of ideas, the stuff of meaning, there is nothing to organize into a publishable form. Temporarily setting aside a concern for writing conventions, form, and sentence order for even a few minutes helps ideas flow without obstruction. Once the ideas are on paper, it is an easy task to organize a well-ordered piece of writing. To accomplish this, I use what I call "color mapping" for collaborative writing. A *color map* is essentially a common clustering technique coupled with a color/number coding system to help organize the form and structure of dictated sentences.

During a response forum with a group of students, I begin by asking open-ended questions, I listen for metaphors, and when I sense that the group is on to a big idea, I write down their words on the back of the Literature Plan chart paper. As mentioned above, their ideas appear randomly, so I write them down in the order they appear, around an empty circle. Once the group indicates that enough ideas have been written down, we think of a word or phrase to use as a title for our cluster of ideas. I write that title in the middle circle.

The next step is to identify similar ideas as related themes. I simply circle similar ideas with a colored felt-tip marker. Generally, two to four themes emerge running through a discussion, so two to four colors will circle the phrases and sentences.

(This is also a time to scratch out written down comments that may have been interesting at the time but that are not pertinent to the themes of the discussion.)

The next step in the color-mapping process is to decide the order of the sentences within a color code theme. The sequence of the sentences is simply numbering them in order with a black pen. The final step is to decide the order of the color-coded themes. I indicate the first set in the center circle with a swatch of color next to the numeral 1; below that, the second color and the numeral 2; and so forth (see Figure 8.7).

The students now have a set of organized ideas to work with in which each color group represents a paragraph. The students can work right from the chart to write up their responses to the book we are reading. In time, the students become so familiar with organizing their ideas as a group that doing the same task in pairs or individually is relatively easy. Usually, the entire process takes about thirty minutes. But occasionally, the group is so engaged in discussing a story that time is taken to follow the students' lead. This kind of flexibility with time can happen because the other groups are generally engrossed in writing, reading, and creative projects.

Conducting Subsequent Response Forums

Having begun the literature-response groups, the literature cycle moves into the body of the Literature Plan development. Over the course of three or four weeks, a rhythm is established of small-group response forums with the teacher, alternating with self-directed work based on the response forums. Approximately every other day, a small group can expect to meet with the teacher unless they request more time to work on a given project. The goal of the subsequent response forums is threefold: (1) to edit first drafts of student writing, (2) to grade and record finished work, and (3) to delve into the more creative ideas that spring from a given piece of children's literature through music, poetry, or imaginative projects.

---

1. Draw an empty cluster map: a circle with lines drawn outward from the edge of the circle.
2. Listen to the students' discussion for a unifying theme. When the theme begins to appear, write down their words in sentence form in random order on the cluster.
3. Once the ideas are written down, ask the students to title the cluster. Write the title in the circle at the center of the cluster.
4. Color-code related themes and ideas by circling them with the same color marking pen.
5. Number the sentences in a logical order within in each color group.
6. Decide the order of the themes and indicate their order in the center circle with the color pens and their corresponding number.

FIGURE 8.7 Steps in color mapping for collaborative writing

Editing First Drafts

There are many elaborate ways to work through editing a draft of writing. Peer editing is popular and requires that training and accountability be built into the process. Simple is better with editing, so I use a simplified system of editorial marks (see Figure 8.8).

To teach students to become peer editors, I use a student's writing draft as a model for a whole-group instruction. I sort the class into pairs, and each pair receives a copy of the student's writing. I also make an overhead transparency of the draft and project it on a screen for modeling purposes. Each student is also given a red pencil for marking corrections. Sentence by sentence, we read through the draft as a group, and I ask the students to tell me where the writing needs to be changed. We mark up the draft, using the simplified system of editorial markings, and we discuss how to improve the writing.

When students peer edit on their own, a degree of accountability must be built in. The peer editor is instructed to write his or her name at the bottom of the draft. Then, when I sit with the student-author to review the work, I ask the editor to sit in and explain the corrections and learn about what the two students missed. The conventions of language are taught directly in context during the editing phase of the writing process. With published work, 100 percent correct spelling is required, and the same goes for grammar and punctuation. Students need to learn conventional English, and they learn it best by crafting their own writing to meet the rigors of conventional writing.

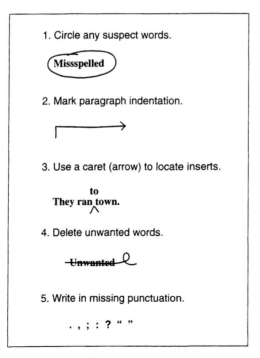

FIGURE 8.8 Simplified editorial markings

Grading and Recording Finished Writing

As we sit together in a response forum, some students hand in final drafts of writing for grading and recording. Having already gone through a two-part editing phase and rewriting, it is generally an easy task to review a final draft of writing. At this point, major revisions or serious problems with a piece have already been discussed, so I focus on the degree to which the student followed the editorial markings on the previous drafts. I assign a grade of (E)xcellent, (S)atisfactory, or (N)eeds improvement accordingly.

The final draft is stapled to the previous drafts to form a concrete documentation of the process the student engaged in. (During the final evaluation phase of the group presentations, I ask the students to give me one or more of their written pieces to put into their student portfolios.) The students keep their completed work in their folders, and the date of completion and the grade are written on the front cover sheet of the folder (see Figure 8.5). I also record in my grade book the E, S, or N grade to maintain a quick reference of the completed work.

Fostering Creative Ideas, Music, and Poetry

It has been my experience as a classroom teacher and teacher educator that teachers often forget, when presenting children's literature, that they are dealing with a work of art, rather than a chapter in a textbook. The students respond aesthetically to this artwork. They experience the emotions of exhilaration, fear, and surprise as they empathize with the characters in the story or identify with a poet's expressiveness. In the words of Rosenblatt (1986),

> The student should be helped to pay attention to the interfusion of sensuous, cognitive, and affective elements that can enter into the process of selective awareness and synthesis. No matter how limited or immature, this can provide the basis for growth. Aesthetic education should be rooted in the individual aesthetic transaction. The student thus can be helped to bring increasing sensitivity and sophistication to the evocation of "works of art," and can learn to bring to bear ever wider contexts for their interplay and study. (p. 127)

The teacher establishes whether the students will spend time exploring their aesthetic responses. Valuable instructional time is rarely taken for aesthetic inquiry. For an unexplained reason, teachers believe they are doing more teaching if the students spend the bulk of their time analyzing story structure or copying vocabulary words. Time spent helping students increase their sensitivity and sophistication to the evocation of "works of art" can only make the students better readers and interpreters of their own world. For this reason, I spend considerable time looking to students for their aesthetic responses and discovering how to represent those responses in poetry, music, and creative ideas.

Karen Gallas (1994), in looking at her own students' languages of learning, asked a second-grade student to explain why she thought she needed to compose a poem to express her thinking. This is what the student said:

> A poem is a little short, and it tells you some things in a funny way. But a science book, it tells you things like on the news . . . But in a poem, it's more . . . the poem teaches you, but not just with words. (p. 136)

There is something deeper here. Art, literature, music, drama, and poetry dig deeper than the surface structure of language and its conventions. Taking time to explore the deep connections that students make by using the media of art, literature, music, drama, and poetry is quality time.

Putting on the Group Presentation

Once the writing, music/poetry, creative ideas, and the various resources have been explored and developed, the group meets to develop a presentation. The group presentation has three phases: (1) individual writing presentation in a small-group rotation, (2) whole-group presentation, and (3) evaluation. The group presentation is an opportunity to practice public speaking, and it provides the students with the opportunity to showcase their work not only to the rest of the class but also to parents. Built into the group presentation is an evaluation component in which students evaluate their own work and that of their peers. The process serves as a culminating activity of an entire study of a book.

Everyone remembers those difficult times as a student, standing up in front of the entire class, with one shot to get a presentation right. That forum is intimidating and sets up students for ridicule. There is a much less imposing way to conduct group presentations. Thinking in terms of individual and group work, I conceive of a presentation in two phases. In phase one, students share their individual writing in a small-group rotation format. In phase two, a whole-group format, students share collaborative projects and songs and answer questions from the audience.

Phase One: Individual Writing

Phase one begins with setting up the room for small-group interaction. I set up the room into three stations (see Figure 8.9). A station is no more than a table surrounded by chairs. I ask the students who are scheduled to present to sort themselves into three groups and to decide which group will be at each station. With a literature-response group of six to eight students, no more than two or three students are at each station. Once the students station themselves in designated areas of the classroom, the rest of the class and visiting parents are sorted into corresponding groups.

My job as teacher is to manage a rotation sequence. I explain that each group has approximately ten minutes to present its writing and to answer questions. I keep track of the time and remind students when it is time to allow for questions about their writing. The rotation gives each student multiple chances in a small-group setting to practice presenting his or her work. It is not a one-shot experience; the students get three run-throughs as the audience rotates from station to station. Other benefits are that the roundtable format lends itself to exchange of ideas and the smaller group is less intimidating.

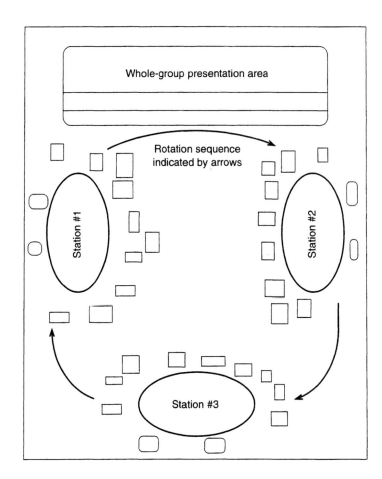

FIGURE 8.9
Classroom layout
for group
presentations

Phase Two: Whole-Group Presentation

Once we have gone through an entire rotation in which everyone has heard the individual presentations at each station, the whole class pulls up their chairs to face the front of the room. It is where the group meets to present creative ideas, hear poetry, and sing songs that were generated from the Literature Plan. This presentation may take the form of a puppet show or a multimedia re-creation of the story. At the end of the group presentation, five to ten minutes is set aside again for questions and answers.

Phase Three: Evaluation

Finally, the students evaluate the presentation. Before we sit down to write out an evaluation, I ask the entire group to talk with each other about what the presenters did well, what was learned, and how the students would do the same projects differently. We talk in pairs first and then share with the whole group orally. This technique gives everyone a sense of what to write in the evaluation and gives me as teacher the chance to emphasize the positive, rather than turn evaluation into a free-for-all for negative criticism.

Once the class has discussed the merits of the presentation, all students fill out the evaluation form (see Figure 8.10). The presenters fill out the front side of the form, describing what they did, what their favorite project was, and how the group could improve in the future. Space is provided for a brief one- or two-sentence response to each question. It is a time of reflection, so quiet conversation is permitted as students fill out the form together.

The students who were the audience fill out a portion of the back of the form, describing what they learned and what they would do differently if it were their project. The value of this time is that students can think about the presenters' cre-

---

Name _____ Date _____

Presenter's Self-Assessment

Directions: For your group, answer the following questions.

Title / Author _____

_____

1. What did you do in the literature group?

2. What was the best project you worked on?

3. How can your group improve?

(front)

FIGURE 8.10a Presenter's self-assessment form

Observer's Group Evaluations

Directions: For each of the other groups, write in the book title/author and answer two questions:
(A.) What did you learn? and
(B.) What would you have done differently?

1. _____   4. _____
   _____   _____

A.   A.

B.   B.

2. _____   5. _____
   _____   _____

A.   A.

B.   B.

3. _____   6. _____
   _____   _____

A.   A.

B.   B.

(back)

FIGURE 8.10b Observer's evaluation form

ativity and get ideas for future projects or see what to avoid doing if the idea was not successful.

It takes two or three days to work through all the group presentations. But once the presentations are done and the students have completed all their work, they turn in their evaluation forms with their folders. I ask each student to flag one of his or her pieces of writing with a sticky note to indicate which one should be placed in his or her portfolio. If I see an additional work to place in a portfolio, I ask the student's permission to put one or both items into the file. I compare the students' work with the records in my grade book and return the rest for their own use.

Calendars and Schedules

Developing Literature Plans from the initial point of selecting books to culminating the plan with the group presentation takes about six weeks. It is a learning cycle repeated throughout the school year. As a general rule, it takes one week to establish literature-response groups, four weeks to work through a Literature Plan in response forums, and one week to plan and present the projects (see Table 8.3 on the next page).

The literature cycle requires large blocks of time during the day to work with ideas in response forums, to read, to write, and to create. Tasks such as composing songs and making creative projects take significant amounts of time for thinking, planning, making, and publishing. The prime time for instruction in any elementary classroom is the morning; therefore, a quality program would reserve those hours for the workshop (see Table 8.4).

TABLE 8.4 Week-long schedule in a third-grade classroom

Time/Days	Monday	Tuesday	Wednesday	Thursday	Friday
8:30–8:45	Opening/ Role	Opening/ Role	Opening/ Role	Opening/ Role	Opening/ Role
8:45–9:40	Read aloud	Read aloud	Read aloud	Read aloud	Read aloud
9:40–10:10	Journals/ Shared reading	Journals/ Shared reading	Journals/ Shared reading	Journals/ Shared reading	Journals/ Shared reading
10:10–10:25	Recess ———▶				
10:25–11:45	Literature conferences, collaborative color mapping	Literature conferences, collaborative color mapping	Literature conferences, editing and revising	Literature conferences, editing and revising	Literature conferences, exploring creative ideas
12:00–12:40	Lunch ———▶				
12:40–1:40	Math/Science instruction	Social studies instruction	Math/Science instruction	Social studies instruction	Math/Science instruction
1:40–2:00	Recess ———▶				
2:00–2:45	Math/Science instruction	Physical education	Math/Science instruction	Physical education	Math/Science instruction

TABLE 8.3 Six-week planner for reader's/writer's workshop

Week 1	▲ Select books or stories (students with consultation from teacher). ▲ Form literature groups around selected books or stories. ▲ Students choose a liaison for each group.	▲ Students make folders. ▲ Teacher provides reading journals.	▲ Teacher meets with each group to start first writing assignment. ▲ Teacher makes color map for collaborative writing.
Weeks 2-4	**Writing** ▲ Teacher conducts whole-group lesson on peer editing. ▲ Students engage in peer editing of first drafts. ▲ Teacher reviews writing, grades final drafts, records in grade book and on reader's folder. ▲ Students produce three or four pieces of written expression.	**Poetry/Music** ▲ Students select appropriate poetry or music to accompany the book or story they are reading. ▲ Students reproduce poetry or music artistically for display and/or performance. ▲ Students individually, collaboratively, or with the teacher compose one or two original pieces of music or poetry.	**Creative Ideas** ▲ Students develop a creative project to express the story within the realm of the visual/performing arts (e.g., painting, sculpture, drama, dance). ▲ Students create a project to connect the story to other areas of the curriculum such as science, social studies, or mathematics in consultation with teacher. ▲ Students and teacher develop computer Hypertext versions of the story.
Week 5	▲ Teacher and students plan presentation. ▲ Students assign roles and responsibilities. ▲ Teacher schedules order of group presentations.	▲ Students finish writing, poetry, music, creative ideas. ▲ Students organize folder of completed work.	▲ Students write an invitation to parents. ▲ Teacher sends home parent invitations. ▲ Student literature groups conduct rehearsals.
Week 6	▲ Teacher sets up classroom in stations for group presentations. ▲ Teacher checks to make sure all groups have necessary props and materials to conduct their presentations.	▲ Students conduct group presentations. ▲ Students read individual written work in rotations. ▲ Students conduct whole-group collaborative presentations of artwork and creative projects.	▲ Students evaluate group presentation (self-assessment and/or group evaluation). ▲ Teacher conducts oral whole-group discussion. ▲ Students complete written evaluations of all presentations. ▲ Teacher and students select work for portfolios—one or two pieces that reflect academic progress.

CONCLUSION

The components of response-centered instruction as they played out in my class-room are summed up in the literature cycle. The literature cycle is designed to max-imize the ripple effect of quality literature among students. The literature cycle is a way of positioning students as authors of their own language and literacy develop-ment. Students involved in the process of a literature cycle form their own litera-ture-response groups based on self-selection of quality children's literature. They share in the reading and discussion of their lived-through experiences, their ideas, and feelings in a response forum. The response forum is an open space for inviting the musings of each student, to tug at their own cultural metaphors, and to map out collaborative writing, individual process writing, song, poetry, and creative projects in the development of a Literature Plan. Students showcase their work in a group presentation for classmates and parents, and they begin the cycle again with the next book they choose to explore.

A Thought from Carole

At many recess and lunch periods, Paul and I discussed what happened during literature groups; several ideas emerged as a result of Paul's teaching and my observing his teach-ing. Time and good books are keys to response-centered instruction in second-language education. It is also very labor intensive. As you saw in Chapter 7, a good discussion lasted an hour and a half. Equally important, the rest of the class sustained interest in their literature group projects without coming to Paul for help, perhaps respecting the sanctity of a really rich literature discussion in progress. They had learned how to use their time, and had learned to help each other rather than constantly come to the teacher for help. This is rather unusual, not the kind of teacher and text-driven literature-based teaching I see frequently in the many hours I spend observing in elementary classrooms.

It is the kind of teaching teachers may only feel comfortable trying with the "top group," rather than those who are struggling or learning English as a second language. Paul generally asks only a few open questions, most often beginning with the prompt, "Talk to me." His students maintain interest in stories and each other's comments without extensive teacher questioning. Paul said, "Talk to me," and waited, and often waited some more, until they did.

The response-centered literature-based teaching in Paul's class includes several components with the potential for generating rich literature discussions supporting second-language development:

Good books.

Aesthetic questions plus lots of wait-time for student responses.

Listening on the part of the teacher.

An open agenda.

Longer blocks of time with group rotation, not daily meetings.

This is not to suggest using a set schedule including these components in some sort of formulaic procedure. These are the components of what happened with good results for Paul. Keep in mind that each literature discussion is unique, a journey not taken before.

THINGS TO THINK ABOUT

1. Teachers teach to their strengths. What are your artistic and creative strengths? How could you use these as a resource in a response-centered classroom?

2. Look back through the chapter. In what ways does Paul foster self-direction with his students?

3. How is accountability built into the management of Paul's classroom?

4. "Whiz Kid," "Scaredy Cat," and "Office Shark" are three metaphors that organize thinking about people. Consider what metaphors are common to the students you are or will be teaching.

5. Read a short story and write down questions that would invite discussion. Trade the questions with a partner. Ask your partner to select the open-ended questions and to comment on which questions would maximize aesthetic responses to the story.

6. To what extent does prior experience, knowledge, and culture influence the reading of a story?

7. Discuss the purpose of assessment in language arts. What is the teacher trying to accomplish by assessing a grade on a work of art?

THINGS TO DO

1. In a small group, share with each other which children's books were favorites as you were growing up. What was it about these books that touched your lives?

2. In a small group, plan out a literature cycle for a favorite children's book. Plan out the kinds of writing you would do—poetry, music, drama. What creative ideas emerge from the story? Present your plan to the rest of the class.

3. Practice using the color-mapping strategy to collaboratively write a story with a small group of three or four other students. Remember to take down ideas randomly and to organize them later by marking similar ideas with the same color and numbering the ideas in sequence.

4. Pick a favorite song. Count the syllables in each line. Rewrite the song with different words that match the number of syllables per line. Sing your new composition.

FURTHER READING

Au, K. (1993). *Literacy instruction in multicultural settings*. Fort Worth, TX: Harcourt Brace.

Faltis, C. (1997). *Joinfostering: Adapting teaching strategies for the multilingual classroom*. Upper Saddle River, NJ: Merrill/Prentice Hall.

Griffiths, R., & Clyne, M. (1988). *Books you can count on: Linking mathematics and literature*. Portsmouth, NH: Heinemann.

Holt, D. (1993). *Cooperative learning: A response to linguistic and cultural literacy*. McHenry, IL: Delta Systems.

Ruef, K. (1992). *The private eye: Looking and thinking by analogy—A guide to developing the interdisciplinary mind, hands-on thinking skills, creativity, and scientific literacy*. Seattle, WA: Private Eye Project. To order, call (206) 784-8813.

REFERENCES

Bergman, I. (1960). *Introduction to four screenplays of Ingmar Bergman* (L. Malmstrom & D. Kushner, Trans.). New York: Simon & Schuster.

Cox, C. (1988). *Teaching language arts*. Boston: Allyn & Bacon.

Cherry, L. (1990). *The great kapok tree*. New York: Harcourt Brace.

Dewey, J., & Bentley, A. F. (1949). *Knowing and the known*. Boston: Beacon Press.

Dyson, A. H. (1990). Weaving possibilities: Rethinking metaphors for early literacy development. *Reading Teacher, 44*(3), 202–213.

Gallas, K. (1994). *The language of learning: How children talk, write, dance, draw, and sing their understanding of the world*. New York: Teachers College Press.

Krashen, S. (1985). *Inquiries and insights*. Hayward, CA: Alemany Press.

Pugh, S. L. (1992). *Bridging: A teacher's guide to metaphorical thinking*. Urbana, IL: National Council of Teachers of English.

Rosenblatt, L. (1986). The aesthetic transaction. *Journal of Aesthetic Education, 20*(4), 122–128.

Word Processing and
Authoring Tools Software

The emphasis in a response-centered classroom is on students as authors, not as passive receptors. Therefore, the selection of appropriate software is limited to word processing and authoring tools: *Children's Writing Center, Bilingual Writing Center, Storybook Weaver, PrintShop Deluxe, Hyperstudio,* and *KidPix.*

The list of titles of software for young children is ever-growing. The current market offers items as diverse as video game type programs and interactive books on CD-ROM. The selection of software mentioned above is specific to word processing, desktop publishing, and multimedia authoring tools. Word processing software includes *Children's Writing Center* and *Bilingual Writing Center.* These two are essentially the same program. Their features include a powerful word processing program with a full range of editing tools, spell checker, and thesaurus. Contained in the program is a full range of clip artwork that students can copy to a page and size, flip, or rotate with a simple click of a mouse button. The difference between the programs is that *Children's Writing Center* is in English, whereas *Bilingual Writing Center* switches from English to Spanish with the click of a button. In *Bilingual Writing Center,* the menu options and commands can be switched from English to Spanish. Additionally, with alternate key strokes, accent and Spanish diacritical marks can be typed into the text.

Print Shop Deluxe and *Storybook Weaver* are desktop publishing programs designed to pull together graphics with text to print out a published work. *Storybook Weaver* is a wonderful program for primary students. It is a simple series of frames for creating a small book, beginning with a title page and following with open frames for text and illustrations. The title page frame guides students to write the title and author name(s) and has an option for creating a variety of colorful borders. Subsequent frames are essentially a split screen with a place for text on the bottom and illustrations on the top. The students either dictate their stories or write them in themselves, and then they can select from a series of backgrounds with different shading to depict times of the day (e.g., dawn, late morning, noon, dusk, night). For the background, students can select and paste story characters, animals, buildings, plants, and other objects to illustrate the text. These pictures can also be sized, rotated, and flipped as desired. The pages are automatically numbered and print out two pages to a sheet of letter-size paper. The students can then cut out the pages and staple them together on the left margin and create their own library of storybooks.

Print Shop Deluxe combines a series of backgrounds, borders, text boxes and writing frames, and a vast array of clip artwork libraries. These items can be used to create greeting cards, banners, signs, stationery, calendars, and so on. The user may also cut and paste items from *Print Shop Deluxe* into other word processing programs as graphic files for adding pizazz to a letter or story.

Multimedia authoring tools are software programs that put the student in an active role as writer and creator. They are programs capable of importing features from other programs; in other words, authoring tools "interface" with other programs. *KidPix* and *Hyperstudio* are the most useful at the elementary grades. *KidPix* and *Hyperstudio* are not for creating hard copy printouts of documents; they operate in the realm of media making. With the tools provided in *KidPix*, a child can make on-screen drawings, record music or voice, write in text, and add sound effects. An effective use of the program would be, for example, to produce an on-screen puppet show with colorful sets, music, sound effects, and text.

Hyperstudio is a more sophisticated interface program that employs the use of "hypertext," importing graphics, digital sound, word processing, a drawing program with animation, and digitized motion pictures. The underlying idea of *Hyperstudio* is that software operates like a stack of cards. On each card, the user creates a background and a foreground with self-made drawings from the built-in draw program or imported pictures from clip artwork libraries or digital photographs. Among the many tools available are text fields that allow the reader to scroll through lengthy passages of writing. Text can be either composed in *Hyperstudio* or imported from a word processing program such as *Children's Writing Center*. Like *KidPix*, voice and music recordings can be added to the card stack, and digital sound effects can also be imported. More sophisticated applications include adding animation to pictures or drawings and importing digitized motion pictures from CD-ROM. A digitized motion picture, sometimes referred to as a "quick-time movie," is simply a brief segment of a motion picture digitally encoded on a computer disk. A digitized movie segment lasts no more than a few seconds because the number of graphics in a motion picture uses up tremendous amounts of computer memory. *Hyperstudio* is the type of program that allows users to create command buttons. All the cards and applications are linked by command buttons in the same way word processing programs use buttons to click on with a mouse to access pull-down menus.

Hyperstudio generates on-screen, interactive, multimedia presentations. With this program, a stack of student-created work could be stored and displayed on a computer. Picture what a *Hyperstudio* stack would look like on-screen:

Begin with a title page of "All About Our Class." The background is a collage of photographs of every student in the class, with their signatures written across each one's picture. At the bottom of the page are three buttons: The left one says "Contents," the right one says "Next Page," and the middle one says "Music." With your mouse, you click on the "Music" button and the computer plays a recording of the students singing a song they composed about their class. After you listen to the song, you click on the "Contents" button and the screen changes. It fades to a table of contents that lists each member of the class and the title of their written work. Next to each name and title is a small photograph of the student. You select a student by clicking on his or her photograph.

The screen fades to another card in the stack. You see an enlarged cropping of the student's picture next to a story in a box with a scroll bar to one side. You can read the story yourself by clicking on the down arrow of the scroll bar and moving down through the text; or you can click on a button labeled with the student's name to hear the student's voice reading his or her own story. Another button labeled "Artwork" is located below the student's picture. When you click on "Artwork," the card appears to lift up and display a screen divided into four quadrants.

The top-left quadrant displays a photograph of a mask the student created out of papier-mâché. The top-right quadrant shows a computer drawing of the student's face, and when you click on the button next to it, the mouth becomes animated and moves from a frown to a smile. The bottom-left quadrant appears empty except for a single button labeled "Top Secret." If you click on "Top Secret," you hear what sounds like a siren and then a voice announces, "Top secret information! No access permitted," and it finishes with a giggle. (It was just thrown in as a joke.) The bottom-right quadrant is a quick-time movie of the student onstage wearing his or her mask. When you click on the button below the picture, the student dances to the tune of the class song. Three additional buttons at the bottom of the page link the card on-screen back to the previous card or to the next student's card or back to the table of contents.

One can review the work of the entire class via this program. It functions like a multimedia portfolio of student-created work. This *Hyperstudio* stack of student-authored stories with photographs, music, sound effects, digitized motion pictures, and drawings with animation is also the substance of on-line Web pages used on the Internet. Providing students with the skills to express themselves by using multimedia tools is a concrete way to prepare them for the future so that they are capable of turning the page for the next century.

The selection of word processing programs, desktop publishing tools, and multimedia applications described above is not intended to be exhaustive. It is a starting place for affordable software that puts the student in an active role as author and imaginative producer of ideas and images. The curse of technology is that what is on the market today is obsolete tomorrow. The programs reviewed here not only are more affordable than some others but also have remarkable staying power and are upgradable. Furthermore, they are readily available in compatible formats for both PC and Macintosh computers.

Index

Abel's Island (Steig), 87
Academic language skills, 32
Acquisition. *See* Language
  acquisition; Second-language
  acquisition theory
Ada, A. F., 72
Additive bilingualism, 33, 34
Adventures of Ratman, The
  (Weiss), 115
Aesthetic questions, 63, 148
Aesthetic stance, 125
Affective fallacy, 24
Affective filter, 31
Alexander and the Terrible,
  Horrible, No Good Very Bad
  Day, 89, 103, 117
"Alligator Pie" (Lee), 84
Alligator under My Bed, The, 58
Altwerger, B., 52, 61
Anna Banana and Me, 55–57,
  85
Applebee, A. N., 50
Art projects, 66
Aschbacher, P. R., 54–55
Assessment
  authentic, 54–55
  of English proficiency, 95–96,
    99, 115

of group presentations,
  182–184
standardized, 51–52
Au, K. H., 73
Authentic assessment, 54–55
Authoring tools software, 161,
  191–193

Baker, C., 29, 34
Basal readers, 50, 51, 55–57
Battle, J., 73
Beach, R., 4, 26
Behavior chart, 129
Behaviorism, 28, 35, 50
Belpré, P., 69, 134, 136
Bentley, A. F., 152
Bergman, I., 172
Biber, D., 71
Big Books, 157, 162
Bilingual class
  classroom setup for, 128–129
  daily schedule of, 8
  language arts/reading
    instruction for, 9–10
  mathematics/content areas for,
    8–9
  reader-response in, 125–148
  room environment for, 6–8

site of, 127–128
teaching with literature in,
  10–19
Bilingualism
  additive, 33, 34
  levels of, 34
  Spanish/English, 109–121
  subtractive, 34
Bilingual Writing Center
  (software), 191
Biographical research, 69
Blanton, W. E., 52
Bleich, D., 26
Bloomfield, L., 27–28
Bookmaking, 66
Bowerman, M., 29
Boxcar Children series, 115
Boyd-Batstone, Paul, 4–19
Breen, M., 29
Britton, J., 26
Brock, C. H., 71
Brooks, C., 24
Brown, M. W., 82
Brown Bear Brown Bear, What Do
  You See? (Martin), 83
Bruner, J., 53
Buddy reading, 61–62
Bullock, A. B., 61

Cactus Hotel (Guiberson), 70, 142, 143

Calendars, 186

Calfee, R. C., 72

California Assessment System (CAS) test, 96

California Mentor Teacher Conference, 4

California State Department of Education, 17

Candlin, C., 29

Caps for Sale, 89, 101, 104, 118–119

Carle, E., 70

Case studies
  bilingual Spanish/English speaker, 109–121
  native English speaker, 81–92
  native Spanish speaker/English learner, 93–107

Cazden, C., 28

Chair for My Mother, A, 90, 103, 119

Cherry, L., 68–69, 174, 176

Children's Writing Center (software), 191, 192

Chomsky, C., 28

Chomsky, N., 27, 28, 29, 127

Classification, 70

Classroom
  description of site of, 127–128
  environment of, 6–8, 61
  language acquisition theory and, 38, 41
  layout for group presentations, 181, 182
  library in, 134
  reader-response theories and, 38, 41
  setup of, 128–129
  text-centered vs. response-centered, 59–60

Clay, 161

Cleary, B., 8, 68

Clifford, J., 25

Cognitive development, 35–37

Collaborative interview, 130–131

Collaborative writing, 176–178

Color mapping, 176–178

Columbus (D'Aulair and D'Aulair), 69, 134, 135

Columbus, Christopher, 59, 69

Communication
  context-embedded, 32–33, 40
  context-reduced, 33

Communication-based approaches, 28–30

Communicative competence, 29

Communicative language skills, 32

Competence, communicative, 29

Comprehensible input, 30–31, 40

Computers
  word processing and authoring tools software for, 161, 191–193
  for writing responses, 66

Connections, personal, 94, 100–104

Constructions, three-dimensional, 66

Constructivist theory of learning, 35–37

Content instruction
  in bilingual class, 8–9
  integrating with literature-based teaching, 67–70, 135–136, 142, 143
  options in, 157–158

Context-embedded communication, 32–33, 40

Context-reduced communication, 33

Cook-Gumperz, J., 29, 41

Cooney, B., 70, 136, 138, 142, 143, 145, 147

Cooper, J. D., 29

Correspondence materials, 162

Costumes, 162

Cox, C., 3–6, 25, 26, 49, 61, 63, 66, 79, 127, 134, 164

Crawford, J., 27

Crossroads, theoretical, 34–41, 123–124

Crowell, C., 21

Cullinan, B., 49

Cummins, J., 5, 27, 29, 31–34, 37, 39, 40, 71

Dahl, R., 129

D'Aulair, E. P., 69, 134

D'Aulair, I., 134

Delfines, Los, 134

Delgado-Gaitan, C., 72, 73

Dewey, J., 25, 35, 120, 152

Dialogical shift, 146

Diaz, S., 72

Doll House series (Wright), 134, 135, 136

Double entry journals, 64

Drafts, editing, 179

Dramatization, story, 65, 82

Drawing materials, 161

Dreams, 58–59

Drills, 28

Dyson, A. H., 125, 152

Edelsky, C., 52, 71

Editing, 179

Education, U.S. Department of, 73

Eeds, M., 62

Efferent questions, 63

Efferent stance, 125

Ellis, R., 29

Encounter (Yolen), 57–59, 70, 74, 134, 135

English
  assessment of proficiency in, 95–96, 99, 115
  bilingual speaker of, 109–121
  native speaker of, 81–92

English as a second language (ESL)
  literature and, 70–74
  Spanish speaker learning, 95–105

English language development (ELD), 100–105

"En Puerto Rico" (song), 136, 137

Environment, classroom
  for bilingual class, 6–8
  for literature-based teaching, 61

Ernst, S., 25

Essays, 156

Evocation, 26

Experts, interviewing, 69, 157

Fallacies, 24

Faltis, C., 29

Family, 81, 82–83, 84, 93, 94–95, 109, 110–111
Farrell, E. J., 25
Fish, S., 26
Fitzgerald, J., 72
Flores, B. M., 52, 61
Fluent-English-proficient (FEP) students, 95–105
Foertsch, M. A., 50
Freeman, Y., 50
Freire, P., 125, 146
Fries, C., 28
Froese, V., 60

Gallas, K., 21, 152, 180–181
Gallimore, R., 125
Gardiner, J. R., 70
Gardner, H., 147
"Gaviota Roja, La" (Belpré), 134, 136
Ghost in the Window, The, 85
Gifted student, 81–92
Giving Tree, The (Silverstein), 112
Goodman, K. S., 5, 17, 25, 50, 52, 53
Goodman, Y., 5
Goodnight Moon, 82
Gough, P. B., 50
Gould, L. J., 71
Grammar-based approaches, 27–28, 29–30
Graphophonic language system, 53
Great Kapok Tree, The (Cherry), 68–69, 174, 176
Great Wave, The, 86
Green, J. L., 37
Groups
  liaison for, 165
  literature, 57–59, 66–67, 74
  literature folder for, 165–167
  literature-response, 154–155, 164–168
  presentations by, 181–186
  shared reading in, 165
  small-group work, 134–143
  whole-group instruction, 129–131
Guiberson, B. Z., 70, 142

Hakuta, K., 71
Halliday, M. A. K., 29
Harding, D. W., 26
Heath, S. B., 37
Held, D., 24
Henry Huggins (Cleary), 68
Herman, J. L., 54–55
Hernandez, J., 142, 144, 145–146, 151, 152–154
Holland, K., 25
Holland, N., 26
Holt, D., 29
Home influences, 81, 82–83, 84, 93, 94–95, 109, 110–111
Home Reading Log, 166
Hoover, W. A., 72
Hudelson, C., 71
Hungerford, R., 25
Hymes, D., 29
Hyperstudio (software), 191, 192–193

Icons, 143
IDEA Proficiency Test (IPT), 95
Imagination, 110, 114, 116–120, 144
Independent reading, 62
Individual space, 131–134
Input, comprehensible, 30–31, 40
Integrated literature-based teaching, 60–70
Intentional fallacy, 24
Interactive journal writing, 131–133
International Reading Association, 4
Interpretation of literature, 138–148
Interviews
  collaborative, 130–131
  with experts, 69, 157
Introduction to Second-Language Acquisition Research, An (Larsen-Freeman and Long), 30
Ira Sleeps Over, 89–90, 103, 119
Iser, W., 26
Isla, La (Belpré), 134, 136

Island Boy (Cooney), 70, 104, 136, 137–142, 143, 147–148
Island of the Blue Dolphins (O'Dell), 129–130, 134

James, W., 25
James and the Giant Peach (Dahl), 129, 130
Johnson, K. E., 71
Journals
  double entry, 64
  interactive, 131–133
  reading, 167
  response, 63–64

Karolides, N. J., 25
Katy No-Pocket, 97
KidPix (software), 191, 192
Knowledge, transmission vs. social construction of, 34–37
Krashen, S. D., 5, 27, 29, 30, 31, 36, 37, 38, 39, 50, 71, 72, 125, 127, 152, 173

LaBerge, D., 50
Langer, J. A., 49, 50
Language
  analysis of, 24
  natural order in, 30
  primary, 31–34, 39, 71–72
  reader-response theories and, 38, 39
  second-language acquisition theory and, 38, 39
  whole, 5, 25, 52–53, 61
Language acquisition. See also Second-language acquisition theory
  communication-based approaches to, 28–30
  grammar-based approaches to, 27–28, 29–30
  learning vs., 30
  literature and, 71–72
Language arts
  for bilingual class, 9–10
  options for, 156–157
Language development
  of bilingual speaker, 109, 111

Language development *(cont.)*
  English (ELD), 100–105
  of native English speaker, 81, 83
  options for, 155–158
  sources for, 158, 159
  of Spanish speaker/English learner, 93, 95–96
Language learning, vs. acquisition, 30
Language proficiency
  assessment of, 95–96, 99, 115
  bilingual, 34
  developing, 95–105
  dimensions of, 32–34
Language skills, 32
Lap reading, 148
Larsen-Freeman, D., 30
Learning
  language acquisition vs., 30
  in text-centered approach, 51
  theories of, 34–37
Lee, D., 84
Lessons
  in response-centered approach, 57–59
  in text-centered approach, 55–57
Lessow-Hurley, J., 34
Library, classroom, 134
Lieberman, A. M., 29
Lieberman, I. Y., 29
Life cycles, recording, 70
Limited bilingualism, 34
Limited-English-proficient (LEP) students, 95–105, 127–128
Lindfors, J. W., 29
Linear model of teaching, 50
Linguistic-experiential reservoir, 39
Linguistic threshold hypothesis, 34
Literacy
  options for development of, 155–158
  second-language, 71–72
  sources for, 158, 159
Literary readers, 50, 51
Literature
  choosing and using, 162–164
  English as a second language and, 70–74

interpretation of, 138–148
  as model for writing, 64–66
  teaching in bilingual class, 10–19
Literature as Personal Exploration (Rosenblatt), 17, 24
Literature-based teaching
  approaches to. *See* Reader-response theories; Text-centered approach
  classroom environment for, 61
  content instruction in, 67–70, 135–136, 142, 143
  growth of, 49
  integrated, 60–70
  mathematics and, 8–9, 67–69, 157–158
  reading in, 61–62
  responding in, 62–66
  ripple in, 60, 66–67
  science and, 69–70, 130–131, 157–158
  social studies and, 69, 157–158
Literature cycle, 147, 154–188
  choosing and using literature in, 162–164
  defined, 154
  forming literature-response groups in, 164–168
  fostering self-direction in, 162
  group presentations and, 181–186
  materials and tools for, 158–162
  preparation and planning for, 154–162, 185–186
  response forums and, 155, 167–181
  ripple effect in, 164
  student role in, 163
  teacher role in, 163
Literature folder, 165–167
Literature groups, 57–59, 66–67, 74
Literature plan, 7, 16–19, 134–135, 136, 142, 168, 169
Literature-response groups, 154–155, 164–168
Lloyd, M., 142

Loban, W., 53
Long, M. H., 30

Mace-Matluck, B. J., 72
Make Way for Ducklings, 88–89, 100, 116
Many, J. E., 4, 5
Maratsos, M., 29
Martin, W., Jr., 83
Mason, J. M., 73
Materials and tools, 158–162
Mathematics, 8–9, 67–69, 157–158
McCloskey, R., 89
McGroarty, M., 34
McLaughlin, B., 29, 30
McLaughlin, T., 52
McLeod, B., 30
Meaning
  in response-centered approach, 54
  in text, 51
Media projects, 66
Mehan, H., 72
Menyuk, P., 28
Merino, B. J., 31
Metaphors, 172–176
Metropolitan Achievement Test (MAT) 6, 96, 99, 115
Mexican American students
  bilingual, 109–121
  English learner, 93–107
Mexico: Splendors of Thirty Centuries (O'Neill), 142
Meyer, L. A., 37
Miss Rumphius, 116–117, 120
Mr. Rogers Neighborhood, 83
Moll, L., 72
Monitor model, 30–31
Moorman, G. B., 52
Morrow, L. M., 50
Mother Goose, 82
Mullis, I. V. S., 50
Murphy, S., 50

Nate the Great (Sharmat), 115
National Council of Teachers of English, 4
New Criticism, 24

Nicest Gift, The, 101, 102, 103, 104, 119

Observation, 70
O'Dell, S., 129–130, 134
O'Neill, J. P., 142
Open-ended questions, 168, 170–172
Opinion survey, 157–158

Painting materials, 161
Papier-mâché materials, 161
Partial bilingualism, 34
Pavlov, I., 34–35
Personal connections, 94, 100–104
Peterson, R., 62
Pflaum, S. W., 37
Piaget, J., 35–37, 39, 52
Pierce, C. S., 39
Piper, T., 29
Planning
  for group presentations, 185–186
  for literature cycle, 154–162, 185–186
  literature plan, 7, 16–19, 134–135, 136, 142, 168, 169
  reader-response and, 143–146
Plays, 65, 156, 157
Poetry, 84, 126, 136, 144, 156–157, 180–181
Politi, L., 104
Pottery materials, 161
Power of Reading, The (Krashen), 71
Primary language
  learning to read in, 71–72
  second-language acquisition and, 31–34, 39
PrintShop Deluxe (software), 191, 192
Probst, R. E., 25
Proficiency. *See* Language proficiency
Proficient bilingualism, 34
Progress Record Sheet, 167
Proximal development, zone of, 31, 36–37
Pugh, S. L., 173

Puppet-making materials, 161
Puppetry, 65, 159–160

Questions
  aesthetic, 63, 148
  efferent, 63
  open-ended, 168, 170–172
  for response journals, 64
  in text-centered lesson, 55–56

Ramirez, J. D., 4, 31
Raphael, G. E., 71
Reader
  emphasis on, 24
  stance of, 25–26, 125
Reader-response. *See also*
  Response forums
  in bilingual class, 125–148
  individual space and, 131–134
  in literature-based teaching, 62–66
  literature cycle and. *See*
    Literature cycle
  literature-response groups and, 154–155, 164–168
  planning and, 143–146
  site of, 127–128
  small-group work and, 134–143
  whole-group instruction and, 129–131
Reader-response theories
  in bilingual education, 23–26
  classroom and, 38, 41
  language and, 38, 39
  open-ended questions and, 172
  other theories, 26
  second-language acquisition theory and, 34–41
  students and, 37–39
  teacher and, 38, 40–41
  transactional theory, 25–26, 37
Reader Stance and Literary Understanding (Many and Cox), 4
Reader's theater, 65
Reading
  buddy, 61–62
  environment for, 61
  family and, 81, 82–83, 84, 86, 93, 94–95, 109, 110–111

feelings about, 86–88, 99, 115
independent, 62
lap, 148
in literature-based teaching, 61–62
for pleasure, 134
second-language literacy and, 71–72
shared, 61, 165
sustained silent, 62
time for, 61–62
Reading aloud, 61, 129–130
Reading instruction, for bilingual class, 9–10
Reading journal, 167
Reese, R., 5
Reflective piece, 156
Research
  biographical, 69
  on historical or scientific background of story, 157
  opinion surveys, 157–158
Response-centered approach, 52–55. *See also* Reader-response
  authentic assessment in, 54–55
  meaning in, 54
  sample lesson in, 57–59
  students in, 60
  teacher in, 60
  text-centered approach vs., 59–60
  whole language in, 52–53
Response forums, 155, 167–181
  conducting, 168–181
  discussions in, 138–142
  first, 168–178
  subsequent, 178–181
Response journals, 63–64
Response process styles
  challenging text, 82, 88–90
  making personal connections, 94, 100–104
  telling own stories, 110, 114, 116–120
Richards, I. A., 24
Richards, J. C., 27
Ripple, 60, 66–67
Ripple effect, 164
Rodgers, T. S., 27

Rosenblatt, L. M., 4, 17, 24–26, 37, 39, 125, 126, 140, 146–147, 152, 172, 176, 180
Rosie's Walk, 89, 100, 103
Rossman, T., 30
Ruddell, M. R., 4, 17
Ruddell, R. B., 4, 17
Runaway Bunny, The (Brown), 82

Samuels, S. J., 50
Santana, C., 120
Scared Stiff, 85
Schedules, 8, 186, 187
Schooling and Language-Minority Children (California State Department of Education), 17
Science, 69–70, 130–131, 157–158
Scripts, 65, 156
Second-language acquisition theory, 27–34
   classroom and, 38, 41
   communication-based approaches in, 28–30
   in education, 29–34
   grammar-based approaches in, 27–28, 29–30
   language and, 38, 39
   monitor model in, 30–31
   primary language and, 31–34, 39
   reader-response theories and, 34–41
   students and, 37–39
   teacher and, 38, 40–41
Second-language literacy, 71–72
Self-direction, 162
Semantic language system, 53
Sesame Street, 83
Shannon, P., 50
Shared reading, 61, 165
Sharmat, M., 115
Shugar, G. W., 41
Silverstein, S., 112
Singer, H., 4
Skinner, B. F., 28, 34, 50
Slobodkina, E., 118
Small-group work, 134–143
Smith, F., 105
Snoopy, 115

Snow, C. E., 41
Snowy Day, The, 95, 100, 116
Social construction, 35–37
Social context, 39
Social interactionist theory, 36–37, 41
Social studies, 69, 157–158
Socratic method, 61
Software, 161, 191–193
Song of the Swallows, 90, 104, 119
Songs, composing, 136, 137, 157, 170–171, 174–176
Sources, 158, 159
Space, individual, 131–134
Spanish
   bilingual (Spanish/English) speaker of, 109–121
   native speaker of, 93–107
Spates, S., 127
Spindler, G., 37
Squire, J. R., 25
Stance, reader, 25–26, 125
Standardized assessment, 51–52
Steig, W., 87
Stinky Cheeseman, The, 115
Stories
   comparing, 156
   dramatizing, 65, 82
   reporting events in, 156
   researching background of, 157
   rewriting, 156
   telling students' own, 110, 114, 116–120
Storybook Weaver (software), 191–192
Storytelling, 65, 110, 114, 116–120
Strickland, R. J., 28
Students. *See also* Case studies
   background and home influences of, 81, 82–83, 84, 93, 94–95, 109, 110–111
   honoring voices of, 72–74
   imagination of, 110, 114, 116–120
   interpretation of literature and, 138–148
   in literature cycle, 163
   reader-response theories and, 37–39

in response-centered approach, 60
   second-language acquisition theory and, 37–39
   in text-centered approach, 60
Subtractive bilingualism, 34
Surveys, 157–158
Sustained silent reading, 62
Swain, M., 28
Syntactic language system, 53

Teachers
   imagination of, 144
   in literature cycle, 163
   reader-response theories and, 38, 40–41
   in response-centered approach, 60
   second-language acquisition theory and, 38, 40–41
   in text-centered approach, 59–60
Teacher's guide, 51
Teacher's Introduction to Reader-Response Theories, A (Beach), 26
Teachers of English to Speakers of Other Languages, 4
Teaching Language Arts (Cox), 5
Teaching Reading with Children's Literature (Cox and Zarrillo), 4–5
Testing. *See* Assessment
Test of Basic Experience (TOBE), 96
Text(s)
   basal readers, 50, 51, 55–57
   challenging, 82, 88–90
   literary readers, 50, 51
   meaning in, 51
   teacher's guide, 51
   transacting with, 25
Text-centered approach, 24, 35, 49–52
   response-centered approach vs., 59–60
   sample lesson in, 55–57
   standardized assessment in, 51–52
   students in, 60

teacher in, 59–60
Tharp, R., 125
Theater
    puppet, 65, 159–160
    reader's, 65
Thematic units, 61
Theme cycles, 61
Theme study, 61
Theoretical crossroads, 34–41,
    123–124
*Theoretical Models and Processes
    of Reading* (Ruddell, Ruddell,
    and Singer), 4
*There's a Nightmare in My
    Closet*, 58
Three Billy Goats Gruff, The, 82,
    85
Time, for reading, 61–62
Tools
    authoring (software), 161,
        191–193
    for literature cycle, 158–162
Tough, J., 29
Transactional theory, 25–26, 37
Transmission model of teaching,
    34–35, 50

Umbrella, 100, 104, 117

Velasco, J. M., 142
Very Hungry Caterpillar, The
    (Carle), 70
Vygotsky, L. S., 31, 36–37, 39,
    41, 53

Warren, R. P., 24
Weiss, E., 115
Wellek, R., 24
Wells, G., 29, 41
What's Whole in Whole Language
    (Goodman), 17
White, E. B., 8
Whitmore, K., 21
Whole-group instruction,
    129–131
Whole-group presentation, 182
Whole language, 5, 25, 52–53,
    61
Widdowson, H., 29
Wilkins, D. A., 29
Winters, L., 54–55
Word processing and authoring
    tools software, 161, 191–193

Workshops, 181–186
Wreck of the Zephyr, The, 58
Wright, B. R., 134
Writing
    collaborative, 176–178
    editing first drafts of, 179
    essays, 156
    grading and recording, 180
    of group presentation, 181
    interactive journals, 131–133
    literature as model for, 64–66
    materials for, 161
    reading journals, 167
    reflective piece, 156
    response journals, 63–64
    rewriting stories, 156
    songs, 136, 137, 157, 170–171,
        174–176

Yolen, J., 57–59, 69, 134

Zarrillo, J., 4, 25, 26, 49, 63, 134
Zone of proximal development,
    31, 36–37